The Far Western Frontier

The Far Western Frontier

Advisory Editor

RAY A. BILLINGTON

Senior Research Associate
at the Henry E. Huntington Library
and Art Gallery

THE NEW EL DORADO;

OR,

BRITISH COLUMBIA

BY

KINAHAN CORNWALLIS

ARNO PRESS

A NEW YORK TIMES COMPANY

New York • 1973

Reprint Edition 1973 by Arno Press Inc.

Reprinted from a copy in The State
Historical Society of Wisconsin Library

The Far Western Frontier
ISBN for complete set: 0-405-04955-2
See last pages of this volume for titles.

Manufactured in the United States of America

Library of Congress Cataloging in Publication Data

Cooke, Philip St. George, 1809-1895.
  Scenes and adventures in the army.

  (The Far Western frontier)
  Reprint of the 1857 ed.
  1. United States. Army--Military life. 2. The
West--Description and travel--To 1848. 3. Mississippi
Valley--Description and travel. 4. Black Hawk War,
1832. 5. Indians of North America--Wars. 6. United
States. Army. 6th Infantry. 7. United States. Army.
1st Cavalry. I. Title. II. Series.
F592.C77 1973   978'.0092'4 [B]   72-9436
  ISBN 0-405-04966-8

THE NEW EL DORADO;

OR,

BRITISH COLUMBIA

STANNARD & DIXON, IMPᵀ

NOON ON THE FRAZER,
OUR BIVOUAC BEYOND THE "FORKS"

THE NEW EL DORADO;

OR,

BRITISH COLUMBIA.

BY

KINAHAN CORNWALLIS,

AUTHOR OF "YARRA YARRA," "HOWARD PLUNKETT," &c., &c.

To the clime of Columbia, Britain's new born,
Where the rays of the sun gladly usher the morn,
  And the landscape deck out with a smile;
Where the hearts of the countless beat hopefully high,
  And gold doth the moments beguile;
Where the frown of the mountains, the blue of the sky,
  Contrast in their beauty with forest and plain;
Where the green perfumed prairie rolls in the breeze,
  And mankind ever struggle for gain;
Where the sight of the ore even fails to appease
  Man's inordinate yearning for gold,—
Still making each eagerly struggle the more
  For the treasure ungather'd—untold.
To that clime go, ye people, ye sons of the west,
  'Tis a land of exuberant plenty and joy;
Go, ye children of cities, by fortune opprest,
  Where gold may be gathered which knows no alloy;
Far and wide doth it lie on that beautiful shore;
  May it gladden and laurel the pathway of time
Left the wanderer to traverse who reaps from its mine.
  'Tis the bauble of earth;—'tis the gift of the clime,
Of millions the spoil,—It is mine—It is thine.

WITH A MAP AND ILLUSTRATION BY THE AUTHOR.

LONDON:
THOMAS CAUTLEY NEWBY, PUBLISHER,
30, WELBECK STREET.
1858.

BY PERMISSION.

PREFACE.

AFTER being long tossed upon the billows of the world, and buffeting with the contending winds of fortune, it is a refreshing season in which the wearied wanderer enters the haven of repose, there to beguile the unconscious moments in a happy contemplation of the past; of dangers braved and hoped for ends achieved. Delicious must be the retrospection of him who can look back upon a career, however short, in which the finger-posts of time point to deeds upon which he can reflect and look upon again without experiencing a shadow of remorse; where the mile-stones of his backward path denote the

manful deeds of heroism and generosity; where
the practice of true religion and philanthropy, the
upholding of the weak and the repelling of the
aggressive, are associated with the never-to-be re-
called events of his manhood, from the contemplation of which he will never have cause to
shrink, when the cold hand of death is stealing
silently yet relentlessly upon him.   Happy, I say,
is such a man.   But thrice happier is he who,
beyond all this, can look forward and see in his
ideal future a welcome reward in some treasured
object of his affection, with whom he may build
up to himself a habitation and found a name;
for how much more noble is it to be a founder
than a parasite, and with her to sail buoyantly
along over the sea of his ambition, and in his
children to see his own life perpetuated, and his
name and fame handed down to generations of
their posterity.

I do not alone speak of the bauble fame of
public life—I speak of the richer fame of worthy
deeds; for worth and heroism dwell in ob-

scurity and the cottage, as noble as ever consecrated kings and riches.

It is these prophetic feelings and objects of a happy future that actuate men in their ardent pursuit of wealth, that impel and sustain them through arduous enterprises, and so lead them to achieve successes which otherwise would never have been. It is the influence of woman that more or less fills the mind of every man with a latent and holy fire, which arms, emboldens, and cheers him through all the great vicissitudes of life; and it is these impulses and these feelings which will send forth to the New El Dorado of 'Fifty-Eight a valorous throng, fresh, eager, and impetuous, to gather gold and plant intelligence in the newly-awakened wilderness of British Columbia. May the light of heaven smile continually upon them from without, and their highest hopes be crowned with the success which enterprise deserves, is my most fervent benediction; and may they, on an ultimate survey of their career, find that the finger-posts and milestones which flank the vista of departed time recall to memory the happy consciousness of noble deeds—for there is a nobility in little things as well as in great ones—and every action of our lives bears witness of our hearts and understanding.

Having thus said, this book I usher upon the world, and again am a mere spectator.

September 4th, 1858.

CONTENTS.

APPENDIX.

INTRODUCTION.

SOCIAL AND POLITICAL.

THE history, brief as yet and marvellous, of the country of our El Dorado, by the wash of the North Pacific, stands alone and unparalleled in the long annals of the world. It has eclipsed California and outshone Australia; it has attracted, by an almost magical influence, tens of thousands to its shores, and flashed upon the universe in alluring fascination. It has sprung into life full armed, as Minerva from the brain of Jove. That which, but a brief period gone, reposed a solitary yet riant wilderness, is now alive with the clamours of a rushing sea of men, and the foundations of cities are already laid far down from the Rocky Mountains to Vancouver, that hilly and forest-clad isle of a thousand beauties and a nation's promise—the England of its ocean.

Gold is the mighty magnet which attracts them—the guiding talisman of their career. For gold has been the absorbing object of their search in the country from which they came, and from which their fellow-men are still rushing in palpitating gladness—a vast and headlong tide—towards its favoured clime. The magic spell of the discovery is being felt throughout the world, and nations have been awakened to the knowledge of another—a new—El Dorado, outvying all beside. And this land, upon which nature has so lavished her treasures, in inviting prodigality, rests beneath the sway of the British sceptre, and its riches are open to all.

Apart from gold, the other resources with which it is endowed are in every way equally bountiful and boundless; while its geographical position with regard to China and the great islands lying to the northward is destined to make it a grand emporium of trade with those countries.* Thus, when such of the restless, thirsty souls as are now amassing the earthy lucre of their ambition and their greed, may choose to embark in a more steady and less exciting career than that of " digging," they will find around them an equally extensive and illimitable field, in which their talents and their industry may be successfully exerted in the building up of an empire, which is destined to be the chief—the ruling power of the southern hemisphere.

It is already, in future promise, the brightest star in the constellation of Her Majesty's colonial dominions ; and the giant march of its progress, swift as the flight of time, is fast out-blazoning even the rapid growth of that once wondrous country of the Sacramento. These men, al-

		Miles.
* From Victoria to San Francisco the distance is		800
,,	Honolula	
,,	Sandwich Islands }	2,370
,,	Japan	4,400
,,	Shanghai	5,800
,,	Canton	6,900
,,	Sidney (Australia)	7,230
,,	Singapore.............	8,200

though possessing an affinity of race and language with ourselves, are, however, alien to us in constitutional government. They are republicans and democrats—we are supporters of a monarchy and an aristocracy; and, therefore, it is desirable that the latter element should be at once infused into the disorderly mass of the Americans now populating the regions alluded to, by emigration from the British islands.

An exodus of this kind would both benefit imperial, social, and individual interests. Firstly, in fortifying our power in these colonies, which are at present so thinly peopled with British-born subjects; and, secondly, in relieving the population of England of a superabundant number of the educated classes, amongst which so much struggling and competition exists, as well as benefiting those individuals by a transplantation into a field where energy and enterprise will be more amply and universally rewarded than are they in these, the crowded walks of the mother country, where, alas! in too many cases, the intellectual labourer may unceasingly toil in the vineyard of professional and daily life, and scarce eke out for himself the means of a bare subsistence.

Moreover, the higher the social element implanted in a new country, the better does it augur for the future welfare, stability, and greatness of that country. Neither the Phœnicians nor the Romans of old, nor the colonizing nations of more modern times, were regardless of the elements which composed the society first founding a new colony. Thus it was that Spain sent her dignified clergy, and her noblest families their sons, to settle in Mexico and Peru. With ourselves, Raleigh retired from the brilliant court of Elizabeth and the highest sphere of political ambition and laid the foundation of Virginia, while Maryland was founded by Lord Baltimore and the highest Catholic families ; and Pennsylvania was the home of Penn, after he had been a courtier. Carolina was similarly occupied, the framing of its constitution being intrusted to John Locke. In connection with Nova Scotia, the title of baronet was first introduced and conferred ; while Cromwell and Hampden both fostered the prospect of a colonial career.

Colonies, to remain long integral portions of

the parent empire, should be composed, to a
great extent, of the elements which govern society there. This gives strength and insures
congeniality; it reflects back, to a great extent,
and in an improved form, the habits and civilization of that nation; and this is exactly what
is wanted in British Columbia and Vancouver,
to counteract the effect of opposite principles and
political tendencies to our own, which exist and
preponderate amongst the mixed and desperate
men who are now, in swelling tide, flocking
over and exploring that country, from the Rocky
Mountains to the Pacific, as well as the neighbouring islands. For the country, so far as its
established laws, customs, and population are
concerned, is still to us a Virginia in the time
of Raleigh, a Massachusetts in the days of the
Pilgrim Fathers; and although society, under
such circumstances, inevitably forms and regu-
lates itself, adapting its uses to its necessities,
still the political helmsman over this newly-
awakened country has a mighty charge in hand;
for he can guide its ultimate destiny, while one
false move might leave nothing but a shattered
wreck to view.

Such is the critical nature of the emergency. The voice of the country is, however, unanimous in its approval of the prompt and liberal policy pursued by the Colonial Minister in the matter; and its successful issue will be sufficient to confer upon him a political immortality as great as that which he has already so deservedly earned in the lofty walks of literature and of learning.

The wisdom of dispatching to British Columbia " a powerful force of the corps of Royal Engineers, provided with everything necessary for the formation of roads and bridges, to open up the resources of the colony ; also to erect blockhouses for the reception and safe custody of the gold which may be disposed of by the miners, and at the same time to form an organised force for the maintenance of law and order,"is deserving of the highest praise. This force is under the command of Colonel Moody, a gentleman who, from his tried talents and his past experience in superintending the formation of the small colony which has existed during the last eighteen years at the Falkland Islands, is in every way adapted for the important service. Great firmness and discretion will be required of him in the performance of the arduous duties he will, without doubt, be called upon to take part in and perform until the ordinary machinery of government, municipal and imperial, is so far introduced and set in motion, as to dispense with the arbitrary rule which he may find himself compelled in the mean time to adopt. Prudent and lenient measures will, however, alone be successful—the rule of equity must be strictly adhered to, else the result might be fatal; for what is a troop of armed, disciplined men in a country where the entire population consists of men equally well armed and disciplined, and infinitely more desperate when opposed, although generous and peaceful when their "rights" are not infringed upon, and the obstacles of nature, which it is their lot to contend against, are not multiplied by the fiscal and other exactions of a too arbitrary and moribund government—I allude to that of the Hudson's Bay Company. And while I so speak I must not omit allusion to the peculiar position and highly commendable personal conduct of Governor Douglas.

Never was man placed in a more awkward position than he was, in having to deal with conflicting interests, to serve two masters, as it were, the Imperial Government and the Hudson's Bay Company, and yet to have to please his new and foreign population rushing down upon him like a whirlwind, and that while the criticising eyes of England and America were upon him, to give, or at any rate be expected to give, satisfaction to both and to all.

Now in forming a correct estimate of the policy which he has and is adopting with regard to the internal regulation of the two colonies of which he is now Governor, this his peculiar and difficult position must be taken into careful consideration; and when such is done, it cannot fail to be said that Governor Douglas has acted, in so far as he judged right, ably and energetically, and moreover has, by his urbanity and liberal feeling, rendered himself popular with the very men who had the first right to complain, when complaint was necessary. The Hudson's Bay Company were fortunate in having so efficient an officer to attend to their interests, for he certainly seems to have done his best in that respect so far as was at all compatible with justice to others. Thus it is that, however much the world may disapprove of the monopoly which he represents, it cannot but be acknowledged that *he has*, so far as he was personally concerned, acted in a manner as agreeable and conciliatory as any Governor of a Colony could have done under the circumstances. Still a Company's officer is in a wrong position as Governor of its Imperial and consequently social interests, and so the Colonists themselves feel it, as was testified in a memorial presented by them to the first Governor, Blanchard, on his retirement, against the anticipated appointment of the present Governor, then chief factor of the Hudson's Bay Company, and in this important respect it is that Governor Douglas has been, and is, singularly unfortunate. He was like the country school-master, who because he felt himself master of his boys, thought himself master of everybody else also, and who did not find out his mistake till he came to London. This was just the case with Governor Douglas : long accustomed to absolute control and discipline over the servants of the all-powerful, half-venerated Company, stationed over the territory; he thought he could, or perhaps took it for granted as a matter of principle, that the same thing could be done with a free and independent population,—but when tens of thousands of armed diggers became arrayed before his vision, his restrictive policy, or rather that of the Company, seems to have recoiled back upon him; he became at once an experienced man, and saw that the diggers, instead of entertaining the anticipated awe and respect for the edicts of the Fur Company, took upon themselves the power of questioning the authority under which they issued proclamations of right and control, entire and universal, over certain territories, and all the inhabitants of such, and is now partly by force of actual circumstances, and partly under the calming influence of Home dispatches, wisely refraining from " enforcing " anything opposed to the interests of the new population. But, notwithstanding his having thus altered his tack, if I may use the expression, he is just as zealous and energetic in behalf of all, as he was when proposing to stop their supplies.

He is an active, talented, and good-intentioned man ; and had he not been harassed by having to defend and sustain the rights, real and supposed, of the Hudson's Bay Company, under the new and unprecedented order of things, he would have been greeted with that unalloyed praise to which his many excellencies would have so well entitled him. As it is, let the monopoly be blamed, and not their individual representative.

Situated, however, as the crown is, with regard to the Hudson's Bay Company, there was no alternative for all this, and therefore we can only remain on guard and wait patiently till the expiration of the term of license in May next, when we may hail the institution of a new and more fitting order of things under the superintendence of a new governor and legislature, and of an organized and distributed force, magisterial and police, to be dispatched from England.

With respect to the levying a license fee and other conditions relating to the mainland, it is certain that Governor Douglas had no Imperial right whatever to do so, having at that time no official control over the mainland, unless as an officer of the Hudson's Bay Company, neither have such exactions been confirmed or acquiesced in by the Home Government; but as they have not been negatived, and as control over the mainland has been since vested in the Governor of Vancouver's Island, and still will continue to be so, Colonel Moody being for the present merely surveyor of crown lands or Lieutenant-Governor of British Columbia, it is left to the power and discretion of that officer (vide Sir E. B. Lytton's despatch of July 1st, in Appendix) as to whether the license-fees may or can be collected. If the diggers rebel against it, instead of as they now do, in many cases, " shirk it," then there is no authority to support him in its enforcement, neither in the prohibition of a free trade,—and very rightly. Ulterior results will be much more safely brought about to British interests and advantage in consequence of the provision of this outlet, and the satisfaction which the liberality and wisdom of its policy has given to the government and people of the United States, from whom a diplomatic agent was promptly sent to the New Gold Region, than would the egregious error of " *enforcing*" " rights " militating against the prosperity of the country, and especially when placed as we are with regard to defences in those regions. It would have been something like tilting against a pyramid.

b

As it is, with much good feeling, more tnan
thirteen hundred miners, nearly all Americans,
had paid the tax up to the 25th of June.   One
measure there was of the Governor of Vancouver which justly deserved the unpopularity
which it met with, and that was the prohibition
of promiscuous trading and the seizing of goods
imported contrary to the terms of his proclamation, claiming, for the Company, the right of
exclusive trade.   This was about as preposterous
and injurious an act as any man in his ignorance
of right and wrong ever committed, and quite
illegal, the Company being unempowered to monopolize any trade, save that "with the Indians"
—(vide Crown licenses of 1838 and August,
1849). But this imposition has, no doubt, by this
time been relinquished by sheer force of necessity,
which there would be no resisting.   Again, the
navigation of the Frazer ought to be free to all
nations ; but Governor Douglas had issued a
proclamation limiting such to " British bottoms" only.   However, it is to be hoped that
this also will remain a dead letter, and that
the would-be tyranny of the Hudson's Bay
Company will be reined in by the wiser policy
of the Home Government.

As respects the treatment of the aborigines,
the universal feeling of friendship which is entertained by the latter towards the servants of
the Hudson's Bay Company, is in itself a sufficient criterion of the kindness practised by
them, the greatest part of that kindness being
in their having left them alone, and in maintaining their trade with them, without infringing
upon their aboriginal habits of life, during the
course of more than a century and a half, so
that up to the present time there was little or
no decrease in the Indian population with which
they trafficked. This in itself is sufficient to
atone for nearly all the past evils of the monopoly, and presents a highly favourable and
striking contrast to the regime and conduct of
the United States Government and people in
dealing with the Indians on their territory, where
the Red Man was uncared-for, and slaughtered
with impunity. It is a melancholy reflection.
Even now there is a war going on in Oregon
between the United States army and the Indians,
a recent result of which was, that the former
were defeated. But of course the attack will
be renewed with a reinforced number of troops,
and the aborigines will inevitably be mowed and

shot down in as relentless and barbarous a manner as ever disgraced California after the gold
discoveries. It is highly probable that on the
resumption by the Crown of Vancouver, that
the Hudson's Bay Company, with their accustomed shrewdness, will put forward their claim
for forts and effects, as also expenses incurred
in colonising the island; and it is already mooted
that the sum is nearly eighty thousand pounds.
Now this is simply preposterous, so far as the
amount is concerned, a twentieth part of that sum
being sufficient to compensate them under any
circumstances; and, moreover, after the unprecedented harvest which the Company are now
reaping, they will be amply repaid without
receiving any retiring grant from the Crown.
It is therefore to be hoped that they will forego
the application for such; but that if it is made,
the eyes of Mr. Roebuck may be employed in
the scrutiny. The ordeal would be a severe
but nevertheless a highly equitable one.

And now to my narrative.

THE NEW EL DORADO;

BRITISH COLUMBIA.

CHAPTER I.

A STARTING GLIMPSE.

NEARLY three years ago—how eventful have
those three years been—and on a certain murky
day in the month of October, I, then a passenger from San Francisco, was emptied out of
a conspicuously huge and clumsy-looking American "stage" into the flimsy township of Sonora,
situate in the heart of a populous mining district of California.

Amongst my fellow-passengers was an individual whose legs terminated in a pair of eagle-topped leather boots, that stretched outside his striped "pants" half-way up to the knee. His head was encased in a white felt wide-awake-shaped hat, encircled by an eagle-buckled band, while a red serge shirt answered the joint purpose of coat and waistcoat. To the maroon-coloured eagle-buckled leather belt which he wore, was also slung a Colt's revolver, and this completed his attire and the appurtenances thereof, as my learned friend Parson Baggs would have said of yore. His countenance was of a sallow, weather-beaten ribston-pippin aspect ; his hair sandy ; his eye keen and piercing ; while, by the nasal twang of his voice, as well as his evident partiality for eagles, he was recognisably and unmistakably Yankee. This man was a miner, and his costume was the common and orthodox one of his class.

During the journey by stage, for the first part of the distance was travelled by steamer, it might have been observed that he found frequent occasion for twisting his body round and jerking something out of his mouth through the window of the vehicle. The reader will understand from this, that my companion

" chawed," as unfortunately somebody else was given to understand during this same trip, who happening to be lounging near where the "stage" passed, received a deluge of the "juice" in the right eye. We all looked back and laughed at the accident, while the thing on wheels rolled up the main street of the town, and shortly pulled up at " Sacramento House," where we alighted. *Apropos* of the tobacco juice, I had witnessed an exactly similar accident from a railway car, twelve months before, in Pensylvania. It was on a Saturday, and during the dry season. The consequence was, that Sonora was flooded with miners from the adjacent diggings, anxious to spend Sunday and their money amidst the attractions of the gambling-houses and hotels, with which the town thickly abounded. The population was chiefly made up of mongrel Mexicans, Frenchmen, and Americans, although Italians, Germans, and a few " Britishers," as my companion termed them, were also to be found. As my object is to introduce territories of more absorbing present interest than this region of California, I shall not enter into its descriptive detail, my intention in selecting this

time and place for my opening chapter being
merely to familiarize the reader, to some extent,
with the men—the reckless but praiseworthy
adventurers whose exodus to the rocky but
diversified shores of New Caledonia, now British
Columbia, has attracted the attention of the world,
and opened to the view another El Dorado, a
second Australia, which bids fair to outvie in
natural treasures even that glittering land.

After dusk, the chief street of the town, in fact,
the town itself, for it is principally made up of
this one street, presented an almost perfect blaze
of light. The "bar" of every hotel and gambling-
house, and almost every house was such, was
brilliantly illuminated. Attractively dressed girls
flaunted behind the counters, and the entire aspect
of the place was one of seductive allurement.
Bands of music, negro and otherwise, played
and resounded in almost every house, and all
was revelry and delight. My companion in the
eagle topped-boots played " Monté" at one of the
gambling-tables, and won ; I did likewise, but
lost. Such is life, such is matrimony—a lot-
tery. After gambling, we repaired to Sacramento House, drank each a flash of lightning

and a gum tickler, drinks of Yankee concoction, and having paid for our beds, received talleys, denoting their numbers.

A little before midnight I set out on a voyage of discovery towards my apportioned bed. After ascending a ladder-like flight of stairs, I found myself emerging, head first, into a sort of hay-loft, faintly lighted by a sickly-looking candle, that sputtered, in an apology for a stick, fastened against the wall, and which light, so painfully contrasting with the glitter and the glare below, revealed to the eye about forty stretchers, that lay in unpicturesque lines right, left, and crosswise, leaving a tangled passage about a foot wide for the purpose of navigating from the trap-door to the respective beds. Snoring, loud and furious, proclaimed it a dormitory. I was perplexed to find number 23, but after considerable groping, shin-striking, and miscellaneous stumbling, I achieved that success. Then, however, to my great discomfiture, I found my appointed stretcher minus both blankets and pillow; in other words, bare of everything but a scanty mattrass; sheets, apparently, not being there in vogue. The

reason of this I soon perceived ; the weather
being cold, those who had preceded me had
helped themselves to additional blankets at the
expense of those who were to follow, so in self-
defence I was compelled to do likewise, and,
moreover, thought myself very lucky in being
able to do so. Thus it was with but little
compunction that I stripped a stretcher a few
yards higher up in the room than my own, and
in addition helped myself to an extra blanket
from another. After that, I followed the ex-
ample of my snoring chamber-mates, and with
my revolver under my pillow, sank to slumber
as happily and contentedly as I had ever done
in regions of elegance and luxury. At about
three in the morning, however, I awoke, feeling
very chilly, a natural consequence, indeed, of
sleeping uncovered. It was dark, and I could
hear nothing, save the snoring of those around
me. I felt that my only alternative was to
dress myself; accordingly I adopted it without
delay, and after that dozed till morning. Of
course I comprehended that the cause of this
midnight interference was the scarcity of blankets amongst those who came last, and who

determined not to be done, pulled them off others, and so established themselves, as their saying went. It was prompt retribution; but Americans are the people, and California is the place for it.

On the Monday morning following, I accompanied my " chawing," twanging, but nevertheless good-hearted companion to his " hole" and tent at the neighbouring mines, for he had two mates, and they had been working while he was away, banking the " dust," and doing " a little on his own hook," at San Francisco.

He was now ready to rejoin them. The history of this man was, that he had been a performer in a circus, a workman in a pegged boot manufactory, a clerk in a store, a barman at an oyster saloon, and several other things respectively in the United States, before setting out for California. This he had done together with six others across the Rocky Mountains, an arduous and perilous undertaking, four years antecedent to this period of my meeting with him. Four only of their number reached San Francisco, three having died through the hardships of the road. These four set to work

digging at " Hell Gate," and their labours were
attended with such success, that in eight months
they amassed sixty thousand dollars. With
this they returned together to San Francisco,
where one of their number was shot in a gambling saloon, and the rest were, to use popular
phraseology, left without a cent, having gam-
bled and extravagantly wasted away their wealth.
After this, the three separated; one went down
to Sacramento,—a city in which during half the
year one-half of the population good humouredly
supports the other half, by reason of the latter
being out of luck,—and was never heard of afterwards; another, who remained in San Francisco,
was lynched, which means that he was hanged for
an attempt at highway robbery; while the third,
my companion, joined a party for the Sonora
Mines, and commenced digging again.

After ten months' hard work his share came
to four thousand dollars, and with this sum he
revisited San Francisco and "started" a store.
Unfortunately he was burnt out " flat"—flat as
a d—d pancake, to use his own expression,
alike with all San Francisco three months afterwards.   On this he resolved to return to gold-

digging, and with this view again joined a party for the same mines, and to this party he still belonged.

We arrived at the tent; two lanky, black-haired, long-bearded men welcomed my companion, and guessed he was serene, and guessed the "stranger," meaning myself, was a Britisher, and hoped I'd "liquor," which I assented to, and so on—all warmth and inquiry. These men had been digging with but indifferent success for sixteen months, that is, they had only paid expenses and put by a thousand dollars a-piece.

They had often stood and worked for days together, as a matter of course, up to the knees in water at the bottom of a hole, and endured wet beds, a windy tent, and rheumatism half the winter round. But the excitement of their free and independent occupation sustained them through all this, and they dug on from day to day with all the undiminished ardour and speculative perseverance of their hopeful nature, for *nil desperandum* is, and ever ought to be, the motto of the unsuccessful and unsatisfied gold-digger—if he but work long enough, he is sure to succeed. It is such men as these that are now flocking over to the New El Dorado. Intent upon speedy gain, they are ready to brave every risk, face every danger, and bear with every hardship and privation. Dauntless, fearless, and restless, they will brook no opposition nor restraint, but with a wild self-dependence of character, plunge, wherever gold attracts them, defying everything, and surmounting all obstacles.

There is a savage heroism in this, which the pampered conservative may denounce, but which, nevertheless, all must admire. It is such men as these that are now populating the new colony on the banks of Frazer River ; they have strength, courage, and enterprise; and although chiefly Americans, they enjoy an affinity of race and language with ourselves, and will no doubt endeavour to preserve those friendly relations with us in British Columbia which ever ought to subsist between two great nations, the one the offspring of the other, and each emulous of higher advancement and the maintenance of a growing prosperity.

CHAPTER II.

THE RUSH FROM CALIFORNIA.

It was on the 20th of April of the present year, that the first rush by steamer of four hundred and fifty adventurers took place from San Francisco to the gold mines on Frazer's River, and between that time and June the 9th, two thousand five hundred people, mostly miners from the interior of California, had taken their departure from San Francisco. It was estimated then that an additional number of five thousand were collected in Puget Sound *en route*.

The exodus continued. All California was in a ferment; the excitement was universal.

Hundreds that would not wait for the steamer, and if they had, could not have been taken by her, set out on the journey overland, starting from Shasta and from Yreka in the north, and travelling through Oregon to the New El Dorado. This is a perfectly practicable route, and the time necessary to the performance of the journey is about eighteen days. From all points squads of miners were to be seen making for San Francisco, and to ship themselves off, or taking the direction towards Oregon. Stock was being driven overland, horses, mules, and cattle through the Puget Sound country. It was calculated that fifty thousand souls would leave California before the end of August. Business in the interior, as a natural consequence, was deranged, suspended, or broken up, rents were diminishing, and all, save San Francisco, was being deserted; the latter city was rejoicing at the great influx of the miners, and still more at the prospect of the new trade with the Frazer River settlement. Storekeepers from the interior were hurrying down to set up as merchants in San Francisco, and all was uproar and delight.

It was on July the 8th that on the order for its second reading, Sir Edward Lytton Bulwer Lytton, Secretary of State for the Colonies, brought prominently, in an able speech, before the House of Commons a Bill for the Government of New Caledonia; of that extensive region, which extends from the Rocky Mountains to the Pacific Ocean, a region which has hitherto been alone trodden by the Red Indian, or the traders of the Hudson's Bay Company in the pursuit of peltries.

The bill proposed to constitute the district of "New Caledonia," on the north-west coast of America, a British colony, saying, " Whereas divers of her Majesty's subjects and others have, by the license and consent of her Majesty, resorted and settled there for mining and other purposes, and it being desirable to provide for the civil government of such territories, it is proposed to enact that her Majesty shall be enabled, by order in Council, to provide for the making of laws for the government of the colony; her Majesty is, as soon as she may deem it expedient, to constitute a local council and assembly, to be appointed or selected, sub-

ject to such regulations as may be considered
suitable to the requirements of the colony." *

The bill does not empower the crown to annex Vancouver's Island to the mainland, but
there is a clause conferring that authority at a
future date, should the legislature of Vancouver
pray for such incorporation, the present object
being simply to provide some form of government, deferring a fuller measure until the colony
is more advanced, and its character and circumstances are more decided than they can be for
some time to come.

The solution of the question, which had from
time to time been raised, as to what should be
done with the territories which the Hudson's
Bay Company have held under royal license
during the last forty years, was forced upon the
cabinet by the gold discoveries.

It is a difficult thing to form any kind of government for such men, desperate, heedless, un-

---

* This measure was to empower the crown for a period
of five years to make laws for the district by orders in
council, and to establish a legislature, such legislature to
be appointed in the first instance by the Governor alone,
but subsequently it would be open to establish a representative assembly.

accustomed to any kind of restraint, and regardless of every consequence, as those, schooled in California, who now people the newly-disturbed wilderness of British Columbia ; yet it seemed necessary to be done, and the co-operation of men of all parties shewed a laudable feeling towards that end. The territory to be regulated and protected is bounded on the south by the American frontier line, forty-nine degrees of latitude, and extends to the sources of the Frazer River, in latitude fifty-five degrees. It is about four hundred and twenty miles long in a straight line, and its average breadth is from two hundred and fifty to three hundred miles; taken from corner to corner, its greatest length would be, however, eight hundred and five miles, and its greatest breadth four hundred miles. Its area is computed at, including Queen Charlotte's Island, two hundred thousand square miles. Of its two gold-bearing rivers, one, the Frazer, rises in the northern boundary, and flowing south, falls into the sea, on the south-western extremity, opposite the south end of Vancouver's Island, and within a few miles of the American boundary; the other, the Thompson River, which rises in the Rocky Mountains, and flowing westward, joins the Frazer, at the " Forks." (See Appendix.) It is on these two rivers, and chiefly at their confluence, that the gold discoveries have been made.

The land on the lower part of the Frazer River is good, but the Thompson's River district is one of the finest countries in the British dominions, possessing a climate far superior to that of countries in the same latitude on the other side of the mountains. Its fisheries are most valuable, its timber the finest in the world for marine purposes. It abounds with bituminous coal, well fitted for the generation of steam. From Thompson's River and Colville districts to the Rocky Mountains, and from the forty-ninth parallel, some three hundred and fifty miles north, a more beautiful region does not exist. It is in every way suitable for colonization. Therefore, apart from the gold fields, this country affords the highest promise of becoming a flourishing and important colony.

When the bill referred to was introduced to the House, the colonial Secretary, who is entitled to the fullest praise of his country for his talented exertions, and expeditious tact in this matter, mentioned that Government had already received overtures from Messrs. Cunard for a line of postal steam vessels, for letters, goods, and passengers, by which it was calculated that the colony might be reached in about thirty-five days from Liverpool, by way of New York, and the Isthmus of Panama.

It is said that there are two sides to every picture; be it so, but the one side is but a shade darker than the other, as respects the country we are dealing with. There are reports which advert to the almost total absence of food supplies, and to the sufferings of the Indian tribes from want and starvation ; that those wild tribes roam over the country, disputing, fighting, and robbing the Americans who venture there, and are at peace only with the free-traders of the Hudson's Bay Company, who furnish them with much of their food. But these reports are not to deter stout hearts, and were only applicable to the first thousand that crossed the frontier. The rivers which run into the Pacific are navigable for some distance into the interior, but then terrific rapids and fearful gorges occur to deter the traveller from further progress. The adventurer in search of gold has to make a path along the mountains, carrying his meagre sustenance with him on a starveing horse, which, food failing, he might have to kill and devour. But such are, and always were, the exceptional experiences of life in a new and mountainous country.

Still when gold allures, what obstacles will not man surmount, what hardships will he not bear. These terrors will not discourage gold-seekers. The men who are rushing to the region to establish " new diggings," are as fierce as the Indians themselves, and will have no hesitation in declaring war to the knife against natives who obstruct their progress.

It is a matter of present doubt whether Vancouver's Island, which is off the mainland, will become an active gold district in itself ; but apart from that, its mere commerce will sufficiently enrich it. It is proposed to be made the principal station of our naval force in the Pacific.

It has the best harbour,—Esquimault—in fact the only good one, northward of San Francisco, as far northward as Sitka, the Russian settlement; there is fine timber in every direction, and coal enough for a dozen navies. It has been said that the Americans will scarcely like the establishment of the new colony, and that we can readily imagine the feeling with which some of the braves among them will contemplate the " location" of Britishers on part of the American continent, which they would like to consider it their exclusive right to possess, while one of the London morning papers accounted for a decline in the funds by referring to an apprehension that the occupation of " New Caledonia " might be considered offensive by the United States.

But all this is idle talk, as the good sense and right feeling of the Americans is sure to be found paramount in the consideration of this question, and that the two nations individually will cheerfully and cordially support each other in the work of colonization.

CHAPTER III.

DAZZLING PROSPECTS.

IT is not my province to endeavour to divert
emigration from its present channels, in favour
of the newly-discovered gold regions of British
Columbia. But it behoves me as a writer, to
describe accurately and impartially the country
with which I have to deal, as well as to express
my own candid and unbiassed belief in the de-
sirability of that country as a place of settlement
for those who, emulous of gain, and intent upon
doing something for themselves, which in England may be of doubtful promise, are willing
to go forth and brave the world amongst a class

of society, which, although crude and unsettled, in its unsophisticated roughness may be found all the more hospitable, and encouraging than in England, where starched and hollow conventionalism curbs, and fetters, and repels, and narrows the souls of men to a methodical routine and a humiliating code, which destroys self-dependence and magnanimity, and, like the desert traveller, lost amid the dust of the sirocco, makes the spirit of enterprize pant for the fresher air of unshackled freedom. In giving this opinion I cannot do otherwise than pronounce Vancouver's Island, and the territory of the neighbouring mainland, as the most desirable fields for the exercise of that talent, and that industry. which the still over-burdened population of this country may send forth.

Although the climate and other natural advantages of British Columbia are not everywhere so great as those which favour the island, still the proximity of both is so close, that each can be made to conduce to the general comfort of man. The climate of Vancouver's Island, although in many respects closely resembling that of England, is very much to be preferred to it. The face of

the country is more radiant—the vegetation is
by far more luxuriant, and during the summer
months, that is from April to September, the
vivifying rays of an unclouded sun, shining
through a tinted but half shadowy sky, gladdens
the earth, and while decking all nature in a
festive array, makes joyful the hearts of men,
and merry indeed the carol of feathered throngs.

Rich and bounteous in its superficial treasures,
it offers to man the solid wealth of gold ; here
can be achieved the sudden gain of what elsewhere millions strive for in vain.

Commerce always follows in the footsteps of
emigration and colonization, and rare will be
the advantages reaped from an influx of people
so great as the countries referred to are now
experiencing, and which tide of immigration
will continue to flow on in augmented greatness
and impetuosity, till the favoured territories
blaze out upon the world in dazzling attractive-
ness and importance, and British American gold
circulates in uncounted millions through the
coffers of civilization.   And while I so speak of
these lands, I cannot but extol the spirit which has
actuated that grand mouth-piece of the British

nation, the *Times* newspaper, in its endeavours
to induce emigration generally, as well as the
publicity which it has given to the new gold
regions of our observation.   The ample resources
which it commands, as well as the magnanimous
feeling of impartiality and philanthropy which
guides its conduct, and which has long placed it
on the highest pinnacle of journalistic fame, have
conduced to the dissemination of more good
throughout Great Britain and her dependencies,
and to an establishment of more thorough and
correct information, than all the other newspapers
of the United Kingdom joined together, and perhaps than all the emanations of the press for the
last fifty years throughout the world.

To some this possibly may seem an exaggerated statement, but can they refute it?   It is
beyond individual power to measure the extent
of good which has resulted from its able advo-
cacy.   Reforms may not have sprung up on the
instant of its bidding, neither have abuses been
always as quickly corrected, but still the effect,
however latent—has been nevertheless as assuredly potent—has worked a marvellous change
in our government, our institutions, and our social

life during the nineteenth century ; and by virtue
of the permanence of such effect in shaping
and influencing the destiny of future ages, and
not only of its own nation, but of the world.
It has gained the ear of humanity, which is
power ; while by the laudable and judicious use
of that power it has contributed to the advancement of civilization, the ends of justice, and the
inculcation of everything calculated to exalt and
fortify ; a power whose sceptre no other journal
was able to wield.   This is public approbation,
and it is that public approbation and confidence
which still keeps it, and promises ever to keep
it, on a pillar of its own, the shining sun of
enlightenment and intelligence, the monitor as
well as the trumpet voice of Britannia, which is
felt and echoed throughout the length and
breadth of civilisation.

Well, indeed, may emigration from the mother country be advocated, while millions of able
and intelligent men and women drag out a feeble
existence, vegetating on the merest pittance
necessary for actual subsistence, and when to
attain that is too frequently a difficult struggle.
Well may emigration be encouraged when thou-

sands are every day being ushered into our jails
for petty thefts for bread. When millions prey
upon each other by the force of sheer hungry
necessity, and are hurried swiftly down the tide
of life and crime into premature graves. When
the widow may wail, and her breadless, home-
less children die on her breast without any helping hand being extended until it is too late.
When monopoly is tyranny sucking the life
blood of the people, and of trade, and men's
hearts are as callous as stones. When the thirst
and the struggle for gold is a work of life or
death amongst the mass of our population, and
the ever unsatisfied yearning and aim of the
wealthy—the moneyed monopolist When the
weak man strong in gold, crushes the strong
man weak in gold, and all the world worship
money. In such an age, and in such a state of
society, is it not the best thing possible to induce
as many of the needy as can procure the means
of emigration to do so with as little delay as is
compatible with their own good interests ? Yes.
The beckoning hand of another El Dorado invites them from their squalid homes and resorts
of wretchedness to participate in the plenteous-

ness of its enduring harvest.   Certain wealth is
spread out before them.   The cry of gold re-
sounds far and wide throughout its territories,
and present riches, with still richer promise,
shine out in alluring fascination, saying, " Come
and partake, ye that are weary and wayworn.
Come, ye children of enterprise and ambition—
all ye that are hungry and desolate, come and
partake of that which ye have long hoped and
struggled for, but never realized."

CHAPTER IV.

THE ENGLAND OF THE PACIFIC.

VANCOUVER, or Quadra and Vancouver, is an island on the west coast of British America, extending from latitude 48 deg. 19 min. to 50 deg. 53 min. north, and longitude 123 deg. 17 min. to 128 deg. 28 min. west. Its length, measured from N.W. to S.E., is 278 miles, its extreme length 290 miles, and in breadth it varies from 50 to 65 miles. On the east and north-eastern side it is separated from the mainland of British America by the Gulf of Georgia and Queen Charlotte's Sound, and on the south from that of the United States by the Strait of Juan-de-Fuca, while on the north and western

side it lies open to the north Pacific.   The interior is highly fertile, well timbered with cedar,
pine, maple, oak, and ash, and picturesquely
diversified by intersecting mountain ranges and
extensive prairies ; the shores are bold, precipitous, and rocky, nearly unbroken on the north-
eastern side, but presenting in other directions
numerous indentations, many of which are so
completely land-locked either by projecting promontories or minor islands stretching across their
mouths as to form excellent natural harbours.
Of these may be mentioned Nootka Sound on
the west, and Camosack, or Victoria Harbour
on the southern side.

The only navigable river hitherto known, is
that of Nimkis in the north east.   In the same
part of the coast, and stretching to a considerable extent inland, an excellent field of coal exists,
and lies so near to the surface that by the aid of
the Indians it has been obtained at an average
cost of four shillings per ton ; the seams, however, although in some places three feet, are
in general only from ten to eighteen inches
thick.   Fogs, remarkable both for their density
and duration, are of frequent occurrence.   The

winter is stormy, and heavy rains fall, particularly during November and December. Frost occurs on the lowlands in January, but is rarely of long duration, and can hardly be said to interrupt agricultural operations.

Vegetation begins to advance in February, makes rapid progress in March, and continues to be fostered by alternately warm showers and sunshine in April and May. The summer heats are excessive, particularly during June and July, and by the end of August the long grass becomes so thoroughly parched as to be easily ignited· Long before the period of the present gold discoveries, the agricultural and farming operations, for the encouragement of which the country is endowed with the most boundless resources, carried on chiefly at Victoria, exceeded in their successful results the most sanguine expectations, and are now being conducted with even greater returns than before. The principal products, in addition to those of the soil, are furs, chiefly those of the bear, beaver, fox, racoon, deer, ermine, squirrel, land otter, and sea otter, while fish, including the sperm whale, abound plentifully on all parts of the coasts.

The Indian population numbers about ten thousand five hundred,* and is divided into twelve tribes; of these the Kawitchen, Quaquidts, and Nootka, are the largest. They are a fine stalwart race, and have since the establishment of the Hudson Bay Company traded with their civilised brethren on the most friendly terms. The property of the whole island was granted to the latter company in 1849, on the express condition of their colonising it, but up to the present time comparatively little progress has been made towards that object.

Vancouver's Island was supposed to form a part of the mainland till the year 1789, when an American vessel sailed through the east channel which separates it. In 1792 it was visited by Vancouver, who named it Quadra Vancouver, the former out of compliment to the Spanish Commandant of Nootka Sound, which, however, has now become obsolete. The agents of the Hudson's Bay Company had long been in the habit of visiting it periodically before the

* Before a parliamentary committee in 1857, Mr. Cooper, an ex-resident on the island, in his evidence, estimated the aboriginal population at from eighteen to twenty thousand.

date of its cedure to them, for the sake of the trade in furs and other commodities supplied by the Indians ; it attracted, however, but little attention till the discussion of the Oregon question brought it prominently into notice. By the boundary treaty with the United States, the entire possession of it was then formally fixed in Great Britain.

Fort Victoria, erected by the Hudson's Bay Company, is situated on the southern extremity of the island, in the small harbour of Cammusan, the entrance to which is rather intricate. The fort is a square enclosure of one hundred yards, surrounded by cedar pickets twenty feet in height, and having octagonal bastions containing each six-pounder iron guns at the north-east and south-west angles ; the buildings are made of squared timber ; they are eight in number, and so constructed as to form three sides of an oblong. This fort is badly situated with regard to water position, the site having been chosen for its agricultural advantages only. Distant from this about three miles, and nearly connected by a small inlet, is the Squimal Harbour, which is very commodious and easily accessible at all

times, offering a much better position, and having
also an abundant supply of fresh water in its
vicinity.   Fields of limestone also abound in the
neighbourhood, admirably suited for building
purposes.

The Straits of Juan de Fuca, which separate
Vancouver's Island from the mainland, are safe
and easy of navigation ; the shores are straight
and bold;   on the south composed of perpendicular cliffs that run backward in high
and ragged peaks, while on the north they are
bold and rocky, and in some places formed of
reddish granite.   The port of Camosack is the
most eligible within the latter straits; it is
hemmed in by a range of plains nearly six miles
square, containing a great extent of valuable
tillage and pasture land, sprinkled here and
there with pine and oak, and intersected by a
canal six miles long, and rivulets well adapted
for the ordinary water-power purposes of flour
and saw mill driving.   The aspect of the country is most picturesque, the climate highly
salubrious, while cattle and the necessaries of
life are abundant.   Clover grows wild with a
rank and luxurious compactness more resem-

bling the close sward of a well-managed lea than the produce of an uncultivated waste.

The following is the synopsis of the basis of the constitution of the Vancouver Island Colony:—

" The Governor is appointed by the Crown, with a council of seven members likewise so appointed.

" The Governor is authorised to call assemblies to be elected by the inhabitants holding twenty acres of freehold land.

" For this purpose it is left to the discretion of the Governor to fix the number of representatives; and to divide the island into electoral districts, if he shall think such division necessary.

" The Governor has the usual power of proroguing or dissolving such assembly.

" The legislature thus constituted will have full power to impose taxes and regulate the affairs of the island, and to modify its institutions, subject to the usual control of the crown.

" Laws will be passed by the Governor, council, and assembly."

There is little to object in the above, but

c 3

when we come to the following we plainly recog-
nise the cause which has hitherto militated
against the colonisation of the island :—

1. That no grant of land shall contain less
than twenty acres.

2. That purchasers of land shall pay to the
Hudson's Bay Company, at their house in London, the sum of £1 per acre for the land sold to
them, and to be held in free and common
soccage.

3. That purchasers of land shall provide a
passage to Vancouver's Island for themselves and
families if they have any ; or be provided, if
they prefer it, with a passage on paying for the
same at a reasonable rate.

4. That purchasers of a larger quantity of land
shall pay the same price per acre, viz. £1, and
shall take out with them five single men or three
married couples for every hundred acres.

5. That all minerals, wherever found, shall
belong to the company, who shall have the
right of digging for the same, compensation
being made to the owner of the soil for any
injury done to the surface ; but that the said
owner shall have the privilege of working for his

own benefit any coal mine that may be on his land on payment of a royalty of 2s. 6d. per ton.

It is needless to offer comment on these impolitic and suicidal regulations, when at the same time, in both Oregon and California, where gold was abundant, land was purchasable at 6s. per acre. The fact was, the Hudson's Bay Company wanted to keep back emigration, for the sake of the furs and other petty traffic with the natives; and so far, as anti-civilisers, they succeeded. By right of charter their territory extends from 49 deg. to 70 deg. north latitude, and from 55 deg. to 135 deg. west longitude, and contains more than three millions of square miles, over which they maintain one hundred and sixty distinct establishments where the fur trade is carried on. In 1838, the charter granted by Charles II. was renewed for twenty-one years, and will consequently expire in 1859, as also that granted in 1848 for Vancouver's Island, when it is to be hoped there will be a dissolution of that monopoly which has since 1670 kept back civilisation for the mere sake of gratifying the wants of the few.

CHAPTER V.

THE GRAND AREA.

BRITISH COLUMBIA is a rugged but highly diversified tract of country in Oregon, west of the Rocky Mountains, stretching between latitude 48 and 57 deg. north, extending about 500 miles north to south, and nearly 400 miles east to west. It is mountainous, and abounds in lakes and rivers, the largest of the latter being the auriferous Frazer. Agriculture has not been prosecuted with so much zeal or success here as on Vancouver's Island, but the natural advantages of the country are in many parts fully equal, if not superior, to it; potatoes, turnips, wheat, and barley, have been long cultivated at the principal posts or stations of the Hudson's Bay Company in the territory, and with much success, especially at Nisqually, where they have fifteen miles of land under tillage, besides large flocks of cattle on pasturage.

The soil varies from a deep black vegetable loam to a light brown loamy earth. The hills are generally basalt, stone, and slate. The surface is generally undulating, well watered, well wooded, and well adapted for agriculture and pasturage. The timber consists principally of pine, fir, spruce, oak (white and red), ash, yew, arbutus, cedar, arborvitæ, poplar, maple, willow, cherry, and tea. All kinds of grain, including wheat, rye, barley, oats, and peas, may be raised in abundance. Fruits, particularly apples and pears, together with every kind of vegetable grown in England, flourish admirably, and produce most abundant crops. The winters are more humid than cold, as from the middle of October to March the rains are almost incessant, and frequently accompanied with heavy thunder and lightning. The winds which prevail at this season are from the south and southeast, and these usually bring rain, while those from the north and north-west bring fair weather and a clear

sky. From the middle of March to the middle
of October, the weather is serene and delightful;
only a few gentle showers fall, but in the morning the dews and fogs are frequent and heavy.
The middle and eastern regions have, from their
elevation, a severer climate.

Nearly at the southern extremity of Puget's
Sound stands Fort Nisqually, where the Hudson's Bay Company have extensive farms and
granaries.* Some of the natives here live in
the plains, and others on the banks of the
Sound. Each of the tribes observe a marked
aversion to mutual incorporation, and confine
themselves to their distinct localities, the plain
tribes not approaching the Sound, and the

* The anchorage off Nisqually is very contracted, in
consequence of the rapid shelving of the bank, that soon
drops itself into deep water. The shore rises abruptly
to a height of about two hundred feet, and on the top of
the ascent is an extended plain covered with pine, oak,
and ash trees scattered here and there, so as to form a
park-like scene. The hill-side is mounted by a well-
constructed road, easy of ascent. From the summit of
the road the view is beautiful, over Puget's Sound and
its many islands, with Mount Olympus covered with
snow for a back-ground. Fort Nisqually, with its outbuildings and enclosures, stands back about half a mile
from the edge of the table land.

tribes bordering on the Sound not extending their rovings into the plains. Their habits and food are in conformity with their condition ; the one are fishers, the other hunters, living principally on roots dried, pounded, and kneaded into cakes, and on deer's flesh. All this country, both maritime and inland, abounds in all sorts of game, — geese, ducks, plovers, partridges, &c. These are not only used by them for food, but are bartered with the Company's servants for articles of use and ornament, such as blankets, tobacco,.ammunition, and trinkets.

From this fort, to obviate the necessity of passing up the Sound, then westward up the Fuca Straits, and thence southward to the mouth of the Columbia, and crossing the bar in a vessel, there is a portage-way across the land, the distance being about ninety miles from this to the banks of the Cowlitz River. This river runs from the northern interior into the Columbia, about forty-nine miles below Fort Vancouver, in a south-westerly direction. At the end of this portage, on the river's banks, there is a British settlement, principally composed of retired Hudson's Bay traders.

Frazer's River rises in the Rocky Mountains, between latitudes 55 and 56 deg. north,
near the source of Canoe River (which is the
first large tributary of the Columbia after the
latter issues from its source), and at first runs
about north-west for a distance of about eighty
miles. It then takes a southerly direction, receiving the waters of Stuart's River, which rises
in one of the chains of lakes that abound in all
Columbia. It continues its southern course by
west, receiving the waters of the Chilcotin,
Pinklitsa, and several other minor rivers flowing
from the lakes or hills of the west, and also the
waters of Thompson's River, Quisnell's River,
and others which flow into it from the east.
In parallel 49 deg. it breaks through the cascade range of mountains, a continuation of the
Sierra Nevada, in a succession of falls and rapids,
and running westward is emptied into the Gulf
of Georgia in 49 deg. 7 min. north. During
this latter part of its course, as far up as Fort
Yale, it is navigable for vessels, after passing its
bar, that draw not more than twelve feet of water.
Its direct length across country is about four
hundred miles. But taking its irregular winding

course into consideration it is nearly nine hundred miles long. The country along its lower section is hilly, and covered with forests of white pine, cedar, and other evergreens, while the soil is generally well fitted for pasturage, and in many places for tillage. But along the other and more southern sections the country is more ungenial and unproductive, being cut up by mountains, ravines, torrents, lakes, and marshes. Yet it is well wooded, yielding all the varieties of trees growing in that region, fir, spruce, willow, cedar, cypress, birch, and alder. The climate is very variable, and the transitions, though periodically regular, are remarkably sudden, if not violent.

During the spring, which lasts from April till June, the weather and the face of the country are delightful. In June there are occasional rains, drifted along by a strong south wind; and in July and August the heat is intense, while the ground, previously saturated with moisture, produces myriads of flies and other insects.

This heat and glaring sunshine are sometimes succeeded in September by fogs of such palpable darkness, that until noon it is seldom possible to distinguish objects at a longer distance than one hundred yards. In November the winter sets in, mildly freezing the lakes and smaller rivers. The cold, however, is not so intense as might be imagined in such a country and climate, being far less severe than that of any part of Canada.

The country is easy of access from Nisqually to the Chetreels River, when the soil changes from gravelly loam to a stiff clay ; and numerous little rivers which overflow their banks and flood the country for an immense distance during the winter and spring freshets, render the land journey to the Cowlitz River difficult ; and during that season, to all, save gold diggers, who are undauntable, almost impracticable.

A few settlers have lately been located on this route, and the Americans had formed a village as far north as Puget's Sound ten years ago. Simultaneously with the latter, a settlement of Canadians was formed on the Cowlitz River, where the Puget's Sound Company had about one thousand acres of land under cultivation. The course of the Cowlitz is irregular and rapid, and at high-water dangerous, but the obstacles are such as the Canadian boatmen can

guard against and overcome.   An establishment
has been formed by the Hudson's Bay Company
at the mouth of this river, in which wheat and
other produce is stored and shipped in large
quantities to the Russian settlement at Sitka,
and to the Sandwich Islands.

Coal abounds over the whole of the north-
eastern territory ; that is to say, from Cheslaker's,
latitude 50 deg. 36 min., to Cape Scott at its
southern extremity.

On the borders of M'Neil's Harbour the coal
juts out above the surface.   The beds are divided by intermediate layers of sandstone, and are
seen most distinctly on the open beach, extending over about a mile in length, generally within
the line of high water ; the mineral having evidently been laid bare by the wash of the sea,
which has frittered and worn away the incum-
bent mould and sandstone.

A fresh-water rivulet which runs across the
bed, in a direction perpendicular to the beach,
has also laid bare a transverse section of the coal
to the distance of nearly a mile from the sea;
shewing that the bed runs in a nearly horizontal
direction as far as that point, beyond which the

depth of the strata has not been reliably ascertained.

The coal can be worked at a comparatively small expense over a field of such extent. Some of it has been brought to England, and answered exceedingly well in forges. Externally it is hard and brittle, interspersed with sulphuret of iron, and it contains but little earthy or incombustible matter ; it, however, burns better in furnaces than elsewhere, and in small quantities.

In the upper and consequently colder regions of British Columbia, the most fertile spots flank the rivers, the thermometer sometimes falls 22 deg. below zero ; but the seasons are milder than in the same parallel east of the Rocky Mountains.

The summer is there never very hot, although fires can be dispensed with from the end of May till the beginning of September. Snow covers the ground from December to April, and at an average depth of two feet.

This elevated part of the North American continent is inhabited by the two great Indian nations of the north—the Takali or Carrier Indians, and the Atnalis or Shouswaps.

The Carriers live principally upon salmon, and prefer their meat putrid; for which end they bury it for months under ground, till it becomes a mass of corruption, when it is eaten and esteemed a delicacy. They are quick tempered, but neither sullen nor revengeful, and are singularly susceptible of ridicule. Their heads present a somewhat oval appearance, owing to the practice amongst them of flattening, during infancy, by artificial means, the craniums of their children.

The Hudson's Bay Company have several river posts, or stations in this upper territory.

The country is too humid for the growth of the finest wool; but much of a coarser nature, and well adapted for commerce, has and may be cultivated with profit.

In Quen Charlotte's Island, which is included in the new colony, gold was discovered in 1850, but only in small quantities.

The discovery of gold on the mainland was first reported to the Colonial Office by a dispatch from the Governor of Vancouver's Island, dated April the 16th, 1856. His words were,— " From experiments made in the Frazer River, there is reason to believe that the gold region is extensive." In that year he granted licenses to dig in the Frazer and Thompson Rivers.

In 1857 the license fees were raised from 10s. to 20s. per month, and persons were prohibited from digging without authority from the colonial goverment. But the prohibition remained a dead letter, as it was found that the Governor had no authority to issue such proclamations, he having no commission as Governor on the main land.

In 1858 the Governor wrote to the Hudson's Bay Company, expressing a hope that her Majesty's government would take measures to protect life and property, otherwise there would be many difficulties; as a large number of Americans had entered the territory, and others were about to follow in rapid succession.

Those who were now hastening to that land only went in search of sudden gain, and it was therefore proposed at home to establish only a temporary government.

On the 29th of July, the bill as originally proposed, for the future government of British Columbia, was read a third time and passed; by this measure the Governor of Vancouver's Island is conditionally empowered, for the period of five years, to appoint such legislature as he may think fit for the due administration of the terms of the new bill (for copy, see Appendix) ; the two colonies in the meantime to remain entirely distinct, unless it should be otherwise enacted by the home government.

Goods may be shipped in London, and carried without transhipment to the western shores of Lake Superior. This has been effected by rendering, among other things, the St. Lawrence navigable by ships of high tonnage. The English are now further across the great continent of America than the Americans themselves.

The line of route from Halifax to Lake Superior exceeds in extent any possessed by the United States ; and it is proposed to carry a railway completely across the continent, so that direct communication would be established between England and Vancouver's Island by way of Halifax.

With the view of opening a communication by railway or canal between Lake Superior and the Pacific, it has been suggested that the system adopted by the United States in the formation of a certain ship canal, might be resorted to by the British government with every likelihood of success. One hundred and eighty thousand

acres of land were set aside in the State of Mi-
chigan, and were given in trust for those who
made the canal, on condition that they finished
it ; and as the work advanced and money was
required, part of the land was sold, and supplied
funds for continuing the undertaking.

It was found that the sale of these lands,
made infinitely more valuable by the proximity
of the canal itself, fully remunerated the share-
holders for their task and outlay of construction ;
and it would not be at all difficult to set aside
reserves of land along the line, from Lake Superior to the Pacific, and apply that to complete
the communication between those two points.

With the exception of a single rapid (which
might be avoided by a canal), the navigation of
the Saskatchewan river offers no impediment.
With this one exception, a vessel of considerable
size could be taken up to the foot of the Rocky
Mountains ; and at this point there is a gap in the
mountains, which would interpose no great obstacle in the way of a junction between the Columbia and the Saskatchewan, whose sources are
but a little distance apart.   Thus a communication with the Pacific would be established.

This colossal design, with the aid of skill and capital, will be, without doubt, eventually achieved unless, indeed, we should become a race of aeronauts, and sail about in balloons, or fly with talismans instead of being drawn over land and ocean by steam.

It is hard to say where the march of improvement may carry us to ; but even calculating by our present standard of inventions, the feasability of the suggestion just made is complete.

With respect to the territory embraced in our El Dorado, over which the authority of the Hudson's Bay Company extends, it is a somewhat peculiar historical circumstance that England herself did not acquire exclusive possession of it until the treaty of Utrecht, in 1713, yet it was given away by Charles the Second, under charter, in 1670. Glancing over the vast regions devoted to the fur trade, the area of which is as large as that of all Europe, the first idea is that of amazement, that so large a portion of the earth's surface, and that under the British sceptre, should have been so long abandoned as a mere hunting ground. Government, however, will not renew the license of the Hudson's Bay Company over any part of

D

the North American territory, which promises
early colonization ; but it is reserved for further
deliberation, whether they will renew it for a
limited period over the more remote and northern
regions, taking care that the government shall
have always the power to withdraw from that
license any land that may be required for the
purposes of civilization ; that they shall retain
all imperial rights to fisheries, and to mines, and
whatever may call forth human industry and enterprise, in pursuits more congenial to our tastes
and wants, than the barren trade in skins, which
carries us back to times without a history.

Already in the large territory which extends
west of the Rocky Mountains, from the American frontier up to the skirts of the Russian do-
mains, Great Britain is laying the mighty foundation of what will become a magnificent abode
for the human race. And now, eastward of the
Rocky Mountains, we are invited to see in the
settlement of the Red River the nucleus of a
new colony, a rampart against any hostile inroads from the American frontier, and an essential arch, as it were, to that great viaduct, by
which it is to be hoped we may one day, and that

not very remote, connect the harbours of Vancouver with the Gulf of St. Lawrence.

With regard to the safety of the Red River settlement from an attack from the United States quarter, the population numbers about eight thousand five hundred, of which two thousand are English, Irish, and Scotch, the remainder consisting of half breeds. They are good shots, and capital horsemen. A local militia of at least one thousand men could be readily embodied at any time. The post is easy of defence, unless against heavy ordnance, which it would be difficult to bring up against it ; but the position might be rendered impregnable.

I have thus made allusion to the Red River settlement, owing to the probability of its becoming an intermediate station, and city of high importance in our future overland traffic between Canada and British Columbia ; as, from its geographical position, it is well adapted for, being without a rival; and as we have before said, the solitary oasis in the wilderness east of the Rocky Mountains.

CHAPTER VI.

HISTORICAL SKETCHES.

IN the year 1497, and under the patronage of Henry VII., when the discoveries of Columbus had awoke the spirit of adventure in England, an expedition was fitted out from Bristol under the command of one Cabot, a merchant. This enterprise resulted in the discovery of Newfoundland, and an exploration of the coast from Labrador to Virginia. Thus the English were the next followers of the Spanish in the new world. This opened the way for other adventurers, and in 1608, the French, under Cartier, penetrated as far as the Island of Montreal, where they founded a colony. After that, the wildest and most seemingly inaccessible country was explored, and a trade at once sprung up between the Indians and the whites.

In 1610, the English, in the person of John Hudson, explored the so-named Hudson's Bay, nine hundred miles in length, by six hundred in greatest breadth. Both nations soon joined in the traffic with the natives for skins and furs, the trade rapidly grew, and immense profits accrued to those engaged in it. The white man plunged into the as yet unknown wilderness, and by the gift of trifling baubles procured all that the Red man could give. Montreal became the chief mart of this traffic.

Hordes of Indians came down periodically in their canoes, laden with the spoils of the hunting season—unloaded their primitive crafts, which they drew up on the beach, and formed encampments outside the town, where, with much show of native ceremony, they held fairs for the disposal of their produce. They would ask an audience of the Governor-General, who would respond to their application, and hold the conference with some pomp, seated in an arm

chair—which for the time being he felt a throne
—while the Indians would squat round him in
a semicircle, smoking pipes. Speeches and
presents would be exchanged, and then the
meeting would break up. When the work of
barter, in which knives, axes, kettles, and blankets took the place of money, was over, the
aborigines would strike their tents, launch their
canoes, and ply their way back into the interior.
At this primitive period a class of men called
Coureurs des Bois, or Rangers of the Woods,
sprung up. These would set out well stocked
with wares suited to the Indian tastes and
wants, and make their way along the rivers far
into the primeval wilderness, and by the attraction of their goods create new wants and habi-
tudes among the natives, assimilating themselves
meanwhile for months to the habits and customs
of the various tribes. They would often clothe
themselves in skins, and travel with Indian
wives. As, however, civilization leaves behind nothing but its vices amongst an aboriginal people,
so these men did not fail in their intercourse
with the red men to contaminate and vitiate
both physically and morally. Subsequently the

French issued orders prohibiting all persons, on pain of death, from trading in the interior of the country without a license; this, however, failed to abolish the traffic referred to, and it therefore continued long after, to the great detriment of the native population, who revelled away in unsightly drunkenness, pitiable victims of " Old Tom," supplied by these outlaws of civilization.

Sixty years later, the Hudson's Bay Company, in the person of Prince Rupert, obtained their charter. In 1794, the United States and Great Britain signed a treaty of commerce and navigation, when an extensive and regular trade, solely in furs, set in with redoubled force between the Americans and the Indian tribes of the Mississippi and Lake Superior. About this period the great North West Fur Company, and subsequently the Pacific Russian-American Fur Company, the latter originated by a wealthy New Yorker, one John Jacob Astor, commenced operations, when fearful rivalry, often involving bloodshed, ensued between them and the established Hudson's Bay Company; the three companies, however, became amalgamated by the intervention of the British government in 1819.

In 1821, an act of Parliament was passed, under which the crown granted to the then amalgamated companies, trading under the title of the Hudson's Bay Company, a license of exclusive trade " over all those tracts that might not be included in the original charter, and also over those tracts which by mutual consent were equally open to the subjects of England and the United States."

It was this license, which, on the 30th of May, 1838, was renewed for the space of twenty-one years, and which consequently terminates on that day 1859.

CHAPTER VII.

THE OASIS IN THE WILDERNESS.

As it is not improbable that the influx of population at one part of the coast will extend its influence to the other settlements of that region, a brief sketch of the Red River settlement, which I visited some years back, may not be unacceptable. Originally established by the Scotch of the Hudson's Bay Company in 1812, it, from its singularity of character and position, lies as an oasis in the vast wilderness of a savage region. It is situated in the fiftieth degree of north latitude, and the ninety-seventh of west longitude, and at an elevation of about a thousand feet above the level of the sea, and near

the confluence of the Red and Assinaboine
Rivers, whose united waters run northward about
thirty miles into lake Winnipeg, which also re-
ceives many other tributary streams. Those two
rivers flow through a vast extent of country,
fertile, and redundant of vegetation, and of salubrious climate. The Red River rises in the
United States, near the sources of the Mississippi,
and runs northward; the Assinaboine flows
from the north-west. The cold season lasts
about five months, from November till April ;
but the ice on lake Winnipeg does not break up
till May. The range of the settlement stretches
upwards of fifty miles along the romantic and
woody banks of those rivers. Their borders
are cultivated to the breadth of more than a
mile ; all the back country remaining to a great
extent in its original state—a vast natural pasture, covered during the greater part of the year
with cattle, and furnishing the colonists with a
considerable quantity of hay for the support of
their herds during the winter.

Horses, horned cattle, hogs, and poultry, are
exceedingly numerous. Sheep introduced from
England and the United States speckle the

landscape, and are reared with great success.
Wheat, barley, oats, beans, peas, maise, potatoes,
turnips, and culinary vegetables thrive well.
Pumpkins, melons, and cucumbers arrive at
maturity in the open air.   Hops, as also flax and
hemp, grow luxuriously.   The most common
sorts of wood are oak, poplar, elm, and maple ;
pines are found towards lake Winnipeg.   On
this lake vessels ply in summer between the
colony and the Hudson's Bay Company's entre-
pôt of Norway House, which is situated at its
northern extremity, where the river navigation
to Hudson's Bay commences, the lake empty-
ing itself into the latter by the Nelson River.

There are two principal churches, the Protes-
tant and Roman Catholic, the latter a bishopric,
and these, together with the jail, the bishop's
residence, the offices of the Hudson's Bay Company, and many of the houses of those retired
officers of the fur trade who prefer remaining
here to returning to their native country, are
built of stone.   The generality of the settlers,
however, live in frame or log houses roofed with
wooden slabs, bark, or shingles, which are for the
most part whitewashed, or painted externally.

Every man, however low his condition, possesses a horse, and each vies with the other in gay curricles, harness, saddle, and fine clothes.

Labour is dear, and produce of every kind sells at a higher price than could be expected in a place so remote and secluded. Domestic manufactures are now lessening the demand for imported goods, and a trade in grain and cattle has sprung up between the colonists and the Americans of the level plains leading to the Mississippi and the St. Peter's; while hides, tallow, wool, hemp, and flax, have already been exported to England. Wind and water mills are as common as in Holland, and Crees and Chippeway Indians have settlements at the lower extremity of the colony.

The Red River Settlement is situated partly on the banks of the Red River and partly on the banks of a smaller stream called the Assinaboine, in latitude 50 deg. and extends upwards of fifty miles along the banks of these two streams. The country around it is a vast treeless prairie, upon which scarcely a shrub is to be seen, but a thick coat of grass covers it throughout its entire extent, with the exception of a few spots, where the hollowness of the ground has collected a little moisture, or the meandering of some small stream or rivulet enriches the soil and covers the banks with verdant shrubs and trees. The banks of the Red and Assinaboine Rivers are covered with a thick belt of woodland, which does not, however, extend far back into the plains. It is composed of oak, poplar, willows, and pine, the first of which is much used for firewood by the settlers. The larger timber in the adjacent woods is thus being rapidly thinned, and very soon the inhabitants will have to raft their firewood down the rivers from a considerable distance. The settlers are a mixture of French, Canadians, Scotchmen, and Indians.

In the year 1826, Red River overflowed its banks and flooded the whole settlement, obliging the settlers to forsake their houses and drive their horses and cattle to the hilly eminences in the immediate vicinity. These eminences are few and small, so that during the flood they presented a curious appearance, being crowded with men, women, and children, horses, cattle, sheep, and poultry. The houses being made

of wood, and only built on the ground, not sunk
into it, were carried away by dozens, and great
numbers of horses and cattle were drowned.
During the time it lasted, the settlers sailed and
paddled among their houses in boats and canoes;
and they now point out grassy and bushy spots
where they dwelt in their tents, or paddled about
the deep waters in their canoes in the year of
the flood. This sounds very antediluvian; and
when you hear a hale, middle-aged colonist tell
you with a ludicrously grave countenance that
so-and-so occurred, or that his house stood in
such a place *a year before the flood*, it is hard
to refrain from grinning—pardon the expression.

Fort Garry, the principal establishment of the
Hudson's Bay Company, stands on the banks
of the Assinaboine River, at about two hundred
yards from the junction with Red River. It is
a square, stone building, with bastions pierced
for cannon at the corners. The principal dwell-
ing-houses, stores, and offices are built within
the walls, and the stables at a short distance from
the fort. The situation is pretty and quiet;
but the surrounding country is too flat for the
lover of the grand and picturesque. Just in

front of the lake glides the peaceful Assinaboine, where, on a fine day in autumn, may be
seen thousands of fish (gold eyes) playing in its
waters. On the left extends the woodland,
fringing the river, with here and there a clump
of smaller trees and willows, surrounding the
swamps formed by the melting snows of spring,
where flocks of wild ducks and noisy plovers
give animation to the scene, while through the
openings in the forest are seen glimpses of the
rolling prairie. Down in the hollow, where the
stables stand, a few horses and cows are always
to be seen, feeding or lazily chewing their cud
in the rich pasturage, giving an air of repose
to the landscape which contrasts forcibly with
the view of the wide plains that spread out
like a sea of green from the back of the fort,
studded here and there with little islets and
hillocks, around which may be seen hovering a
watchful hawk or solitary raven.

The climate of Red River is salubrious and
agreeable. Winter commences about the middle of November, and spring begins in April.
Although the winter is very long and extremely
cold (the thermometer usually varying between

ten and thirty degrees below zero), yet from its being always a dry frost, it is much more agreeable than those accustomed to the damp, hazy weather of Great Britain might suppose. Winter is here the liveliest season of the year, as it is in Canada. It is then that the wild, demi-savage colonist leads the blushing, 'half-breed' girl to the altar, and the country surrounding his house rings with the joyful music of the sleigh bells. It is at this season that the hardy *voyajeurs* rest from their toil, and circling round the blazing fire, recount many a tale of danger, and paint many a wild, romantic scene of their long and tedious voyages among the lakes and rapids of the far interior, while their wives and children gaze with breathless interest upon their swarthy, sun-burnt faces, lighted up with animation as they recall the scenes of other days, or with low and solemn voice relate the death of a friend and fellow-voyajeur, who perished among the foaming cataracts of the wilderness.

Generally speaking, the weather is serene and calm, particularly in autumn, and during that delicious season peculiar to America, called the Indian summer, which precedes the com-

mencement of winter. The scenery of Red
River is neither grand nor picturesque, yet when
the sun shines brightly on the waving grass, and
glitters on the silver stream, and when the distant and varied cries of wildfowl break in plain-
tive cadence on the ear, a sweet, exulting feeling
of happiness steals upon the mind, comforting,
grateful, and refreshing, making the beholder
feel that even the so-called oasis in the wilderness of North America is not without its charms,
and that life may be enjoyed wherever content-
ment prevails, and hope-buoyed enterprise holds
sway.

CHAPTER VIII.

OVERLAND RAILWAY AND OTHER COMMUNICA-
TION BETWEEN CANADA, THE UNITED STATES,
AND BRITISH COLUMBIA.

As to the probability of a railway being constructed from Canada to some point of British
Columbia, through the natural gap in the Rocky
Mountains between Mount Hooker and Mount
Brown, or elsewhere, there can be but little
doubt. The commerce of the two countries
demands that such a communication should be
established, and that with the least possible
delay. Various suggestions have been made,
having reference to the line of route; that

through the Red River settlement being the most feasible as well as the most desirable, both on account of the termini being in British territory, as well as on account of the ulterior advantages likely to accrue to us from its being constructed by means of British capital, and under the auspices of the British Government. It is necessary, however, that a company should be forthwith organized for the undertaking, otherwise it is not only likely, but certain, that American enterprise will be usurping the privilege, and we shall have an iron way stretching across the mighty wilderness, not from Canada, but from the territory of the United States.

With respect to present overland communication between the latter and British Columbia, St. Paul, Minnesota, near the Canadian border, appears to be the most desirable starting point; it has also the advantage of being situated on the chosen highway between England and the Red River settlement. But as to whether it will become the seat of the proposed railway, in the event of the Americans taking the lead of us in that respect, is a matter for future deliberation. In the meantime, the following par-

ticulars of the line of waggon route and natural
features of the country may not prove uninte-
resting :—

As we are all aware, it is now established that
a district of British Oregon, holding a relation
to Puget's Sound similar to that of the Sacramento Valley to the Bay of San Francisco, contains rich and extensive gold placers.

The upper waters of Frazer River, including
its principal tributary, Thompson River, are
eagerly sought by adventurers from Oregon and
California, and all accounts concur that the
surface minings are as successful as those of
California and Australia have been.   Geologists
have anticipated such a discovery, and Governor
Stevens, in his last message to the Legislative
Assembly of Washington Territory, claims that
a district south of the international boundary is
equally auriferous.

The southern boundary of Minnesota is in
latitude 43½ deg. north.   St. Paul and the
Falls of St. Anthony are about 45 deg., and
the northern boundary, coterminous with the
international line, is partly on the parallel of
49 deg.   The Frazer River mines will probably

be explored from latitude 49 to 55 deg. ; therefore, if an overland emigrant route thither is practicable from Minnesota, it will be an important consideration in favour of such a route, that the valleys of the upper Mississippi and the Red River of the north are on the most direct line of communication from Canada and the States north of latitude 40 deg. to the Frazer River district.

An overland route through Minnesota, ascending the course of the Saskatchewan, and crossing the Rocky Mountains in latitude 54 deg. to British Oregon, would traverse a region of North America hitherto withheld from colonization, but soon to be surrendered by the Hudson's Bay Company for civilized settlements. West of the Rocky Mountains that company claim no chartered rights, and their license of Indian trade will expire in May, 1859. The British Parliament have published a " Report of a Select Committee of the House of Commons," which exhibits a disposition on the part of the company to withdraw from an immense district, reaching west of Lake Winnepeg to the Pacific, if thereby a recognition of the exclusive privileges hitherto enjoyed by them within the remainder of their chartered limits can be obtained. Even such a compromise is vigorously opposed by the people of Canada, but the citizens of Minnesota would have reason to be satisfied if their north-western connection with Assimboia, Saskatchewan, and British Oregon should be placed on the footing of such an adjustment. Henceforth no other relation than "reciprocity" is possible between British America and the adjacent States of the American Union. The latter especially welcome the assurance that Victoria, the capital of Vancouver's Island, is to be selected as the naval station of England in the Pacific, perhaps to become, under the influence of an international railroad, the Liverpool of the Pacific coast.

As to the " adventurers of England trading into Hudson's Bay" (so the stockholders of the company are technically called in the charter of incorporation), they can with the, as yet doubtful, consent of Parliament, turn their partial defeat into a victory. The map of Arrowsmith exhibits their posts at every advantageous locality between the lakes and the Pacific, and between latitudes 49 and 56 deg. Open that immense belt of country to European and American colonization — extend over it the benefits of reciprocity—adopt the American system of land-surveys and land-bounties to settlers, and the members of the Hudson's Bay Company if they are to have another lease of life over the upper territories not yet discovered to be auriferous, would receive more advantage in ten years as proprietors of cities and towns, than would be possible for them as fur traders in a century. But if they do get a partial renewal of their charter, let it be granted on the absolute condition of their adopting measures calculated to foster, and not as hitherto, to repel and keep back colonization.

Encouraged by the London Geographical Society, if not by the government, Capt. Palliser has led an exploring party to the sources of the South Saskatchewan, and the passes westward through the Rocky Mountains. Colonel Elliott, at the head of fifty engineers and as many soldiers, has recently arrived at Van-

couver Island, and, accompanied by a hundred
voyagers, will thence move eastward through
British territory, definitely locating a railroad
route as he advances. Simultaneously, a joint
commission of the American and English governments are engaged in running the international boundary from Puget's Sound to Lake
Superior, commencing at the Pacific terminus.
And now comes the gold discovery of the
north west, which will probably renew, if not
outvie, in that direction, the wonderful history
of California and Australia.

An overland route from St. Paul, on American territory, to Puget's Sound, or through the
Saskatchewan basin to Frazer River and Vancouver's Island, is central to an immense and
fertile area, which, at no remote day, must
connect with the channels of the Mississippi
and the St. Lawrence, within the limits of
Minnesota. From lat. 44 to 54 deg., and from
longitude 92 to 112 deg. (west of Greenwich),
or between Lake Superior and Winnepeg on
the east, and the Rocky Mountains, there is
comprised an area of 631,050 square miles.

Extend these lines of latitude to the Pacific, in longitude 124, and we have a further area of 378,636 square miles, or an aggregate of 1,009,686 square miles, equal in extent to France, Germany, Prussia, Austria, and that portion of Russia which lies south of St. Petersburg and west of Moscow. A district 10 degrees of latitude wide by 32 of longitude in length, would comprise twenty-four states of the size of Ohio.

Our present inquiry, however, is confined to the upper half of this vast region, or exclusively north of the boundary of forty-nine degrees; and since an emigrant route to Frazer River is under consideration, a general view of the districts to be traversed by such a route, or closely connected with it, will first be presented. Those districts of British America west of the lakes, which by soil and climate are suitable for settlement, may be thus enumerated :—

	square miles.
Vancouver's Island	16,000
Frazer and Thompson Rivers	60,000
Sources of the Upper Columbia	20,000
Athabaska District	50,000
Saskatchewan, Red River, Assineboin, &c.	360,000
	506,200

E

Under these geographical divisions—whose area would constitute twelve States of the size of Ohio—I propose to give the results of a parliamentary investigation, recently published, into the affairs of the Hudson's Bay Company, so far as they are descriptive of the foregoing districts :—

VANCOUVER'S ISLAND.

This island is fertile, well timbered, finely diversified by intersecting mountain ranges and small prairies, with extensive coal fields, compared by one witness to the West Riding of Yorkshire coal, and fortunate in its harbours. Esquimault Harbour, on which Victoria is situated, is equal to San Francisco. The salmon and other fisheries are excellent; but this advantage is shared by every stream and inlet of the adjacent coast. The climate is frequently compared with England, except that it is even warmer. The winter is stormy, with heavy rains in November and December; frosts occur in the lowlands in January, but seldom interrupt agriculture; vegetation starts in February, rapidly progressing in March, and fostered by alternate warm showers and sunshine in April and May —while intense heat and drought are often experienced during June, July, and August. As already remarked, the island has an area of sixteen thousand two hundred square miles, and is as large as Vermont and New Hampshire.

FRAZER AND THOMPSON RIVERS.

Northward of Vancouver's Island, the coast range of mountains trends so near the Pacific as to obstruct intercourse with the interior, but it is a fine open country. This is the valley of Frazer River. Ascending this river, near Fort Langley, a large tract of land is excellently adapted to colonists; while of Thompson River, it is one of the most beautiful countries in the world, with a climate capable of producing all the crops of England, and much milder than Canada. The sources of Frazer River, in latitude fifty-five degrees, are separated from those of Peace River, (which flows through the Rocky Mountains eastwardly, into the Athabasca,) by the distance of only three hundred and seventeen yards.

E 2

SOURCES OF THE COLUMBIA.

A glance at the map will show how considerable a district of British Oregon is watered by
the Upper Columbia and its tributary, the
McGillivray or Flat-bow River. It is estimated
above as twenty thousand square miles, and has
been described in enthusiastic terms by the Catholic Bishop of Oregon—De Smet— in his " Oregon Missions." The territory of the Kootonais
Indians would seem, from his glowing description, to be divided into favourable proportion
between forests and prairies. Of timber, he
names birch, pine of different species, cedar, and
cypress. He remarked specimens of coal, and
" great quantities of lead," apparently mixed
with silver. The source of the Columbia seemed
to impress him as " a very important point."
He observes that " the climate is delightful"—
that the extremes of heat and cold are seldom
known, the snow disappearing as it falls. He
reiterates the opinion, " that the advantages nature
seemed to have bestowed on the Columbia, will
render its geographical position very important
at some future day, and that the hand of civi-

lized man would transform it into a terrestrial paradise."

It is an interesting coincidence that Father De Smet published in a St. Louis (American) paper, a few months since, a similar description of this region, adding that it could be reached from Salt Lake City, along the western base of the Rocky Mountains, with waggons, and that Brigham Young proposed to lead his next Mormon exodus to the sources of the Columbia river. Such a movement is not improbable, and would exhibit far greater sagacity than an emigration to Sonora.

Already the Mormons — obnoxious though they be—have established a flourishing half-way post on the Salmon River, (a branch of the Columbia); and as De Smet has had many opportunities for ascertaining the designs of the Mormon hierarchy, the next scene of their zeal and industry—should they still exist—may be under the protection of the British crown.

THE ATHABASCA DISTRICT.

The valley of the Peace and Athabasca Rivers, which occupy the eastern base of the Rocky Mountains from lat. 55 to 59 deg., share the

Pacific climate in a remarkable degree. The Rocky Mountains are greatly reduced in breadth and mean elevation, and through the numerous passes between their lofty peaks the winds of the Pacific reach the district in question. Hence it is that Sir Alexander Mackenzie, under date of May 10, mentions the " exuberant verdure of the whole country," trees about to blossom, and buffaloes attended by their young. During the late Parliamentary investigation, similar statements were elicited. Dr. Richard King, who accompanied an expedition in search of Sir John Ross, as " surgeon and naturalist," was asked what portion of the country he saw was available for the purpose of settlement. In reply, he described as a " very fertile valley," a " square piece of country," bounded on the south by Cumberland-house, and by the Athabasca Lake on the north. His own words are as follow: " The sources of the Athabasca and the sources of the Saskatchewan include an enormous area of country;—it is, in fact, a vast piece of land surrounded by water. When I heard Dr. Livingston's description of that splendid country which he found in the interior of Africa within the equator, it appeared to me to be precisely the kind of country which I am now describing. . . . It is a rich soil, interspersed with well wooded country, there being growth of every kind, and the whole vegetable kingdom alive." When asked concerning mineral productions, his reply was, " I do not know of any other mineral except limestone; this is apparent in all directions. . . . The birch, the beech, and the maple are in abundance, and there is every sort of fruit." When questioned further as to the growth of trees, Dr. King replied by a comparison " with the magnificent trees round Kensington Park, in London." He described a farm near Cumberland-house under very successful cultivation— " luxuriant wheat " — potatoes, barley, pigs, cows, and horses.

THE SASKATCHEWAN, ASSINEBOIN AND RED RIVER DISTRICT.

The area of this continent, north-west of Minnesota, and known as the Saskatchewan district, is estimated by English authorities to comprise three hundred and sixty-eight thousand square miles. North-west from Otter-fall Lake, the

geographical centre of Minnesota, extends a vast
silurian formation, bounded on the west along
the eastern base of the Rocky Mountains by coal
measures. Such a predominance of limestone
implies fertility of soil, as in the north-western
states, and the speedy colonization of Saskatchewan would be assured, if the current objection
to the severity of the climate was removed.   On
this point I shall offer a few illustrative facts.

The Sea of Azof, which empties into the
Black Sea, forming the eastern border of the
Crimean peninsula, freezes about the beginning
of November, and is seldom open before the beginning of April. A point less than one hundred miles north, but far down in Southern
Russia, namely, Catherineoslay, has been found,
from the observation of many years, to be identical in summer and winter climate with Fort
Snelling. Nine-tenths of European Russia, therefore—the main seat of population and resources
—is further north than St. Paul.   In fact,
Pembina is the climate equivalent of Moscow,
and for that of St. Petersburg, (which is sixty
degrees north) we may reasonably go to latitude
fifty-five degrees on the American continent.

Like European Russia, also, the Saskatchewan district has a climate of extremes—the thermometer having a wide range ; but it is well understood that the growth of the cereals and of the most useful vegetables depends chiefly on the intensity and duration of the summer heats, and is comparatively little influenced by the severity of winter cold, or the lowness of the mean temperature during the year. Therefore it is important to observe that the northern shore of Lake Huron has the mean summer heat of Bourdeaux, in southern France, or seventy degrees Fahrenheit, while Cumberland-house, in latitude fifty-four degrees, longitude one hundred and two degrees, on the Saskatchewan, exceeds in this respect Brussels and Paris.

The United States' Army Meterological Register has ascertained that the line of 70 deg. mean summer heat crosses the Hudson river at West Point, thence descends to the latitude of Pittsburg, but westward is traced through Sandusky, Chicago, Fort Snelling, and Fort Union, near latitude 49 deg., into British America. The average annual heat at Quebec is experienced as

E 3

far north as latitude 52 deg. in the Saskatchewan country.

It is justly claimed that, not only all the vicinity of the south branch of the Saskatchewan is as mild in climate as St. Paul, but that the north branch of that river is almost equally favourable, and that the ameliorating influence of the Pacific, through the gorges of the Rocky Mountains, is so far felt on M'Kenzie's river, that wheat may be grown in its valley nearly to the 65th parallel.

I have quoted the foregoing details in order to exhibit the general features and advantages of the country which extends between Minnesota and the gold regions of the North Pacific. It now remains for me to arrange the facts relative to the journey thither by the route of Pembina and the Saskatchewan

The journey from St. Paul to Pembina is familiarly known and easy of travel. From Pembina to the junction of Moose river with the Assineboin there is a well-defined track over a plain, such as Sir George Simpson describes on the way to the same point from Fort Garry. Under date of July 3d, he says :—" On the east,

north, and south there was not a mound or a tree
to vary the vast expanse of the greensward,
while to the west (it would be to the north of
our advancing party) were the gleaming bays
of the Assineboin, separated from each other by
wooded points of considerable depth."

Gov. Simpson, with relays of horses, made
the journey to Carlton-house in thirteen days,
about forty-six miles per day. Commencing
with his diary of the third day from Fort Garry
(at the point where a party from Pombina would
intersect his trail), such extracts I shall make as
seem to embody useful information.

July 5.—On resuming our journey we passed
among tolerably well-wooded hills, while on either
side of us lay a constant succession of small lakes
—some of them salt—which abounded in wild
fowl. In the neighbourhood of these waters the
pastures were rich and luxuriant; and we traversed two fields (for so they might be termed)
of the rose and the sweet briar. On reaching
the summit of the hills that bounded the pretty
valley of the Rapid River, we descried an encampment, which proved lodges of Saulteaux Indians
We spent an hour in fording the stream. No

assistance from the Indians, but unmolested by them.

July 6.—A good supper of wild fowl, which were very numerous in the small lakes still along the route—a large salt lake — hilly and well wooded district—complaints of mosquitoes.

July 7.—Passed Bird's Tail Creek, a rapid flowing tributary of the Assineboin—beyond this stream an undulating prairie of vast extent—bands of antelopes—ferried over the Assineboin to Fort Ellice in the batteau, swimming the horses — leaving the fort, passed through a swampy wood, forded the Qu Appelle or Culling River, and surmounting a steep hill, encamped on a level meadow of several thousand acres in extent.

July 8. — Extensive prairies, studded with clumps of trees — considerable inconvenience with regard to provisions, from heat of the weather — antelopes in sight — in the afternoon the country swampy and beset with underwood.

July 9.—Prairie harder and more open—grass withering under recent drought—more antelopes—circuit of a swamp near Broken Arm River, losing a few hours.

July 10.—Forded White Sand River with the mud up to the bellies of the horses—hitherto weather dry, clear, and warm, but a cool rain fell afternoon and night—saw a red deer.

July 11.—During the night a serenade by wolves and foxes—an early start and a glimpse of an object eagerly looked for—the Butteaux Chiens, towering with a height of about four hundred feet over a boundless prairie as level and smooth as a pond — evidently once the bed of a lake, with the Dog Knoll as an islet in the centre—and which was covered with an alluvial soil of great fertility.

On leaving the Dog Knoll, the party traversed about twenty miles of prairie among several large and beautiful lakes. The cavalcade now consisted in all, of nineteen persons, fifty horses, and six carts, with the following order of march:—the guide was followed by four or five horsemen to beat a track; then came the carts, each with a driver, and lastly followed unmounted animals under the charge of the rest of the party.

July 12 — Followed for twenty miles the shores of " Lac Sale," having water as briny as the Atlantic. The most curious circumstance with respect to these saline lakes is, that they are often separated from the fresh water only by a narrow belt of land. For three or four days the soil had been absolutely manured with the dung of the buffalo, but the animal had not been met.

July 13.—Marched until ten o'clock in a soaking rain. In the afternoon travelled a long distance through a picturesque country, crossing the end of an extensive lake, whose gently sloping banks of green sward were covered with thick woods.

Here the party fell upon the trail of emigrants from Red River to Columbia, and thence followed the well-beaten track made by them for both horses and carts.

July 14.—In this part of the country we saw many sorts of birds, geese, loons, pelicans, ducks, cranes, two kinds of snipe, hawks, owls, and gulls; but they were all so remarkably shy, that we were constrained to admire them at a distance. In the afternoon we traversed a beautiful country, with lofty hills and long valley full of sylvan lakes, while the bright green of the surface, as

far as the eye could reach, assumed a foreign
tinge under an uninterrupted profusion of roses
and blue bells. On the summit of one of these
hills we commanded one of the few extensive
prospects we had enjoyed. One range of heights
rose behind another, each becoming fainter as it
receded from the eye, till the farthest was blended
in almost indistinguishable confusion with the
clouds, while the softest vales spread a panorama
of hanging copses and glittering lakes at our
feet.

July 15.—The travellers had now reached the
Bow River, on the south branch of the Saskatchewan, " which," says Simpson, " takes its rise
in the Rocky Mountains near the international
frontier, and is of considerable size, without any
physical impediment of any moment. . . . . . .
At the crossing place the Bow River was about a
third of a mile in width, with a strong current,
and some twenty miles below, falls into the main
Saskatchewan, whence the united streams flow
towards Lake Winnepeg, forming at their mouth
the Grand Rapids, of about three miles in
length."

A smart ride of four or five hours from the

Bow River, through a country very much resembling an English park, brought the party to Fort Carlton, on the Saskatchewan—latitude 53 deg., longitude about 108.

The Saskatchewan, Governor Simpson remarks, is here upwards of a quarter of a mile wide, presenting, as its name implies, a swift current.   It is navigable for boats from Rocky Mountain House, in longitude 116 deg., to Lake Winnepeg, upwards of seven hundred miles in a direct line, but by the actual course of the stream nearly double that distance.   Though above Edmonton the river is much obstructed by rapids, yet from that Fort to Lake Winnepeg it is descended without a portage alike by boats and canoes, while even on the upward voyage the only break in the navigation is the grand rapid already mentioned.

July 17. — After forty-eight hours at Fort Carlton, Governor Simpson's party resumed its journey along the north or left bank of the Saskatchewan.   The first day's route lay over a hilly country, so picturesque in its character that almost every commanding position presented the elements of a picturesque panorama.

July 18.—The hottest day; inconvenience from thirst—encamped at 9 P. M. on a large lake.

July 19.—Overtook the emigrants to the Columbia. In this connection so many particulars of interest are given that I make a liberal extract: — These emigrants consisted of agriculturists and others, principally natives of Red River Settlement. There were twenty-three families, the heads generally being young and active, though a few of them were advanced in life—more particularly one poor woman, upwards of seventy-five years of age, who was tottering after her son to his new home. This venerable wanderer was a native of the Saskatchewan, of which, in fact, she bore the name. She had been absent from this, the land of her birth, for eighteen years; and on catching the first glimpse of the river from the hill near Carlton, she burst, under the influence of old recollections, into a violent flood of tears. During the two days that the party spent at the fort, she scarcely ever left the bank of the stream, appearing to regard it with as much veneration as the Hindoo regards the Ganges. As a

contrast to this superannuated daughter of the
Saskatchewan, the band contained several very
young travellers, who had, in fact, made their
appearance in this world since the commencement of the journey.

Each family had two or three carts, together
with bands of horses, cattle, and dogs. The
men and lads travelled in the saddle, while the
vehicles, which were covered with awnings
against the sun and rain, carried the women and
the young children. As they marched in single
file their cavalcade extended above a mile in
length, and Simpson's party increased the length
of the column by marching in company. The
emigrants were all healthy and happy, living in
the greatest abundance, and enjoying the journey with the highest relish. Before coming up
to these people, evidence had been seen of the
comfortable state of their commissariat, in the
shape of two or three still warm buffaloes, from
which only the tongues and a few other choice bits
had been taken. This spectacle gave the explorers
hopes of soon seeing the animal themselves, and
accordingly it was not long before they saw their
game on either side of the road, grazing or

stalking about in bands of between twenty and a hundred, to the number of about five thousand in all.

July 20.—The first complaint of the scarcity of water—only one supply, from Turtle River, during thirty-six hours. Game abundant — buffalo, beaver, and deer, besides wolves, badgers, and foxes. Returned to the immediate valley of the Saskatchewan, reached Fort Pitt about dark.

July 21.—Crossed to the south bank of the Saskatchewan, and travelled about thirty miles through bolder scenery than formerly. At night, first apprehensions of Indians, expressed by hoppling horses and mounting guard.

July 22.—No water till eleven o'clock, and again in the afternoon; passed over a perfectly arid plain of about twenty-five miles in length, encamping for the night at the commencement of the Chaine des Lacs, a succession of small lakes stretching over a distance of twenty or thirty miles. The journal adds, " During the afternoon we saw our first raspberries ; they proved to be of large size and fine flavour. Two days previously we had feasted on the service-berry or misasquitomis, a sort of cross between the cranberry and black currant, and before leaving Red River we had found wild strawberries ripe."

July 23.—Encamped on the confines of an extensive forest, a tongue of which, stretching away to the northward, is known as Le Grande Pointe. In the afternoon we had come upon a large bed of the eyeberry, or cos quisikoomina, very nearly resembling the strawberry in taste and appearance. It grows abundantly in Russia, and flourishing as it does in the same soils and situations as the strawberry, it would doubtless thrive in England. Nights chilly, dews heavy.

July 24.—Reached Edmonton House. In the vicinity is an extensive plain, covered with a luxuriant crop of the vetch, or wild pea, almost as nutritious a food for cattle and horses as oats. The Saskatchewan here is nearly as wide as the Carlton, while the immediate banks are well wooded, and the country beyond consists of rolling prairies. Coal also is found on its banks.

Governor Simpson's further route was along the eastern base of the Rocky Mountains, to

the sources of the Bow River, or South Saskatchewan, whence he crossed to the head
waters of the McGillivray, or Flat Bow River.
He left his carts at Edmonton, making the
journey to Fort Colville with pack-horses; but
a party destined to Frazer and Thompson
Rivers would find a direct route, but not for
waggons, through the Athabasca Portage to the
Boat Encampment on the Upper Columbia.
This pass is between Mount Hooker and Mount
Brown, and on its divide a small lake, called on
some maps " Committee's Punch-Bowl," sends
its tribute from one end to the Columbia, and
from the other to the Mackenzie.

A witness before the Parliamentary Committee, Mr. John Miles, states that from the
Boat Encampment it is " two days' level walk"
on the head waters of the Columbia before
reaching the mountain—" a good day's walk,
and hard work, too," to reach its summit, and
three days' before getting out of the mountain
ridge altogether.   It seems reasonable to suppose from this testimony that a party might
traverse the Rocky Mountains from Edmonton

House to the head waters of Thompson River
in about twelve days.

The distance from St. Paul to the eastern
border of the gold mines is computed to be
1,650 miles, as follows:—

	Miles.
St. Paul to Pembina	450
Pembina to Carlton House	600
Carlton to Edmonton	400
Edmonton to Thompson River	200
Total	1,650

In view of the facilities afforded by the face
of the country, and a continuous line of Hudson
Bay Company's posts, this journey can be
accomplished in seventy days.

The distance from St. Paul to the gold mines
of Frazer and Thompson Rivers may be put
down as.follows:—

	Miles.
St. Paul to Pembina....................	450
Pembina to Carlton House	600
Carlton to Edmonton .... ·	400
Edmonton to Boat Encampment..........	150
Boat Encampment to Thompson River	50
Making a total distance from St. Paul of	1,650

Estimate of the expense necessary to equip and fit out a party of ten from St. Paul for six months :—

	Dollars.
10 bbls. flour, cost 4 dols. per bbl.	40
5 bbls. pork, cost 18 dols. per bbl.	90
450 lbs. sugar	54
40 lbs. tea, cost 60c. per lb.	24
Sundries	100
Powder and lead	100
10 pairs blankets	100
Goods and implements	100
Teams and vehicles	1,200
Total cost	1,808

St. Paul, Minnesota, has the advantage of three distinct routes, and those more easy and direct than any south of its latitude, viz.: 1. By Pembina, Carlton, Edmonton, Athabasca portage, and the Boat Encampment of the Columbia. 2. By the South Saskatchewan and the Kootanar's Pass to Fort Colville; and 3. By Governor Steven's well-known route on the American side of the international boundary. Each of these routes is more alive with game, better timbered, and bettered watered, as well as being less difficult of travel, than either of those leading

from the Missouri River. Faithful guides are
to be had easily over the entire distance, and
there is no danger of molestation from the
Indians.

CHAPTER IX.

SKETCHES OF INDIAN LIFE — INVASION AND
EXTERMINATION — THE GLORIOUS FUTURE
OF BRITISH COLUMBIA.

THE natives inhabiting the district of Cape
Flattery, the southern entrance to the Straits of
San Juan de Fuca, are the Clatset tribe. They
are numerous, tall of stature, and finely formed.
Their food consists principally of salmon and
wild fowl, of which there is always an abundance. They manufacture their blankets from
the wool of the wild goat, which they weave
with great skill. The sea otter abounds on
this coast, and great numbers are captured by
the natives, who pursue them in their canoes.

F

They have a habit, similar to the members of many tribes of Australia, which is that of thrusting fish bones, bone rings, and other ornaments through the lower division of the nose, and they flatten their heads in a manner similar to the Chinooks and the Indians of the lower Columbia.   They build their huts under the shadow of pine-trees, frowned upon by high and craggy mountains, whose summits are crowned with perennial snow, and they besmear their bodies with salmon-oil and vermilion clay. Further along the straits, and on the north-east side of Vancouver's Island, are to be found the Coquilths.   Further on still, and at the northern extremity of the island, the Newette tribe, a miserable remnant of their former number, hold dominion.   They have been principally reduced in consequence of the inroads of the Indians from the mainland, who, when on their fishing excursions, kidnapped and subsequently enslaved them.

Many years ago, an American vessel was driven ashore at this part of the island by stress of weather, when all hands were murdered, with the exception of the armourer and sail-maker. These the Indians spared, and compelled to join in their war parties. Some months afterwards, one of them died, but the other continued to live on with them for several years before he succeeded in making his condition known to one of the American ship captains who came in to trade. The latter then, fortunately for the other, succeeded in enticing several of the native chiefs on board, where he detained and threatened them with death unless the white man was given up to him. Thus intimidated, they soon had the poor fellow sent on board, to the great delight of the ship's company, who heartily greeted and sympathised with him.

The chiefs often, in the winter months, give feasts to their people; the food consists of dogs flesh, seal, and whale blubber, with berries and various roots, including potatoes, which they cultivate.

They manufacture blankets from the inside bark of the cedar tree. This is soaked in the water for several days, and then beaten between two pieces of bone. They then set the thigh bone of a deer, or a bone of similar size and strength, firmly in a stand, the position being horizontal. On this they lay a large piece of the bark, and keep beating it until it becomes soft like hemp. It is then woven together and dyed with various figures; the colours being extracted from various roots. Each blanket takes two women ten days to complete.

Three distinct tribes occupy the coast opposite Vancouver's Island. They have prominent and regular features, and are each equally well-made and valiant. They have the same partiality for daubing their hair with fish-oil, and their bodies with vermilion clay, as all the tribes of this region. They also paint and otherwise adorn their children, who run about like miniature clowns
—— in dazzling gorgeousness.

The fish spawn which they gather is dried by them on sea leaves, and stored for winter provision. They also take the tender rind from the inside bark of the hemlock tree, and pound it into cakes, which they dry in the sun. Salmon they split down the back, and then smoke and dry it for the same provident purpose. Blankets are made by the women from cedar bark, in the same way as those made by the

Coquilths. They have several villages that they
shift to, at various seasons of the year. Their
winter villages are strong-built houses, particularly those belonging to the chiefs. Here, as
well as in Johnson's Straits, the chiefs entertain
at a public feast the members of their several
tribes. On these occasions the men sit on
benches ranged on one side, while the women
are ranged opposite them. They also give
entertainments to the chiefs of more inland
tribes.

In their marriages, the Indian taking a wife
generally makes her friends presents; a war canoe,
dressed elk skins, beaver skins, and English goods,
such as blankets, ammunition, and trinkets, being
the principal articles, receiving presents in return.
On the wedding day they have a public feast, at
which they dance and sing; sometimes in separate groups, but generally altogether men and
women. In their singing, which is a sort of
irregular chant, they all keep to the same key,
and therefore it is not easy to distinguish any
individual excellence amongst them. In their
dances they throw their bodies into a variety of
fantastic attitudes, and move their hands, keep-

ing time to the music On these occasions
they are decked off in their best dresses and
ornaments.

They have one curious custom in their dances,
which is, that, at stated periods, they keep puff-
ing from a painted tube, one end of which is
inserted in the mouth, the other pointed
upwards, quantities of fine down which flies
about their heads, presenting the imitation of a
snow shower.

During the winter months, these as well
as the neighbouring tribes assemble in great
numbers in the chief's house, for the purpose of
witnessing his personification of various spirits.

He puts on at intervals different dresses, and
large masks entirely covering his head and neck.

The masks are made to open at the mouth
and eyes, by means of secret springs invisible to
the spectators. He dresses for each character
behind a large curtain, drawn quite across the
hut like the drop in a theatre, and then comes
forth and stands on a sort of stage in front of it,
uttering strange noises, and moving the eyes and
mouth horribly, while the spectators, ranged on
benches along the side walls, gaze in alternate

awe and merriment. In one of his characters the rising sun is personated, which the natives describe as a shining man, wearing a radiated crown, and continually walking round the earth, which is stationary. He wears on this occasion a splendid dress of ermine and other valuable furs, and a curiously-constructed mask, set round with seals' whiskers, and feathers, which gradually expand like a fan, and rise and fall like the quills of the porcupine; while from the top of the mask, swans'-down is shaken out in numerous and varied flakes, according to the movement of his head. The expanding seals' bristles and feathers represent the sun's rays; and the showers of swans'-down, rain and snow; meanwhile the gathered Indians chant, in measured order and subdued tone, a song of reverence, awe, and devotion.

There is one very remarkable peculiarity of their religious customs, which deserves notice. The chief who is supposed to possess the "right divine" of governing, and to be the intermediate agent between some vague Spirit and his creatures below, retires at times, whenever he fancies himself summoned, from the tribe, without giving them any previous intimation of his mission, and takes up his abode in the lonely woods and mountains, bearing with him clandestinely a small stock of dried salmon for sustenance.   When he is missed, the report is soon spread abroad, and it becomes known that he is gone to hold communion with the Spirit.   The Indian who saw him last on the day of his departure gives his testimony as to the direction which he took, and by that it is judged as to the district to which he has repaired ; a boundary line is then drawn, beyond which it would be heinous to venture, as the region in which the chief is supposed to be, is held sacred till the period of his return ; any violation of this law is death, at the hand of the chief himself or of the tribe.

The duration of his absence on this mission is irregular—often three weeks, and in general he selects the most barren and dreary region for his pilgrimage. He returns at last to the vil-lage, the most hideous object in nature, with matted hair, shrunken cheeks, blood-shot eyes, and parched lips—his blanket, which is his sole covering, hanging in shreds about him, torn by boughs and brambles—his face begrimed with filth, and himself animated with all the unnatural ferocity of a demoniac. His return is by night, and as uncertain as his departure. In general he does not repair first to his own house, but rushes to some other, according to the blind caprice of his wildness, and instead of entering it by the door, he ascends the roof, tears off one of the cedar-board coverings, and plunges down into the centre of the family circle; he then springs on one of the full-grown inmates like a famished wolf, and wrenches with his teeth a mouthful of the flesh from his limbs or body, which he convulsively bolts down without any process of mastication, but barely chopping the lump once or twice for the purpose of easier deglutition.

No resistance is made, for the sufferer thinks that he has been ordered by the Spirit to yield up a certain portion of his anatomy in sacrifice to the chief. The latter then runs to another hut, and makes the same sort of hurried repast. He continues this process into other houses, until in a few hours he becomes exhausted from the quantity of human living flesh which he has devoured. He is then taken home in a state of torpor, and thus remains like an overgorged beast of prey for a day or two afterwards.

So much importance and pride do the Indians attach to these lacerations, that the young men who have not experienced the luck of being thus fed upon, apply lighted gunpowder to their limbs, and use other means to produce the effect of a bite.

In the neighbourhood of Seal Harbour dwell the Sebassa tribe. They daub themselves entirely over with vermilion, and wear large rings through the nose. When a relative or parent dies, they put themselves in mourning by cutting the hair quite close, and blacking the face and neck for some months. Both sexes have large holes bored through their ears, from which they suspend plaited red worsted, hanging down about eight inches. They also wear bracelets of brass wire. The old women disfigure themselves by having a slit cut right through their lower lip crosswise from one end to the other. They then have a piece of hard wood or bone made the length of the cut, rounded at the end, about two inches long, half an inch broad, and a quarter of an inch thick. This is inserted in the slit inside, between the lip and gum, making the lower lip project about an inch beyond the upper, which of course is hideous.

The Nass tribe adjoin the latter, and much resemble each other in many respects. They, the Nass, however, burn their dead, and deposit the ashes in a box in a secluded spot in the woods When a chief dies, he is, before the roasting takes place, dressed up in his ermine—his face painted—and placed in a sitting posture in a canoe, and paddled round the maritime village looking almost alive again. The magicians, or doctors, wear very long hair; they carry images of their gods in a box, which is kept sacred from the eyes of the multitude. The natives stand in great awe of them, as they think them endowed with the power of charming away life. The natives along the entire coast speak, to some extent, broken English, owing to their traffic with Americans and Europeans.

There can be no doubt but that civilised man is the worst enemy of the savage. Vice and extermination invariably and eventually attend

his presence amongst the primitive children
of the wilderness, and the remaining tribes of
North American Indians are as surely fated to
extinction as were the Mohicans who peopled
the banks of the Hudson, as are the Choctaws,
the Poncas, the Pawnees, and the Pottowat-
taines of the same continent, whose remnants
still drag out a fettered and miserable existence
on the usurped lands of their primogenial inheritance.   The discordant din of civilization
is now heard far and wide over the grand
extent of the land of the prairie and the lake;
and where the song and the war-cry of the red
man alone resounded through the mighty solitude of forest and of plain, now the busy clamour of a million tongues strike harshly upon
the ear from the midst of a city of bricks, and
alas! the red man is no more.   But is society
in a healthier state than when nature reigned in
undisturbed, unmolested sovereignty; when the
savage was lord of all, and he rang out in
strains triumphant the thrilling whoop of victory, the enchanting and unsophisticated song
of freedom, unconscious of a blighting future;
when his native glee was boundless, and the

thought of a world beyond his own never broke through the sunlight of his imagination, nor darkened the horizon of his happiness. No; civilization preys upon itself. It creates wants, and it supplies them ; but in that creation and supply we have involved an amount of strife, contention, and infamy which, in a more primitive state of society, would never have had existence.

A mixture of vice and effeminacy, it has given us an inheritance of woe, and built up around us a complex network ever destined to thwart and repel, struggle and toil as we may in our passage through the chequered labyrinth of life. It has made human nature base and sordid, and rendered the whole world one vast vortex of sin and iniquity. It has extinguished the spark of more than brotherly love which nature and nature's God primevally ordained, and has made callous the heart of man. This is an age, however, corrupted though it be, when might is right, and all the world worships Mammon ; when gold is more fascinating than wisdom or virtue, and money is indispensable to power. Thus it is that invasion is

nothing worse than the other crafts and wiles of
our complicated machinery, in which the stronger
tyrannize over the weaker, and every deed and
word is shackled by the hollow mockery—the
giant hypocrisy—of conventionalism. It is in
England that humanity is most shackled, and
curbed, and oppressed by the offspring codes of a
narrow civilization, rather than to endure which
it would be a happier lot to sniff the woodland
perfume of the primeval wilderness, and make
nature alone tributary to our individual wants,
far away from the pale of civilization, where the
white man as yet hath never trodden. Fain
would I echo the words of the last of Wau-
waurrong, and exclaim—

> Give me the fierce wild wassailry of yore,
> Now but remember'd in my country's lore;
> Give me a gunya, I should spurn a throne,
> And cherish more a boomerang my own,
> Than all the pomp conventionalism I see
> Gather'd around from which I long to flee,
> (E'en as the eagle doth in search of prey),
> And plough the distance lone and far away,
> Far as the desert by gay Kordofan,
> Or farther still, where never yet trod man.
>
> Give me a free, wild, boundless solitude,
> With panthers for companions and food,

Where lions and hyænas prowl awide,
And stealthy tigers spring and leopards hide,
For I would rule them with an eye of fire,
And tame them with the music of my lyre.
Give me the quick Red Indian's thrilling whoop,
The hungry vulture's swift unerring swoop.
These are the things I love to hear and see,
But better still to be alone and free
On some wild cragland where the ocean's roar
Blends up with wind-mouth'd caverns and the shore
Is desolate of man, there would I dwell,
And build my gunya in some covert dell.

That, however, which next approaches such a
state is the enterprise which impels a man into
a strange and distant country, there to combat
with the rude hand of nature, and build up to
himself a habitation, become a founder of a
new nation, the basis of whose social structure
may rest on more independent ground than
does the tinsel fabric of his mother country, and
whose children may deck his memory with
laurels. Such a career, gilded with wealth and
attended by all the excitement and pleasures of
dazzling promise, is open to any and every son
of enterprise, who, discontented with his present
lot and endowed with physical energy, may
go forth to the New El Dorado of the

North Pacific, where the banner of England flaunts in the breeze, and Hope ever smiling, " leads on to fortune ;" where millions may revel away in luxurious delight, and the sun of liberty will ever shine..

CHAPTER X.

ABORIGINAL AND DESCRIPTIVE.

FORT ST. JAMES, the depôt of British Columbia, erected by the Hudson's Bay Company, stands near the outlet of Stuart's Lake, and commands. a magnificent view of the surrounding country. The lake is about fifty miles in length, and from three to four miles in breadth, stretching away to the north and north-east for about twenty miles; the view from the Fort embraces nearly the whole of this section of it, which is studded with beautiful islets, that repose like bouquets of flowers upon the bright and smiling face of the living waters. The western shore is low, and indented by a number of small bays formed by wooded points projecting into the lake, the background rising abruptly into a ridge of hills of varied height and magnitude.

On the east the view is limited to a range of two or three miles by the intervention of a high promontory, from which the eye glances to the snow-clad summits of the Rocky Mountains, that loom far in the distance, an imposing panorama of the bold and beautiful, hewn out in rugged grandeur, stern and picturesque. There is an Indian village, situated in a lovely spot, at the outlet of this lake. The houses, however, are few, and of very slight and simple construction; they are formed of stakes driven into the ground, a square slab of wood being placed horizontally along the top of the wall made by the stakes, to which the latter are fastened by strips of willow bark. This enclosure, which is of a square form, is roofed in by placing two strong posts at each gable, which support the ridge-pole on which the roof-sticks are placed, one end resting on the ridge-pole and the other on the wall, the whole being covered with pine-tree bark. There is, in general, a door at each end, which is cut in the wall after the structure

is erected : these apertures are of a circular
form, and about two and a half feet in diameter,
so that a stranger finds it very awkward to pass
through them.   In effecting an entrance you
first introduce a leg, then bending low the body,
you press in head and shoulders ; in this position you will have some difficulty in maintaining
your equilibrium, for if you draw in the rest of
your body too quickly, it is but a chance that
you will find yourself head undermost.   The
natives, however, glide through them with the
agility of a weasel.   A little further on, over a
somewhat flat country, and in latitude 53 deg.
north, stands Fort Alexandria, on the banks of
Frazer's River, so called after the celebrated
traveller, Sir Alexander Mackenzie.   The timber in this district is chiefly poplar, alder, and
birch; there is also some wild fruit scrub in
the neighbourhood, furnishing abundant and
grateful crops of berries to the natives.   Rock
crystal, cobalt, talc, iron, marcosites of a gold
colour, granite, fullers' earth, black marble, and
limestone have been found about here, probably
owing to their having been forced down the
beds of rivers from the mountains.

The tribe of the Talkotins inhabit this immediate region.   They are, however, alike with the
Slowercuss, Dinais, Nascud, and Dinnee tribes,
inhabiting the upper part of Frazer's River,
as also, the entire tribes of British Columbia,
merely divisions of the great Carrier tribe, and
speak ostensibly the one language, although
broken up into various dialects.   They entertain great affection for their dogs, which are
of diminutive size, resembling those of the Esquimaux, with the curled-up tail, small ears
and pointed nose.   The natives here are very
friendly and hospitable, and on the most peaceful
terms with the whites.

The salmon, the so-called British Columbian
staff of life, ascend Frazer's River and its tributaries from the Pacific, in immense shoals, proceeding towards the sources of the streams, until
stopped by shallow water.   Having deposited their spawn, their dead bodies are to be
seen floating down the current in thousands;
few of them ever return to the sea; thus it is
that in consequence of the old fish perishing in
this manner, they fail in this quarter every fourth
year.   The natives display a good deal of inge-

nuity in catching them. Where the current and depth of water permits, they bar the stream across by means of stakes driven into the bottom with much labour, and standing about six inches apart; these are strongly bound to a piece of timber or plate running along the top, stays or supporters being placed at intervals of ten or twelve feet, and the upper end bearing against the plate so as to form an angle with the stream. Gaps are left in the works of sufficient size to admit the baskets in which the fish are taken. After the whole is finished, square frames of wicker work, called keys, are let down against the upper side, to prevent the fish from ascending, and at the same time to allow the water a free passage.

The keys require to be kept entirely free from obstruction, such as branches and leaves, otherwise the whole works would soon be swept away from the force of the current. The baskets are of a cylindrical form, about two and a half feet in diameter at the mouth, terminating in a point of four or five inches. When the fishing is over, all the materials are removed, and replaced the ensuing year with equal labour.

In order to preserve the fish for future consumption, the back is split up, and the back bone extracted; it is then hung up by the tail for a few days, when it is taken down and distended on splinters of wood; these are attached to a sort of scaffold erected for the purpose, where the fish remains till sufficiently dry for preservation. It is rather a singular circumstance that at each periodical failing of the salmon, rabbits should swarm over the country in far greater numbers than at the other, and plentiful seasons; but such is the case; without which the natives would experience little short of famine.

When the salmon return, the rabbits disappear, being destroyed or driven away by their greatest enemy, the lynx, which gradually swarm, also retiring, however, with the rabbits.

The primitive custom amongst the natives here, as well as of the other unsettled tribes, is to burn their dead. The process is rather revolting than anything else; so I shall not enter into its minute detail. If a male, the relatives of the deceased as well as of the widow are present, and stand up armed while a funeral pile is erected. On this the body is placed, after which the widow immediately sets fire to the pile, and stands by it during the entire process of blazing demolition, which lasts several days.   After the burning, the bones and ashes are collected in a box and given in charge to the widow, who carries them about on her back until the time of the appointed feast day to his memory, when they are taken from her and deposited in a small hut, or placed on the top of a wooden pillar neatly carved, as their final resting place.

These people have no idea, primitively, of a deity, nor of a future state; it is therefore a popular error amongst Christians, promulgated chiefly by missionaries, that of supposing that there exists no nation on earth who are entirely strangers to the belief in a Supreme Being, or a resurrection of the dead.

This opinion has been disseminated and strengthened by the representations of superficial, hearsay travellers, who have but imperfectly conversed with the aborigines of a country, and that *after* their intercourse with disciples of Christianity.

The Indian, as well as the untutored mind generally, is too ready to catch at novelty to

allow anything to pass unnoticed, or even without enlarging upon it, and making it applicable
and tributary to himself; and so it was and is
that the savage, in whom poetry is innate, has
conjured up to himself superficial images of
Divine agency, without knowing why or where-
fore, but simply at the prompting of missionaries,
and just as readily as a parrot may be taught to
speak and the monkey to mimic, with this
exception, that the Indian, having a keen intelligence and perception, readily fastens upon and
comprehends a new idea ; he delights in the ideal
—he is a creature of imagination, and so far as
his thinking faculties go, he strives for emulation ;
for anything else save the chase, and absolutely
aboriginal occupations, he is disinclined; and hence
his inadaptability for civilisation, and the certain
destruction that succeeds to it.

" Sees God in clouds, and hears him in the storm,"

is a poetical phantasy — true he hears the thunder and he sees the lightning, but with the same,
only keener, effect as the buffalo and the deer.
The God, which the poet mentions, is with him
vague and undefined ; the commotion of the

elements he considers, and rightly, to be the effect of natural causes. He never ponders over the creation of these things. He considers himself aloof, as he really is, entirely disconnected from their great workings He accepts the moon and the stars as a part of this vast system, but he never associates himself with these things, and he never hopes for anything beyond the grave.

I have conversed with New Zealanders, Australians, Kaffirs, Esquimaux, and other aborigines, but could never deduce from their testimony that before they were submitted to the indoctrinating influence of Christianity in the persons of the missionaries, they ever pictured to themselves a resurrection or a life hereafter; and even now their belief, if such be at all entertained, is too vague and empty to influence their hopes or actions.

Even at the present day the Takelly or Carrier Indians never allude to the deity; in fact the Takelly language has not a term in it expressive of either deity, spirit, or soul—heaven or hell,— or anything approaching such.

The Takelly says, " The toad hears me." When a Takelly is asked what becomes of him

G

after death, he replies, " My life shall be *extinct,*
and I shall be dead." Not an idea has he of
the soul, or of a future state of rewards and
punishments.

Fort Alexander is agreeably situated, as
before mentioned, on the banks of Frazer's
River, on the outskirts of the great prairies.
The surrounding country is beautifully diversified by hill and dale, grove and plain; the
soil is rich, yielding abundant successive crops
of grain and vegetable, unmanured. The
charming locality, the friendly disposition of the
Indians, and the prolific abundance of vegetable
and animal life, render this settlement one of
the most pleasing in British Columbia. In
spring the country swarms with game, pheasants
and curlew, ducks and geese. Fort George,
an outpost of Alexandria, stands higher up on
the right bank of the same river. Its situation
is exceedingly dreary, having in front a high
hill that shades the summit late in the morning,
while the forest, deep and far, hems it in and
clothes it in a somewhat melancholy gloom; yet
the soil is as prolific and the other products of
the farm and the dairy are as abundant as at
Alexandria.

The Takelly, or Carrier language, is a dialect of the Chippewayan ; and it is rather a singular fact that the two intervening dialects of the Beaver Indians and Tsekanies, kindred nations, should differ more from the Chippewayan than the Carrier; the two latter nations being perfectly intelligible to each other, while the former are but very imperfectly understood by their immediate neighbours, the Chippewayans.

I may here mention that a popular error is extant relative to the number and variety of languages spoken by the North American Indians. There are, in reality, only four radically distinct languages from the shores of Labrador to the Pacific: Sauteux, Chippewayan, Atna, and Chinook. The Cree language is evidently a dialect of the Sauteux, similar in construction, and differing only in the modification of a few words. The Nascopies, or mountaineers of Labrador, speak a mixture of Cree and Sauteux, the former predominating.

Along the communication from Montreal to the foot of the Rocky Mountains, following the Peace River route, the Sauteux are first met with ; their region extends from the lake of the

Two Mountains to Lake Winnipeg; then come
the Crees as far as the Isle à la Crosse; after
them Crees and Chippewayans as far as Athabasca; and along the banks of Peace River
the Beaver Indians occupy the lower, and the
Tsekanies the upper part. The Chippewayan
is evidently the root of the Beaver, Tsekany,
and Carrier dialects. On the west side of the
Rocky Mountains, the Carrier language is succeeded by the Atna, which extends along the
Columbia as far down as the Chinooks, who
inhabit the coast. The Atna language, in its
variety of dialects, seems to have as wide a
scope as either the Sauteux or Chippewayan.

The climate of British Columbia is exceedingly variable at all seasons of the year. During some winters the weather continues mild
throughout. These vicissitudes of temperature
are owing to local causes,—proximity to, or
distance from, the glaciers of the Rocky Mountains, the direction of the winds, the aspect of
the place, and such other causes.

Fort St. James is so situated as to be completely exposed to the north-east wind, which
wafts on its wings the freezing vapours of the

glaciers. The instant the wind shifts to this quarter, a change of temperature is felt ; and when it continues to blow for a few hours, it becomes so cold, that even in summer small ponds are frozen over.

The surrounding country is mountainous and rocky. Frazer's Lake is only about thirty miles distant from Fort St. James (on Stuart's Lake), yet there the climate is beautiful. But then the Fort stands in a valley open to the south-west, a fine champaign country, of a sandy soil, and is protected from the north-east winds by a high ridge of hills. The winter consequently seldom sets in before December, and the navigation is generally open at the end of April. Few countries present a more bold and beautiful variety of scenery than British Columbia, where towering mountains, hill and dale, valley and plain, forest and lake, all blend together in picturesque antitheses, and can be taken in at one meandering glance.

There is nothing, I think, better calculated to awaken the more solemn feelings of our nature than these noble lakes, studded with innumerable islets, suddenly bursting upon the

traveller's view as he emerges from the sombre
forests of the American wilderness. The clear,
unruffled waters stretching out to the horizon,
here embracing the heavy and luxuriant foliage
of a hundred wooded isles, or reflecting the
wood-clad mountains on its margin, clothed in
all the variegated hues of autumn; and there
glittering with dazzling brilliancy in the bright
rays of the evening sun, or rippling among the
reeds and rushes of some shallow bay, where
hundreds of wild fowl chatter as they feed, with
varied cry, rendering more apparent, rather than
disturbing, the solemn stillness of the scene.

This region is still rich in fur-bearing animals,
especially beavers and martens, owing to their
finding a safe retreat among the fastnesses of the
Rocky Mountains, where they multiply undisturbed; there are also others, chiefly musk rats,
minxes, and lynxes. Of the larger quadrupeds,
bears only are numerous; they are, however, to
be met with in all their varieties, black, brown,
chocolate, and grizzled. When I write the
word grizzled, I am led to a vivid remembrance
of a very narrow escape that I once had from
one that I had wounded when out shooting

alone in California.   On that occasion I had to run a considerable distance, with the bear in close pursuit, before reaching a tree, my only chance of preservation.   No sooner, however, had I sprung and clambered up to the second branches, than I perceived Bruin had reached its base, and moreover, was on the point of climbing up after me.   Fortunately the tree was an awkward one for him on account of its slender trunk, but was nevertheless climbable and strong enough to bear his weight.   Without a moment's hesitation, and with all the deliberate impetuosity of desperation, I commenced loading my double-barrel piece, balancing myself meanwhile astride a branch, with legs depending and my left shoulder leaning against the trunk.   I had not a moment to lose, the tree shook violently with the efforts of my grizzly enemy to ascend ; and no sooner had I capped my charge, than up he came with stealthy but savage strides.   He was within two feet only of me when I fired straight into his skull, upon which he fell half reelingly to the ground, and died within five minutes.— However, back to our El Dorado.   A most

destructive little animal, the wood rat, infests
the country, and generally nestles in the rocks,
but prefers still more human habitations. They
domicile under the floors of outbuildings, and
not content with this, force their way into the
inside, where they destroy and carry off everything they can. There is no way of securing
the property in the stores from their depreda-
tions but by placing it in strong boxes. When
fairly located, it is almost impossible to root them
out. They are of a grey colour, and of nearly
the same form and size as the common rat, the
tail excepted, which resembles that of the ground
squirrel. The birds of British Columbia are the
same as in Canada, excepting that more frequently
than in the latter country, immense flocks of
cranes are to be seen in autumn and spring flying
high in the air; in autumn directing their flight towards the south, and in spring towards the north.

Most of the lakes abound in fish ; the principal varieties are trout, carp, white fish, and pike.
Sturgeon weighing from one hundred to five
hundred pounds, are sometimes caught. A beautiful small fish of the size of an anchovy, and
shaped like a salmon, is found in a river that

falls into Stuart's Lake ; it is said they pass the winter in the lake, and ascend their favourite stream in the month of June, where they deposit their spawn. They have the silvery scales of the large salmon, and are exceedingly rich, but the natives preserve them almost exclusively for their own use. There are four varieties of salmon, distinguished from each other by the peculiar form of their head ; the largest species seems to be the same as abounds in the rivers of Britain, and weighs from ten to twenty pounds ; the others do not exceed half that weight.

The Takellies, or Carriers, do not use canoes on their hunting excursions, so that they are necessitated to carry all their conveniences on their backs ; and it is astonishing to see what heavy loads they can carry, especially the women, on whom the transport duty generally devolves. Amongst this nation, however, the women are held in much higher consideration than amongst other Indians ; they assist at the councils, and some are even admitted to the feasts. This consideration they doubtless owe to the efficient aid they afford in procuring the means of subsistence.

G 3

The one sex is as actively exployed as the other during the fishing season.   The men construct the weirs, repair them when necessary, and capture the fish; the women split them up, a most laborious occupation when salmon is plentiful, suspend them on the scaffolds, attend to the drying, and other processes connected with their preservation.   They also collect berries, and dig up the edible roots that are found in the country, and which are of great service during the years of scarcity.   Thus the labour of the women contributes as much to the support of the community as that of the men.   The latter are passionately addicted to gambling, staking everything they may possess, and continuing at it night and day until compelled to desist by sheer hunger.   Their games are played with a few small sticks neatly carved with a certain varying number of marks upon them, which being tied up in a small bundle of hay, the players draw out successively, throw up and catch in their hands until all are drawn, when they are taken up one by one and dashed against a piece of skin parchment and rolled up again in the hay; the process being repeated after the manner of our card dealing.

They sing in chorus during the play, and manifest much merriment.

The Takellies are a sedentary people, remaining shut up in their huts during the more severe part of the winter. A native encampment may then be approached without any sign being perceived of its vicinity, until their well or one of the salmon catches is arrived at. They are very social, congregating at each other's huts, and passing their time either in talking or sleeping. When awake their tongues are ever in motion, all bawling out at the same time, and creating a babbling uproar highly ludicrous to hear.

There is much variety and melody in the airs they sing. They dance in circles, men and women promiscuously, and while holding each other by the hand, and keeping both feet together, they hop sideways with a sudden jerk of the body ; this movement is difficult of execution, excellent time is, however, kept, while the blending together of the voices—male and female—in symphony, has an effect which cannot be called other than delightful.

They are extremely hospitable, cheerfully

sharing their last morsel with the stranger who may be in want. Hospitality, however, is a virtue which civilisation never improves.

British Columbia has hitherto been the richest district in the vast domain of the Hudson's Bay Company: its annual returns averaged about 8,000 beavers, with a fair proportion of other valuable furs.

When first settled, the goods required for trade were brought in by the winterers from Lac la Pluie, which was their depôt. The people left the district as early in spring as navigation permitted, and returned so late that they were frequently overtaken by winter ere they reached their destination. Cold, hunger, and fatigue were the unavoidable consequences experienced; but the enterprising spirit of the men of those days—the intrepid and indefatigable adventurers of the North-west Company—was undauntable, and vanquished over every difficulty.

It was that spirit that opened a communication across the broad continent of America; that penetrated to the frost-bound regions of the Arctic circle; and that established a trade with the natives in this remote land, when the merchandize required for it was in one season transported from Montreal across the wilderness, to within a short distance from the Pacific. Such enterprise is now dead so far as the fur trade is concerned. The Hudson's Bay Company's outfit stores have been hitherto sent out from England, via Cape Horn, usually to Fort Vancouver; thence they are conveyed in boats to Okanagan, tl en transported on horses' backs to Alexandria, the lower post of the district on Frazer's River, whence they are conveyed in boats onward to Fort St. James.

Over these tracts of country once ranged the hardy mountaineers,—the trading trappers who scaled the vast mountain chains of North America, and pursued their hazardous vocations amidst their wild recesses—moving from place to place on horseback, piercing the rugged defiles and threading the narrow gorges of the mountains, bounding across plains and valleys, whose pure and exhilarating atmosphere seemed to make them both physically and mentally a more lively and mercurial race than their fellow men— lithe, vigorous, and active; extravagant in word, deed, and thought; heedless of hardship, daring

of danger, prodigal of the present, and thought-
less of the future ; hardy, self-dependent, and
game-spirited, they pursued a career whose
romantic wildness was only surpassed by its vicissitudes.

Accustomed to live in tents, or to bivouac
in˙the open air, the mountaineer despised even
the comforts of the log hut, and preferred
shooting his own game, lighting his own fire,
and cooking his own repast *al fresco*.   With his
horse and his rifle he felt himself independent
of the world, and spurned all its restraints.
There was a nobility in this, more sterling than
the peerage, which could not but command
admiration.

No class of men on the face of the earth led
a life of more continued peril, exertion, and
excitement, and were more enamoured of their
occupation than these free trappers of the west.
No toil, no privation, no danger, could turn the
trapper from his pursuit.   His passionate excitement at times resembled a mania.   In vain
might the most vigilant and cruel savages beset
his path ; in vain might rocks, and precipices,
and wintry torrents oppose his progress ; let

but a single track of the beaver meet his eye,
all thoughts of danger were banished, all difficulties defied. At times he might be seen
with his traps slung over his shoulder, buffeting
his way across rapid streams, amidst floating
blocks of ice; at other times, with his traps
swung on his back, clambering the most rugged
mountains, scaling or descending the most
frightful precipices, searching by routes inaccessible to the horse, and never before trodden
by white man, for springs and lakes unknown
to his comrades, and where he might meet with
his favourite game. Such was the mountaineer,
and such he still may be; but he has changed
his field of enterprise, he has gone still higher,
and still further from the haunts of civilization,
and he is but seldom seen, and few indeed is
the number of his once wild band. There was
a fascination in savage life for these men—
many of them shunned the haunts of civilization, ever after plunging beyond its pale,
and so marrying native women, whom they
became as attached to as they could have
been to women of their own English, French,
Canadian, or American race, transmitted to

posterity the "half-breeds" who so plentifully
abound over the northern continent. It was
a matter of emulation with them to adopt the
manners, habits, dress, gesture, and even
walk of the Indian. Their hair, suffered to
attain a great length, was carefully combed
out, and either left to fall carelessly over
the shoulders, or plaited neatly, and tied up
in otter skins or parti-coloured ribbons. A
hunting shirt of ruffled calico of bright dyes, or
of ornamented leather, fell as far down as the
knee, below which curiously-fashioned leggings
ornamented with strings, fringes, and a profusion of hawks' bells, reached to a costly pair
of mocassins of the finest Indian fabric, richly
embroidered with beads. A blanket of scarlet
or some other bright colour hung from the
shoulders, and was girt round the waist with a
red sash, which held the customary pistols,
knife, and the stem of an Indian pipe. His gun
would be lavishly decorated with brass tacks
and vermilion, and provided with a fringe
cover, occasionally of buckskin, ornamented with
feathers. His horse, the noble minister to his
pride, pleasure, and profit, was selected for his

speed, spirit, and prancing carriage, and held a
place in his estimation second only to himself,
sharing largely of his bounty and of his pride
and prowess of trapping, caparisoned in the
most dashing and fantastic style; the bridles
and crupper weightily embossed with beads and
cockades, with the head, mane, and tail inter-
woven with an abundance of eagles' plumes,
that fluttered in the wind; while, to complete
his grotesque equipment, the proud animal was
bestreaked and bespotted with vermilion or
white clay, whichever presented the most
glaring contrast to his real colour.   These
tastes were and are still exactly those of the
Indian, who prides himself as much upon his
horse as upon his wife, and when thus gaudily
caparisoned, is in his highest glory.

CHAPTER XI.

THE FUTURE GOVERNMENT OF BRITISH COLUMBIA.

LET the colony of British Columbia be constituted on the same basis as was New South
Wales. Why talk of ever annexing it to Canada?
The plan did not answer with regard to Victoria, whose geographical position with respect
to New South Wales was far more favourable
than is that of British Columbia with Canada;
and if worse did not befall it, the yoke would
be even sooner thrown off by the settlement
under consideration, than was that of the colony
alluded to.

Let a provisional government be formed, and
sent out, if necessary, to administer the affairs

of the colony until such time as a fitting legislature might be provided, but by all means let it remain independent, and tributary alone to the mother country.

For Canada to exercise surveillance over it would be at once fettering and obnoxious; moreover, the work would be but inefficiently performed with so wide a distance between the seat of government and the local staff. For a rapidly rising country such as British Columbia, which has sprung into giant manhood, as it were, in a day, the ruling power must be on the spot; the time which would necessarily elapse in communicating from the one country to the other would be too great to suit the exigencies and requirements of a community and a territory so peculiarly situated as this.

It must have a special governor and legislature of its own; it would be a dangerous experiment to try to dispense with such; whereas their presence will contribute more to the safety, stability, and good order of the place amongst the sea of aliens for whom we have to legislate, than any other measure which the British Government might organize. To make it

a mere undignified parasite of Canada would be
the greatest blunder of statesmanship ever committed ; the probable consequences of such a
course I shall not presume to mention ; suffice
it to say, that the representatives of the elder
colony would be as little respected by the heedless population who are now swarming from
Puget's Sound to Thompson's River, as the
laws they might be instructed to enforce.   It is
therefore to be sincerely hoped that the result
of present and future deliberations upon this
important subject which has so prominently
engaged the minds of our politicians, and in
which our present colonial secretary, Sir Edward
Bulwer Lytton, has taken so leading and praiseworthy a part, will be such as to obviate the
hazardous evils which would inevitably arise
from a union at any time of Canada with British
Columbia, and to ensure the safe keeping of
a land so extensive and bountifully supplied with
the requirements of man, and upon which Nature
has lavished her treasures with so inviting a
prodigality.

CHAPTER XII.

THE MAGIC SPELL.

IT would be hard to describe in colours and language sufficiently vivid, the tremendous excitement which is now raging, and the exodus that is now going forward from California to the new El Dorado of the North Pacific. Since the middle of the month of April the fever has been increasing with an almost maddened pulse, and its climax is far from reached. The San Francisconians are rejoicing; the halcyon days of 1849 were supposed to have gone by for ever; but suddenly they have awoke again— with their rush, their clamour, and their gold.

As she looked ten years ago in the first flush
of her prosperity, now looks she again. Red
and blue woollen shirted men, rough and stalwart, now throng and lend renewed animation to her streets, ranging about in squads,
with picks, shovels, pans, blankets, and primitive
looking rockers on their shoulders. It is
nearly nine years since such scenes were
witnessed there before. Shopkeepers are overrun with customers they never dreamt of
seeing at their counters. This is owing to
San Francisco being the grand rendezvous for
miners from all parts of the interior, *en route*
for Frazer's River. They, of course, require to
replete their " kit " before starting, with the
substantial addition also of a second revolver.
Thus, it will be seen, that although anticipating
it, they are not to be deterred by danger; although it is to be hoped that order will prevail,
and the sacrifice of human life be avoided. So
far as this refers to the Indians, it is sincerely
to be desired; unfortunately, however, a chief
and another were shot, during a disturbance
in the vicinity of Fort Hope, on Frazer River,

when the whole tribe was with great difficulty appeased by the agent of the Hudson's Bay Company.

It is said, that men who have worked for years in the mountains of California, know how to manage the red men better than any regulars in the world; but it is to be deplored, that their management is conducted too much at the revolver's mouth to be in accordance with true philanthropy, or yet the views of the Aborigines' Protection Society. Civilisation, however, is a pestilence, and aboriginalism is as fated to fall before its inroads as, to use a scriptural simile, the sparks fly upward. Alas, that it should be so! but we are driven, in self-defence, to seek sustenance in lands hitherto alone roamed over by the primitive rulers of the earth. Even in civilised society each preys upon the other—the stronger upon the weaker—and in this crushing of barbarism under the foot of civilisation, we have nothing worse than is being despotically enacted every moment of our lives in our cities and our homes.

No longer is it doubted, or disputed, that a new

gold country awaits development in the North as rich, or even richer, in its resources as was California or Australia.   The magic spell of the discovery is now being experienced throughout America, and its influence cannot fail to spread far and wide over the whole dominion of civilisation. Even up to the 20th of June, 14,800 souls had embarked from San Francisco alone, by steam and sailing vessels, for the new El Dorado; and it was fully anticipated that during the ensuing two months an equal or greater number would depart, and that the entire exodus from California, during the first six months of the Frazer's River fever would reach the enormous figure of 50,000.   The rapidity and extent of the emigration now going forward has never been paralleled.   On the 19th of June, when the steamer Republic, from Frazer's River, was telegraphed as coming up the bay about half-past two o'clock, the town was quite taken by surprise, as she was not expected till the 21st.   The sensation which swayed the city was tremendous.   Excitement and anticipation had been at a high pitch for two entire weeks, as no steamer had come down in the interim

with later news than the Panama brought on
the 5th of the same month; the Pacific had
arrived on the 8th, but her dates only corre-
sponded with those of the Panama. This was
a long period of suspense ; but faith in Frazer
River had never once flagged among the great
body of the people of California, although more
than one of the leading San Francisco journals
had seemingly wavered, and striven to check
the swelling tide of the northward bound. In
less than an hour after the Republic had reached
the wharf, several extras, *i.e.* evening editions
of newspapers, were issued, as also the Evening
Bulletin flooding the city with the eagerly
sought intelligence. The result was, that confidence and assurance became doubly sure, and
those who had hitherto hesitated and held back,
haûled down their colours, and went in pell
mell with the enthusiasm common to fresh con-
verts.

The question was no longer, " Are you
going ?" but " When do you get off ?"

All was animation and florid excitement,
while gin slings and cocktails were in greater
demand than ever. All the letters received

H

from the various ports on Puget's Sound (American territory) and the diggings furnished corroborative testimony as to the extent and richness of the new placers.

The impression of all who have gone is, alike with my own, unanimous and conclusive as to the grand fact of the new El Dorado being the seat of even greater treasures than have made famous the name of California.

Up to the 22nd of June no steamer had returned with more than a dozen passengers, and these had come down to obtain supplies either for themselves or party, with the intention of returning by the next steamer; saying, however, that nothing would be lost by not reaching there before the beginning of August, as the rivers will remain flooded till that time. But this information has no effect in retarding the people of California; on they rush, making every sacrifice, and caring for nothing save a passage to the glittering land.

Impatient of the day, they rush on with resistless speed and palpitating gladness—attracted as the magnet to the steel, they fly to the demon of gold.

Between the 5th and the 20th of June the following vessels sailed from San Francisco for Victoria (Vancouver's Island) and ports on Puget's Sound :

June   5, Barque, Gold Hunter.
—   7, Steamer, Republic.
—   9,   „   Commodore.
— 10, Schooner, Giulietta.
— 12, Steamer, Panama.
— —, Ship, Georgiana.
— —, Barque, Adelaide.
— —, Sloop, Curlew.
— 14, Ship, William Berry.
— 15, Barque, Live Yankee.
— 17, Steamer, Cortez.
— —, Schooner, Kossuth.
— 18,   „   Osprey.
— —, Barque, Madonna.
— 19, Steamer, Santa Cruz.

The above is one fortnight's list, according to the clearances at the Custom-house, besides which several vessels in the regular coasting trade to those ports left, each taking a full complement of passengers; about 6,000 took their departure between the dates named.

On the 22nd of June the steamer Republic took her departure for the north again; the Oregon on the 23rd, and the Commodore on the 24th; while, at least, twenty vessels were on the berths announced for immediate despatch; some of the smaller vessels to take passengers through to Fort Langley, stopping at Victoria to obtain permits to pass up Frazer's River, at the mouth of which the British steamer, Satellite, is stationed to guard against unlicensed egress. The price of a first-class cabin passage to Victoria by steamer is sixty-five dollars, and thirty-five dollars in the steerage. The sailing craft charge from sixty down to twenty-five dollars. Nearly all the Californian emigration has hitherto landed at Victoria, owing to Governor Douglas not granting licenses elsewhere.

From the 1st of May to the 15th of June, 9,500 passengers left Sacramento for San Francisco, against 5,800 during a previous period of six weeks. The excess of travel over the different stage routes to Sacramento and Folsom since the fever set in was 3,674. What the emigration by the San Joaquin has been was not computed; but the rush from the southern mines was even more general than from the middle and northern sections. The arrivals by up-river steamers in San Francisco during the week ending the 20th of June averaged 500 nightly of those bound to the New El Dorado, while the departures for the latter were of about the same daily average.

The roads in the interior and across the mountains presented, meanwhile, an appearance similar to the retreat of a routed army. Stages, express waggons, and vehicles of every character, were called into requisition for the immediate emergency, and all rolled along crowded, while whole battalions were pressing forward before, behind, and alongside, either on horse or mule-back, or on foot, all eager for the fray. New life has been infused into the blood of the vast mining population of North America, and on they roll in one resistless tide,

To gather gold where ghastly hunger hies.

However, plenty will follow in their train,

And gold will gild what nought but wealth could build.

May happiness crown their hopes is my most enthusiastic wish.

Of course, the shipments of merchandise from San Francisco were very large to keep pace with this sudden transmigration of thousands to a region totally unsupplied with the commodities necessary for their use and subsistence, but the supply was still unequal to the demand.

Recurring again to San Francisco, the rush and excitement are by no means confined to miners, but seem to have operated on all classes alike. Even newspaper men, the most inveterate and pertinacious of all, were about leaving in considerable numbers. A lively business—very lively it is to be presumed—was reported to be doing in the hardware and clothing lines as well as in provisions—very indispensable, *we guess.* Nearly all those from the interior require a new fit out in whole or in part. Revolvers, rifles, shot, guns, and knives; pickaxes, shovels, and hoes, rocker iron drills and rifle boxes, flannel shirts, thick coats and pants, waterproofs, oilcloths, and water-boots—eagle-topped ones, of course—were all in high demand. So great is the rush, that hundreds are unable to procure an immediate passage, while thousands were waiting their turn at Sacramento and Stockton for conveyance to San Francisco. Scarcely one leaves the latter city without disbursing more or less money, and more than a million dollars were calculated to have been added to the daily circulation of the place since the rage set in. Such is the unparalleled effect of the discovery of our New El Dorado—the golden realm of thrice ten thousand hopes.

CHAPTER XIII.

THE FINGER-POST.

THE difficulties which present themsemselves at first sight in the way of reaching our El Dorado, are obviously greater than those attending a transmigration direct to the shores of the Australasian isles ; these, however, upon examination, will be found either easy of obviation or such as may be readily surmounted by those endowed with the spirit of enterprise, and possessed of that subordinate but necessary qualification, their passage-money.

The readiest mode which the traveller can pursue is to take passage to New York, from

which city he can travel with a through ticket
to San Francisco viâ the Isthmus

From San Francisco steamers ply to Frazer's
River, up which he can proceed without delay in
boats and canoes.   California may be reached at
a minimum expense of twenty-five or thirty
pounds only from England, from which the adventurer can either proceed overland on foot and
horse viâ Puget's Sound, or by steamer, at a chance
fare, to the nearest navigable point of the new gold
diggings. Frazer's River lies seven hundred miles
north of San Francisco, yet it is still one or two
degrees south of the latitude of London; and
although at a distance of one hundred and fifty
miles from the shores of the Pacific, there stands
a barrier of mountains, whose rugged and lofty
summits are ever snow-capped; still the average temperature throughout the year between
that and the coast is fifty-four degrees Fahrenheit, while snow is seldom lodged on the ground
for more than three days throughout the entire
winter.   Fruit-trees blossom in April, and salad
goes to seed early in May.   Wheat yields from
twenty-five to thirty bushels per acre.   The trees
are gigantic, while iron, copper, and other

minerals intersect the rich and flowery pasture
lands.   From Frazer's River down to Peru the
rivers all bear down treasures of a natural wealth
perfectly inestimable; thus demonstrating the
vast resources, collateral and direct, of that land
where Fortune stands beckoning, and lavishes
her bounteous gifts upon all who come.   There
is a strong and growing demand for all kinds of
labour at almost fabulous rates of remuneration.
There are the finest openings for trade speculations that ever existed.   Credit, of course, as in
all new countries, is, and will continue to be
abundant, thus dispensing with the necessity for
capital ; all that is required being the wide-
awake faculty,—a stout heart and a strong arm.
Men who have been groping in the hazy squalor
of poverty for years in this country, and might
remain so for ever, may at once make a plunge
into the arena of wealth and all its attendant
glory, by embarking for the golden shores of
our dazzling El Dorado.

There are 500,000 square miles of the richest
and most splendid country in the world, even
looking at it in an agricultural point of view
only, spread out before him, when he stands on

the auriferous region of which we speak. The salubrity of the climate sustains health and prolongs life, as is universally testified by those who have resided there, and who have displayed and borne out their good opinion of it by making it their final home—this is especially applicable to the retired officers of the Hudson's Bay Company. Of course, it is the grand object and interest of the latter monopoly to make the world believe the territory which they hold is a barren and rocky wilderness, unfit for anything but fur-bearing animals and those red warriors of the soil with whom they have so long trafficked in toys; but the Hudson's Bay Company must remember that geographers and the world know to the contrary of what they would make believe, and that at least the 500,000 square miles already mentioned of their three millions of square miles of terri-tory are highly fertile and cultivable, and that the new and unprecedentedly rich gold fields which have just eclipsed Australia, and made California look pale, form the central gem of this vast and wealthy domain, where the Red Indian is now being driven before the rush of civilization,

which in its influence, alas! cannot fail to be
otherwise than blasting and exterminating to
him, but which will build up cities in the wilderness where the waving of the prairie and the
solitude of the mighty forest before only inspired
the explorer with awe—regions of Indian romance—unchronicled—forgotten.

CHAPTER XIV.

USEFUL AND PICTORIAL.

TAKING steamer from Liverpool or Southampton, the passenger will find himself in all probability the cabin-chum of some trading German,
or Yankee, returning home after his travels. If
he should have the misfortune to come in such
close proximity with the former, I can only wish
him married,—anywhere but berthed under or
over a Dutch-bottomed lager beer-drinker.

Yankees themselves are usually pretty smart,
agreeable sort of fellows ; although when a
revolver has been pointed at a man's head by
one, as was the case with myself, I might be
expected to speak differently. However, if the

adventurer—I use the term in its most ennobled dignity—keeps clear of the alloy of " loafers" and card sharpers, which so plentifully abound amongst the American community, he stands a good chance of being fairly dealt with.

The American character, on the whole, is highly to be commended ; they are extremely good-hearted, frank and obliging, and their faults, if in our egotism we so denote them, are rendered more conspicuous owing to their freedom from cant and treachery.

A set of empty-headed, starched, convention-alists have gone to the United States and written books about a people of whom and their institutions they were all but entirely ignorant, and so have impressed John Bull with some odd notions of Jonathan, which, however, the latter is well able to defend and repudiate, were it worth the trouble ; the Yankee, however, is too mag-nanimous to heed or to retaliate—he can afford to stand the brunt of a few stray shots from such nurselings of vanity as have wasted their feeble strength in still more feeble satire and malignation.   So much for the nation which report tells us has threatened to lick *all* creation,

and something else—but I forget what—into
the bargain.

From the foot of Canal Street, where the
principal steam wharf lies, in the city of New
York, the passenger may proceed to any of the
hotels—I prefer the Metropolitan—in the car-
riages of the latter, which he will find in attend-
ance.   He had better do this if he wishes to
avoid exorbitant cab fare, and is unwilling to trust
his luggage to hand porters and himself to his legs.

His first duty after arrival should be to
repair to the Aspinwall and Pacific Steam Company's offices, and engage his passage through
to San Francisco. Afterwards, and up to the
time of his departure, he can amuse himself to his
perfect satisfaction ; for what with the continual
eating and drinking going forward at the hotels,
the most magnificent in the world, which charge
at the uniform rate of two dollars and a half a
day—the bustle of Broadway, and the thousands
of pretty—I should say lovely—women that are
there to be seen—the morning and evening
amusements at Niblo's and other theatres and
places, —he cannot fail in making matters agreeable to himself.   The life and animation of the

Broadway is unparalleled in any other city of the world ; there is an excitement in merely looking at it. Moreover, there is a frankness and hospitality of manner and feeling about the people, that to any, save a narrowed and prejudiced mind, is pleasing and comforting. For my own part I should prefer living in New York to any other place I have ever seen, both on account of its society, liberality of opinion, which I term general magnanimity, and the beauties of the island city itself, as well as its contiguity to Brooklyn, the most delightful place of residence in the new world.

After embarking, the passenger will find himself one of a thousand as regards the number on board, and in order to enjoy the voyage, he must blend in with the multitude, and guess and talk with them. This is an easy and congenial task, and one from which he may derive much information of the country to which he is bound, that is so far as California is concerned, there always being miners and traders on board, who have made the voyage there and back more than once before.

When he gets to Panama, after crossing the

Isthmus from Aspinwall, it will well repay him
to make a visit to the island of Taboga, which
lies at a distance of five miles from the city. It
is highly picturesque, as well as being the old
resort of the Gulf pirates, and the present
dock-yard of the Pacific. The exuberant density
of the foliage is presented to the eye in every
direction, and the island having a hilly and
undulating surface, the effect is very fine and
imposing, mountain rising on mountain, as it
were, of luxuriant forest and mangrove trees,
whose unfading and perennial green ever invites
the eye of the traveller down the lovely Bay of
Panama. When I was there, three years ago, a
much-to-be-deplored tragedy was enacted. A
carpenter by trade, who resided with his wife in
a cottage near the beach, was known to have
amassed some money, and he was about to leave
the island. This was also known,—his cottage
was broken into at two o'clock on one morning
in June ; his throat was gashed at the hand of a
rude assassin as he slept. His wife, who was in
bed with him at the time, miraculously escaped
from the house in her night dress, with her
throat also half dissevered. She ran through

the forest and the night to the nearest habitation — the "Verandah Hotel;" an alarm was
given, but the murderers had fled when the
scene of bloodshed was reached. During the
day, however, two suspected men were captured
and hanged by the populace; one from the
bowsprit of an old ship, stranded on the beach,
the other from the bough of a tree.

This was Lynch law with a vengeance. Their
bodies were afterwards thrown into the bay,
where they were quickly devoured by sharks,
which there abound in large numbers. A short
period after that, a melancholy catastrophe
occurred, by the upsetting of a boat on her way
from Panama to Taboga, which resulted in the
loss of six lives, and of which the following lines
offer a more graphic description than any other
I can afford :—

Returning to that island yet once more,
The breeze-impelled swift-coursing cutter flew
On o'er the rock-strewn waters tow'rds the shore
Of high Taboga, picturesque to view.
The wind blew fresher, and the rampant waves
Lash'd the bare breakers as we passed them by
In plunging haste. Here ocean often raves,
And sharks disport and winds blow fierce and high ;

The blue above turns black with sudden change,
And all is wild commotion, till the squall
 Passes away, and then with lengthy range
The eye can mark the mountains dark and tall,
That flank the main five thousand miles along,
 From this the Gulf of Islands, to that strait
Cours'd by Magellan once.   But to my song.
On plunged the boat, she bounded to her fate--
One moment more a sunken reef was struck,
(The sailors cursed their own and vessel's luck);
She filled, she sank, and left eight struggling souls
To battle with the elements or die—
To flee the sharks which now swam up in shoals,
Or be devoured.   But whither could they fly ?
An island lay not far from where she sank,
So all dashed forward, madly, tow'rds its bank,
But of the eight, two only gain'd the shore,
The rest were gorged or mangled as they swam.
And on those waters, save some crimson gore,
No sign of those who'd peopled the " Wig-wam"*
Was left.   Woeful their fate ! sad, thrilling, yea,
Too wild to tell.   Alas that island bay !

From Panama to San Francisco across smooth
water, and with the balmiest of sea breezes, the
passenger will observe nothing unusual to strike
his attention, or mark the voyage with more than
ordinary incident; on nearing the Gulf Strait of
San Francisco, however, the bold and picturesque

* The name of the sunken boat.

scenery of mountains and coast cannot fail to excite his admiration.

The Bay is separated from the sea by low mountain ranges, looking from the peaks of the Sierra Nevada. The coast mountains present an apparently continuous line with only a single gap, and that resembling an Alpine pass. This is the only water communication from the coast to the interior country. Approaching from the sea, the coast presents a bold and declivitous outline, with undulating shade, here sharp and rugged, there almost smokelike in its softness.

On the south the bordering mountains come down in a narrow ridge of broken hills, terminating in a precipitous point, against which the sea breaks heavily. On the northern side the mountains present a stern and imposing promontory, rising, in a few miles, to a height of two or three thousand feet. Between these points lies the strait, about a mile broad in the narrowest part, and five miles long from the sea to the bay.

Passing through this so-called Golden Gate, the bay opens to the right and left, extending in each direction about thirty-five miles, having a total length of more than seventy miles, and a coast of two hundred and seventy-five miles.

It is divided by straits and projecting points into three separate bays, of which the northern two are called San Pablo, and Luisoon bays. Within the view presented lies a mountainous country, the bay resembling an interior lake of large extent, lying between parallel ranges of mountains.

Islands, which have the bold aspect of the shores, some mere masses of rock, others verdant and moss clad, rising to the height of from three to eight hundred feet, break its surface, and enhance its picturesqueness

Directly fronting the entrance, and a few miles back from the shore, are to be seen a lofty range of mountains, rising about two thousand feet above the water level, and crowned by forests of gigantic cypress trees. Behind, the rugged peak of Mount Diavola, nearly four thousand feet high, overlooks the surrounding country of the bay, and the San Joaquim. The immediate shore of the bay derives, from its proximate and opposite relation to the sea, the name of Contra Costa, or Counter Coast.

It presents a varied character of rugged and broken hills, rolling and undulating land, and rich alluvial shores, backed by fertile and wooded ranges, here and there marked with villages and farms.

A low alluvial bottom land, several miles in breadth, with occasional open woods of oak, borders the base of the mountains around the southern arm of the bay, terminating in a breadth of twenty miles in the beautiful valley of San Joseph; a narrow plain of rich alluvial soil, lying between, ranges from two to three thousand feet high.   The valley is thinly wooded with groves of oak, free from under-brush, and after the spring rains is covered with grass.   Taken in connection with the valley of San Juan, with which it forms a con-tinuous plain, it is fifty-five miles long, and from one to twenty broad, opening into smaller valleys amongst the hills.   At the head of the bay it is twenty miles broad, and about the same at the southern end; where the soil is beautifully fertile, covered in the summer with four or five varieties of wild clover.   In many places it is overgrown with wild mustard, growing ten or twelve feet high, in almost impenetrable fields, through which roads are made like lanes.

On both sides, the mountains are fertile, wooded, or covered with grass and scattered trees. On the west it is protected from the chilly influence of the north-west winds by the Wild Cat ridge which separates it from the coast. This is a grassy timbered mountain, watered with small streams, and wooded on both sides with many varieties of trees and shrubbery, the heavier forest pine and cypress occupying the western slope. This range terminates in the south in the Anno Nuevo point of Monterey Bay; and in the north declines into a broken ridge of hills about five miles wide, between the bay and the sea; and having the city of San Francisco on the bay shore near its northern extremity, sheltered from the cold winds and sea fog.

The slope of alluvial land continues around the eastern shores of the bays, intersected with small streams, with good landing-places and deep water.

The Strait of Carquines, about a mile broad,

connects the San Pablo and Suisoon Bays. The latter is connected with an expansion of the river, formed by the junction of the Sacramento and the San Joaquim, which enter San Francisco Bay at the same latitude nearly as the Tagus at Lisbon. A delta of twenty-five miles in length, divided into islands by channels, connects the bay with the valleys of the Sacramento and the San Joaquim, into the mouth of which the tide flows, and which water the bay together as one river.

Such is the bay of San Francisco and its bounding coast land. It lies as a sea in itself, connected only with the ocean by a defensible neck, or gate, opening out, between seventy and eighty miles to the right and left, upon a breadth of fifteen, deep enough for the largest ships. The head of the bay is about forty miles from the sea, and there connects it with the noble valleys of the Sacramento and the San Joaquim.

Fascinating as is the scenery just described, it is, however, more probable that the traveller will have his thoughts more engrossed by the land he is nearing, and the wealth it has in store for him, than in the contemplation of forest and mountain, flood and plain; and he will more eagerly canvass the pilot's news, and join in the clamour of enquiry and conversation about the latest from the diggings on Frazer River, than he will about the geographical prospect within his view.

However that may be, it is to be hoped, that he will not omit the survey on his return, when his mind has been rendered more calm by the realization of his hopes: for there is no excuse for a man who has wealth in gold, and consequently entertains no fear of sheriff's officers, not enjoying the beauties of Nature wherever he be. So much for the picturesque.

CHAPTER XV.

THE DIGGINGS.

It is a pleasing sight to stand on the here rocky and there moss-clad banks of that picturesque but unpoetically-named river, the Frazer, and watch canoe after canoe glide past at regatta speed, laden with the gold-thirsty adventurers of eclipsed California. There is a romance in the lot and career of each of those weather-beaten daring sons of enterprise who launch forth into the wilderness to brave danger and endure hardships far away from the homes of their childhood, to which many of them are assuredly never destined to return. There is

something noble in the self-dependence they
manifest, and the hope and perseverance which
fires and actuates them in their arduous struggle
for the necessary bauble of earth. But those
who have felt the pains of poverty and the
insults of debt, will at least in spirit join with
them in their quest for gain, for this is an age
and a world in which we must have money or
sink; and if we die in its pursuit, we scarcely
share a worse fate than would have awaited us
had we remained passive. All the world worship Mammon, and woe unto him who does
not gain and lives; better to perish; to be unsuccessful is to be socially damned. Such is the
barren code of English life and opinion. Get
me out of it, say I, and may millions echo my
words and sentiment.

The Frazer was navigated as far as Fort Hope,
one hundred and fifty miles from its mouth, on
the 4th of June, by the steamer Surprise, and for
the first time, Fort Langley having hitherto been
considered the highest navigable point. It is
now known that Fort Yale, which is still higher,
may be reached by sea-going vessels. The Surprise, together with others, was regularly steam-

ing between Victoria (Vancouver's Island) and Fort Hope, in connection with the Pacific Mail Steam Packet Company's steamers from San Francisco to the former port.

The Hudson's Bay Company's steamer the Otter, together with the Seabird, owned by a private party, were also engaged in the same traffic, each charging the same fare, viz. twenty dollars from the island, or any of the sound ports, to Fort Langley, and the ports beyond.

Between the 27th of May and the 5th of June, fifty canoes had reached the latter-named fort, each containing an average of six persons. The governor of the Hudson's Bay Company, together with four directors, and the captain of the British steamer Satellite, proceeded to Fort Yale on the 22nd of May, where they appointed Custom House officers. They were cordially received by the miners on the various bars along the river, and appointed magistrates from among them. After the 1st of August Governor Douglas will, to the best of his ability, enforce strictly the terms of his late proclamation, requiring every man to take out a license, for which he is to pay five dollars per month. The edict that no freight shall be taken into the interior on the steamers or otherwise, except that shipped by and belonging to the Hudson's Bay Company, is hardly likely to be strictly enforced for the time being. Miners were being allowed to carry full supplies for themselves, but none for trade. The up-river steamers were prohibited carrying any male passenger without his having a digging license. The sale of ardent spirits to the Indians was also prohibited. Already some have violated these regulations, and are to be severely dealt with in consequence.

One American trader from Bellingham Bay had two thousand dollars' worth of goods confiscated by the Hudson's Bay Company for trading near Fort Langley. It will be well, however, when such exasperating tyranny as this is done away with, and when that monopoly and impediment, the Company referred to, are dispossessed of the territory on which at present they form the grand stumbling-block of civilization. They would fain make each of their skin-buyers an autocrat, and constitute each digging community a serfdom; but they

will find the strong arm of rebellion lifted up
against them, if they persist in too arbitrary a
mode of government during their small remaining reign in that region.   The American and
the gold-digger will brook no infringement of
the law of right and equity; with him it is
justice or death.

Gold is found everywhere along Frazer's
River; and even during its extreme height parties were averaging fifteen to thirty dollars per
day digging in the bank or on the upper edge
of the bars, nearly all of which were overflowed.
Big strikes of from fifty to two hundred and
fifty dollars were common.   The miners were
chiefly congregated between Forts Langley and
Yale, and for some twenty or thirty miles above
the latter, stretching along a distance of more
than one hundred miles.   A few were digging
on Harrison River and other tributaries, where
the gold abounds in larger particles.   Those
who were mining on the forks of Thompson's
River showed still richer yields, but were compelled to leave, owing to the absence of provisions and the high stage of the water.   The
god upon the bars of the river, where the great

body of the miners are at work, is found in little particles like sand. No quicksilver had been used; but when that is attainable, the yield will be greatly augmented.

At Hill's Bar, those at work averaged fifty dollars per day during the whole time they had been there. The Indians are as rich in gold and as excited as the whites.

While the river remains at its height, trails have to be resorted to above Fort Hope, and these are difficult. When the water falls, the river is navigable for canoes almost to its source, with the interruption of a few short portages.

CHAPTER XVI.

FROM LONDON TO SAN FRANCISCO.

IT is well to keep to facts—bald facts in a work of this kind — and therefore the reader will fix his reliance more upon what is said than turn over the leaves, seeking the amusement of a romance, or the fun of comedy.   This book may shape the destiny of hundreds, pardon my egotism, therefore it behoves me to consider of the responsibility of my task, and, however sprightly may be my step, not to stumble into the ditch of error.   Let us then proceed, reader, arm in arm—that is to say —with our spades and pickaxes, up the. golden river of our hopes.   Anything for money ; we cannot do without it, and that is the reason we pay our sixty per cent. for money, and half that swallowed up in gilt *jewelry*, and—deliver us, ye gods—a picture. However, Moses must suffer a postponement ; if the diggings pay, he's sure to be glad to see us again—in the mean time creditors' proceedings must be adjourned till our return to town—next year but one. Moses will like that. Unanimously resolved that we go to the diggings, and take our petty cash with us instead of into the Queen's Bench. Let us fancy ourselves off, whizzing across country, under arches and over bridges, past the brightly gleaming light — the red flare of the Lancashire furnaces, bang into the Lime Street station at Liverpool. Then far away over the dancing waves of the merry Atlantic to the Parian spires and the islet-strewed bay of New York—the city of bricks and marble, of beautiful women and fried oysters—of gorgeous hotels and flirtations. Then away with the rabble, nine hundred at least, to the Isthmus, where Aspinwall lies as flat as a pancake half hid in a swamp, and looking most blistered and brown. By the way at Jamaica, the steamer may call to take

I 3

in her dinner of coals, when women alone to the
feeding are set, while the lords of creation sit by,
and bamboo-faced Englishmen tear about town
as though they were treading Dundee, when of
course all the time it is as hot as Bombay, and
as dusty as Melbourne in May.   From Aspinwall, starting by railway, you go with a mountain
of forest in view, built up on each side in im-
pervious growth, rank and gigantic and wild.
Ten to one but we shall have to get out before
we are half way across, to give the engine a push
along.   Such is travelling across the Isthmus.

Panama is an old tumble-down city, with
ancient and defenceless walls and narrow streets,
but possessing, however rocky and treacherous
it may be, a picturesque and lovely bay, decked
out with flower-clad isles, and overlooked by the
mighty Andes, that loom far and high in the
enchanting distance.

After the arrival of the train all Panama will
be tramped over and blockaded by the eight
hundred live Yankees ; all the cafés and bar-
rooms will be overcrowded, and Panama will
seem to writhe under the din and weight of the
sacrilegious strangers.   A gun is fired—all rush

down to the beach—a tender takes us off batch after batch to the steamer yonder; away we go. A sudden squall springs up, we career gaily over, and sing and drink amidst the clamour of nearly a thousand voices. There is scarcely moving room on board, yet there is a life-belt slung up for every soul of us—happy consolation—where's mine? It is all eating, drinking, and anticipation till we reach San Francisco. They don't care so much about our arrival now as they do of the El Dorado ships, but still they are very glad to see us in their way. It is the twenty-ninth of May. On shore we go, leaping like so many frogs from the whole side-length of the steamer. Here we are; what a hubbub! We drink cocktails and gum-ticklers to amuse ourselves. We go with the crowd to "book" for the next steamer to Victoria — we have to wait our turn—there are at least five hundred before us, and just as many coming up behind. Glorious country! We have reached it at last.

Once more I stand on the shores of California, and the bay of San Francisco.

It is the rosy month of Juue. On three

sides the glorious waters are spread out to the view, bounded by shores beautifully diversified with bold headlands, verdant promontories, and shaded islets, where the streamlets stealing down from the sloping hills commingle with the blue waters of the Pacific, while towering above are lofty mountain ranges, amongst which the half shadowy crest of Mount Diavola stands in towering pre-eminence, forming a striking background, holding the bay and its contiguous shores in their embrace, like a large inland lake; the broad expanse of its rippling bosom picturesquely relieved by the sight of many a sail-spread craft, with here and there a steamer, and the naked rigging of the anchorage ground.

San Francisco itself is all life and animation, full of revelry and delight; the very streets and wharves seem to groan beneath the weight, and the hotels and saloons swarm with the daring adventurers destined for the El Dorado, hardy sons of toil and enterprise, ready to penetrate even to the North Pole, in their eager, fevered pursuit of gold. Down the Sacramento pours night after night a torrent of future British

Columbians. It is useless to attempt to stem the tide: in the rush, the words of advice and the voice of reason are equally unheeded. The fever rages with a virulence that defies description, and those who have become infected with it will hear nothing, listen to nothing, think of nothing, dream of nothing but Frazer River and its golden sands. Even newspaper men, the last and least credulous in the world, are making off, — all seem determined upon exploring for themselves. They cannot be stopped even for a moment in their excited career; and although those who are now there, from whom letters have been received, advise intending emigrants not to start for a month till the river falls, yet every steamer, clipper ship, or barque, which sets sail for the north, is filled with passengers, and hundreds have to be left behind for want of accommodation-room for them. For the rest—to my narrative.

CHAPTER XVII.

I EMBARK FOR VANCOUVER, AND SUBSEQUENTLY
MAKE USE OF MY GEOLOGICAL SHOVEL.

IT was a bright and beaming morning in early
June on which I embarked on board the steamer
Cortes for Victoria, Vancouver's Island; all
things to me wore a riant and festive aspect, for
my spirit was elate with hope and buoyed up
with the pleasures of anticipation; to my eyes
all was gold and glitter, and all that glittered
gold. Ardent and impetuous, with a daring
love of enterprise, danger, and excitement, I felt
ready to plunge wherever the hand of fate or
fortune beckoned, and, being reckless of consequences, wherever destiny determined.

I stood upon the deck of that vessel as she
slowly moved from her place at San Francisco

wharf, one of nearly fifteen hundred passengers, and I blended up my voice with the farewell of that mighty crowd in a hearty, hopeful cheer to those collected on shore, although I had no friend there to respond. I was alone—I had been alone in life before—but I make friends with all mankind, and I never expect to find one more true to me than another till I am smiled upon in Holy —, my friend Parson Baggs will fill up the blank, by her whose love and every pleasure may be mine.

The cheers of those on shore died faintly away in the distance, as the paddle-wheels flew round ; the waving of hats ceased, and the broad bay, with its bounding and picturesque coast-lands, lay out before our view. The bright glare of the sun lent a golden tinge to the rippling waters, and all nature seemed clad in her most brilliant array. The majority of those on board were, like myself, alone in California, and had forsaken the city we were so fastly receding from, without compunction or regret, without a shade of sorrow at parting from any beloved object, or a qualm of conscience for the past ; but some there were whose anxious, lingering looks proclaimed the inner working

of the heart, and as the wharf became entirely
hidden from the view, seemed to utter within
themselves a benediction on those whom they
had left behind—wives and children dear to
them—for the gold-digger is a man of deep
and generous feelings ; his avocations foster
affection and endear the remembrance of home,
and as he rocks away at his cradle-rocker,
and gathers the glittering treasure presented
to his eye, he thinks of those to whom he is
endeared, and contemplates it more for the
sake of the good it will be productive of to
those whom he loves, than he does for the mere
sake of gratifying his taste for gain.   Away
sped the ship, her sails pouting in the gentle
breeze ; soon we cleared the strait, and the
ocean, calm and expansive, lay spread out before
us, with here and there a sail coursing along
the horizon, not " small by degrees and beautifully less," but

> Slowly expanding as we nearer drew,
> 'Neath and above the ever-rolling blue.

There were several companies on board, num-
bering from three to six men each. Some of these
had brought whaleboats with them, in which
they intended making the voyage up-river from

Victoria, and all were tolerably well stocked with
mining tools and provisions.   Swarthy, restless
fellows, they walked backwards and forwards,
and guessed and calculated, either on deck or in
the cabins, from early morning till midnight.
The same restlessness of tongue and manner
manifested itself during the consumption of
their usual meals, when pork and beans, pickles
and molasses, were thrown together on the one
plate, and hurried into obscurity with all the
impetuosity of an ardent gusto and excitement
peculiar to themselves.

At length, and on the morning of the sixth
day from San Francisco, the bold shore of the
destined island was presented to our longing
view, and in two hours afterwards we anchored
within the harbour of Esquimault, Victoria.

We all went ashore immediately, that is as fast
as boats could be had to carry us, so that very
shortly the streets of the island town presented
an appearance of human traffic not dissimilar to
that of Panama after receiving a similar freight.
We lost no time in repairing to the government
gold license office, where we tendered our five
dollars each, in exchange for a monthly voucher,
privileging us to dig, which also was our neces-

sary passport to travel up river, for without it
we could not have proceeded along the mainland.   This tax was frankly paid, but heartily
denounced.   The town wore a highly flourishing
and pleasing appearance, the most noticeable
feature in the shop and trading line being the
scarcity of anything like hotels ; there were five
places, however, where liquor was sold, the proprietor of each having to pay the Hudson's Bay
Company a license fee of no less than £120 per
annum for the privilege.   For my own part, I
strolled a little way inland along green Jamaica-
looking lanes, running like channels through a
continent of cultivation ; acres of potatoes, wheat,
maize, .barley, and gently-waving rye, were successively presented to my admiring view.   The
fertility of the soil was everywhere apparent.
Limestone-built villas here and there decked the
suburbs, and cottages festooned with a profusion
of blossoming creeping plants flanked the road a
little to the westward of Government House,
which from its elevated position seemed to hold
presidence over all the lesser architecture around.

The sun with his golden radiance was shed-
ding floods of light over the varied landscape,
casting the shadow of the Indian on the placid

water of a lagoon, which wound like a river in a gently-shelving valley beyond, and giving a glow of life and animation to the bending corn-fields and the parian habitations of men. The birds were joyfully caroling away in sweet and hope-inspiring unison; the herds at pasture lowed plaintively, and the bleating of sheep and lambkin broke audibly to life as I passed by natural hedges of wild rose and black-berry bushes, and fields redundant of grass and clover, whose aroma was borne on the breeze far away to the uplands, where the wild man still holds sway, and civilization hath scarce or never trodden.

At five o'clock on the same day I embarked on board the American steamer Surprize,—(which had just returned from Fort Hope with Governor Douglas and suite. He is a fine old, jolly looking Scotchman, very gentlemanly and agreeable; his wife is a half breed lady, and he has issue a daughter, recently married, as beautiful and valiant as ever sprang to life in North America) —for the highest navigable point of the Frazer River; the passage-money being twenty dollars without distinction, whereas the San Francisco steamers' fares varied from thirty to sixty-five

dollars.   We passed and saluted the steamer
Satellite, as we entered the mouth of the river,
after crossing, or rather rounding, the Strait of
San Juan de Fuca, which separates the island
from the mainland, and after that, threaded our
way amongst the canoes past Fort Langley and
the mouth of the Harrison River, towards Fort
Hope, which we reached early on the morning
of the second day afterwards ; having sailed a
hundred and sixty miles in all from Victoria.
The slowness of our progress was owing to the
strong down-river current ; had the supply of coal
not been limited, she would have advanced' as
far as Fort Yale.   Here I disembarked.

The weather was delightful, and tended to
enhance the merry excitement of the gold-
hunters.   The right bank of the river on either
side of the Fort and the Que-Que-alla River,
was dotted with miners, each stooping and
busy, rocking, digging, or scooping up the gold.
Gold glittered amongst the sands on the beach ;
I stooped down and gathered a few grains, and
finding the bait too tempting to resist, I set
manfully to work, turning over the sand with a
geological shovel I had brought with me from
San Francisco.   I was but an amateur, and had

entered on the Frazer River journey more for the sake of seeing a young nation spring into life than anything else, although I do not disclaim having turned digger for the time being, an avocation too remunerative and independent to be considered *infra dig*. True, I had dug for gold at the Sonora mines and at Ballaarat, on two respective occasions of half-an-hour each, and found a little, but still, as the Yankees would say, I was green at the business ; yet, in spite of my greenness and geological shovel, I realized, to use another of their expressions, in the space of three hours, no less than fifteen dollars and sixty cents.' worth of particles. I thought myself in for a run of luck, and resolved to set to work on the next morning in the same place ; in the meantime, however, I met with several of the red-shirted community, who rather made small of my day's earnings and geological shovel than otherwise, and guessed if they hadn't realized more than that 'ere they'd be looking tarnation down flat on their rockers.

" I guess, I calculate pretty correctly when I say that I've realized three hundred and seventy-three dollars and fifty-eight cents this ar week," said a gaunt, sleek-haired man with a black beard

and restless eyes, and with two revolvers slung
to his belt.   He stood in front of a large tent
used as a boarding house, the only concern of the
kind nearer than Fort Langley, and in which I
had engaged residence at a charge of three dollars
a day, being half a dollar in excess of the charge
at the hotel-palaces of New York.   It was
supper time and seven o'clock, so I sat down
with my successful double-revolvered friend, and
commenced with considerable gusto the work of
tea-drinking, mutton-chop eating, and speculation as to the probable yield of gold both during
and after the freshets.   There were fifteen of us
in all, including our German host, who had only
just set up his canvas hotel, having run down
from San Francisco on the previous steamer to
the Cortes, for the purpose of boarding and lodg-
ing the miners in the octagonal tent he brought
for the occasion.

" I guess he's realizing a pretty considerable
sum," remarked a party with only one revolver,
but a terrific pair of moustachios.   I nodded
assent, guessing at the same time that we
should have to sleep on the ground.   My companion guessed likewise, but accompanied it
with the ejaculation " skins " and a significant

point of the head and the eye towards the tent wall; seeing nothing there, I guessed the skins alluded to were outside for the time being. I was right; they were lying *al fresco*, and were destined to constitute our only beds. After dark, the skins were brought in and spread along either side of the tent, leaving a space of about half a foot for the purposes of navigation. They were soon covered with the lounging and recumbent bodies of the miners, who kept on talking and medicinal-brandy drinking till about ten o'clock, when silence supervened or rather snoring was substituted for talking. All slept with their revolvers and gold under their variously improvised pillows, and I did not form an exception to the rule. The host slept in the middle of his pantry, surrounded and almost hidden by pots and pans, and occasionally making commotion amongst his scanty supply of crockery ware. I did not very readily yield to the embrace of slumber, for the novelty and excitement of my new life kept my thinking powers awake. It was a little past midnight, and the sickly oil lamp which swung from the tent roof still shed its hazy light. Suddenly I heard a rustle and a hissing noise, something between that of a hostler currycombing and

stifled laughter.   I lifted my head, and directing
my eyes towards the tent's opening, beheld a
Red Indian, more than six feet in height, holding
the canvas drop up, and grinning with evident
delight, while the heads and eyes of two or three
of his fellows were to be seen peering in the back
ground.

"Hillo !" I involuntarily exclaimed : two or
three awoke at the signal, and sprang upon their
legs as they heard the glee shouts and tramp of
the Indians, who bounded off at the instant.   At
least a dozen awoke and asked "What's up ?"
but after ascertaining that it was all over, went
to sleep again, including our host, who upset a
mustard pot over his whiskers, in his sudden
endeavour to attain the perpendicular, and
dropped flat on a gridiron when he proceeded
to resume the horizontal.   At about five o'clock,
several began yawning, and recommended " the
bolt upright."

" I guess, mate, you've had a pretty good
hiding ?" said one jocularly, in allusion to a
good night's rest on the skins.

" Guess I have, it's done me a tarnation deal
more good than a cow-hiding," was the response.

" What was that about Indians ?" some one

asked ; and so they talked, meanwhile assuming the bolt upright, and adjourning outside the tent to make their slight and hasty toilet. After that, gold was the sole and absorbing theme, the great order of the day.

Already miners were at work along the river's banks, and the lurid sun shot out his rays of fire in dazzling brightness, and hope-inspiring efful-gence far and wide, over the river and over the grass land, lighting up the mountains in beauty of many shades, and displaying the mighty fo-liage of the forest in gilded loveliness—giving gaiety and animation to everything ; and while buoying up the hearts of men, making all nature glad and rosy. It was such a morning—the first after my arrival—when I again set to work with my geological shovel, not half a mile from the tent, and about three miles above Fort Hope.

The river was a little lower than on the previous day, and miners were busy, either singly or in twos, rocking the washing stuff ; it requires two to work a rocker well, one to dig and the other to wash and collect the " bits." Some who had not brought rockers with them, were engaged in making them out of green timber ; the bot-

K

tom, however, a thin metal plate punctured with holes, had to be purchased, and at an exorbitant price—one of my fellow boarders have given forty dollars for one ; a thing that in England would cost about eighteen pence, and in San Francisco two dollars and a half. But the necessity for a rocker in wet diggings is all but absolute. For my own part, I gave four dollars for a pan, and worked that in lieu of a rocker, making about four bits each washing, equivalent to two shillings sterling : this continued throughout the day, so that by nightfall I had realized " pretty considerable," which means more than two ounces of clean gold. In spite of the proverb of a rolling stone gathering no moss, I was impelled by force of reports coming down river of great yields nearer the mountains, as well as by seeing the canoes making their way past me for a higher part of the river, to join in the purchase of a canoe for eighty dollars, with five others ; and accordingly, everything connected with the Yankee-California and gold-hunting element being done with a rush, we set off at seven o'clock on the next morning for Fort Yale, afterwards to advance as we deemed best. Two or three miles below the latter, however, at a point called Hill's Bar, a sandy flat about five hundred yards in length, we went ashore, having heard reports before starting, of good returns there. We found the place crowded with Indians, at least five hundred of them, men, squaws, and children; with about eighty miners at work on the bar. These were averaging from fifteen to twenty-five dollars a day each man. Provisions were exceedingly dear and scarce, flour selling at eighty dollars the barrel, bacon at seventy-five cents per pound, and butter at a dollar per pound. A party of twenty miners had set out on the previous day to prospect for dry diggings in the interior, under the guidance of a batch of Indians, who said there was plenty (hihew) of gold to be found, but no tidings of their success had yet been heard of. The population were subsisting chiefly upon deer's flesh and salmon, both of which were abundant. My companions went "in for a dig" as they termed it, at this place, but being anxious to explore new spots, did not remain beyond noon on the day following, during which time I ate a "green bear" steak—the first of the kind I had ever partaken of, and

K 2

worthy of being ranked with the shark cutlets,
and pieces of a whale's tail, not omitting the
morsel of horse-flesh, which I had previously
demolished in other regions of land and water.

About half-a-mile higher up than Fort Yale
the river rushes between huge and naked rocks,
belonging to the Cascade range, the sides being
almost perpendicular.   Here a portage has to be
made along an Indian track-way, and over
rugged ground ; the scenery on either side, however, is highly picturesque and mountainous.

We ascended the river under the pilotage of
an Indian, whom we had engaged at eight
dollars a day wages, about sixty miles above
this fort, passing the " Forks," the junction of
the Thompson and Frazer, on our way, and
making about a hundred and seventy miles
in all from the river's mouth.   During the
journey we had to stem and round a rapid
where the water fell and swilled rather heavily
over rocky shoals; this was about five miles
below " Sailors' Diggings," and twenty above
Fort Yale, consequently about forty miles from
where we now found ourselves.

There were not more than half-a-dozen

miners to be seen along the shore in either
direction; and these were stragglers, or rather
prospecting explorers from the Thompson and
Sailors' Diggings lower down, and reported to
be very rich, but which our party were eager to
"beat," and outvie by fresh discoveries.

On shore we jumped, pell mell and excited,
for there is ever an excitement about gold
digging; and blunted must be the suscepti-
bility, and torpid the soul of that man who
can gather naked gold and not feel a throb of
delight and an ever unsatisfied longing for more,
which keeps alive every faculty of the human
mind, and makes imagination picture joys and
comforts to be bought, and perhaps castles to
be built, with that same lucre.   Thus, practical
as is the labour of the "digger," it is the
strongest incentive to romance of thought, as
well as the most ambition firing of any of the
manual occupations of the age.

My companions of the canoe were soon hard
at work: three were single-handed, that is, without partners; the other two were in partnership,
and had a rocker between them, one filling, the
other rocking.   I set to work, after a salmon

dinner, with my geological shovel and my tin pan, and washed away with all the gusto of a veritable digger. At about sunset I was interrupted by a hoarse "Hillo, mate!" from one of my canoe brethren, an Anglo-Saxon Californianized pick and shovel handler.

"The yellow fever's pretty high with you, I guess," he observed.

Of course I comprehended his metallic joke, and retorted by the ready calculation that it was the same with him.

"Sartinly," was his reply, "it's raging up here awful strong."

After this interesting exchange of feverish ideas we joined the rest of our party, and found that each man, during the six hours we had been working, had realized from three to five ounces, or in other words, from forty-eight to eighty dollars; the market value of gold being sixteen dollars the ounce.

These were good earnings, and as satisfactory as any we had heard of lower down the river; but still the mania was for advancing further still, by making a land portage with the canoe to avoid the rapids a few miles higher

up, as the miners had the impression, and truly
so, that whatever the yield here might be, it
was sure to be still greater higher up; for it
was evident that the grains became more plentiful and larger the more we advanced; thus
demonstrating that such, during the course of
time, had been washed down from the mountains,
or other highly auriferous regions adjacent,
which, when reached, would far outvie the most
sanguine expectations. We looked forward
to fields of gold; and our imaginations transformed the very mountains into gold, which we
should find in unportable abundance. We
thought of gold as a collier does of coal; but
still we treasured every grain we gathered, and
would have defended it at the revolver's point
as desperately as life itself. Such is Mammon.

As for provisions and habitations, at this
stage, they were both equally scarce. We had
to run down river three miles, towards Sailors'
Bar, before we arrived at a newly constructed
store of green timber, where flour was selling
at a hundred dollars the barrel; molasses, seven
dollars a gallon; pork, a dollar per pound;
tea, four dollars per pound; sugar, two dollars

per pound; beans, one dollar per pound; picks at six dollars each, and shovels three dollars each; and where we were taken in for the night at three dollars a head.

For the benefit of the unsophisticated, who know as much about dollars and cents as those who live in Buffalo do about the falls of Niagara, I may as well mention that five go to the sovereign; the dollar Yankee being here worth forty-eight pence British currency.

The Indians at this spot were straggling in their numbers, but were as well stocked with gold as the white men. They carried it about with them in skin pouches and bags containing from one to five hundred dollars' worth, and manifested the most friendly feelings towards us, frolicing about in the highest glee imaginable; and giving ejaculatory utterance to a more complicated amount of Chinook than I could possibly comprehend. They "absquatulated" as the evening closed in, and sought rest, or revelry, as the case might be, in their encampment, which lay at the distance of a mile or so inland.

As for myself, I "turned in," or rather on

to a wooden bench covered over with a bear skin, at about ten o'clock, and so passed the night together with about twenty others, who were variously located about the store, which, of course, consisted of one room only; most of them occupying positions on the tops of boxes of merchandize, surrounded by varieties, raw and manufactured, in a manner similar to the German boarding-house keeper amongst his crockery; and constituting in all a perfect chaos of legs, arms, provisions, and hardware.

No Red Indian disturbed our slumbers during this night, which, to speak poetically, was beautifully radiant with moonbeams that penetrated with welcome light (through the place where the windows " ought to be ") into our chaotic dormitory, where molasses and butter were the silent witnesses of our unconscious repose, and where nails were our sharpest bedfellows.   By-the-bye, speaking of nails, they were here selling at a rate equivalent to a shilling each, thus placing their famous brethren, the so-called Ninepennys, completely in the shade.

We were up and at work by six o'clock, and

K 3

on one of the most lovely mornings that the
month of June ever ushered into existence—the
air at once warm and fragrant of the forest and
wild clover, was just sufficiently stirring to prevent
the heat feeling oppressive, while the enchanting
rays of the rising sun decked out the prospect in
magnificent array, brightening the more prominent parts of the mountains hundreds of miles
away, and leaving the recesses lost in a deeply contrasting shade, while far and high in the back-
ground the lofty snow-capped summits shone in
crystal purity, white and dazzling in the midst
of a sky of tranquil blue; further down, the picturesque shores of the river enhanced the beauty
of the scene, and as the eye ranged far and wide
over the landscape of forest and prairie, gentle hill
and sloping valley, admiration could not fail in
taking possession of the beholder, and imbuing
the most imaginative with feelings of delight,
and making even the most practical of gold
diggers feel that he stood up within view of a
perfect paradise of scenery—a land as rich and
as beautiful, a clime as golden and luxurious
as any upon which Nature ever lavished her
inviting treasures.

CHAPTER XVIII.

OUR ASCENT OF THE FRAZER.

NOT finding the yield equal to expectation, and being myself equally, or even more, anxious than my partners in the canoe to press on higher up the river, we set out with a newly-engaged Indian, with the view of passing the upper falls, either by land portage or skilful steersmanship; the latter, however, we were warned against trusting to, as two miners and an Indian had been drowned in the attempt to pass through, their canoe being also smashed to pieces, five days previously.

While speaking of calamities, I may as well mention that, on the 12th of May a miner from this place, who had followed his mate down river, under the impression that the latter meant to "absquatulate" on French leave with their joint earnings which he had in his possession, met him not far from the mouth of the river, and shot him dead. He was subsequently arrested, and imprisoned at Whatcom under government order.

In the vicinity of Fort Hope an American ill-treated an Indian chief, which resulted in a return of hostilities, the former drawing his revolver and shooting the chief through the left side, from the effects of which he died almost instantly. This aroused the wrath of the Indians standing near; one of whom being also armed, returned the fire, and shot a miner through the heart, from which he fell dead. The murderer of the chief then made his escape; and some days of commotion and anger elapsed before the Indians were pacified by the agent of the Hudson's Bay Company, who very laudably exerted himself in the re-establishment of peace, and the work of condolence, after so diabolical an injury received at the hands of a rude assassin.

On reaching the falls we disembarked, each man carrying his own " kit," and our Indian pilot the canoe. Had it not been for the un- usually high state of the river at this particular time and season, we could have easily avoided making the portage, but as the river ran, it was the wisest thing we could do to abstain from trying it. Still the American character— and four out of the five were Americans—is more apt to study dispatch than safety ; as for instance, a go-a-head Yankee would sooner travel by a train that was likely to take him to his destination an hour quicker than another one, although the chances were in favour of his having his neck broken on the journey. The American is eager, pushing, and impetuous; he is fond of risk, if there is the remotest chance of gaining anything by it ; and in under- takings of a hazardous and uncertain nature he is without a rival in his achievements. He will " drive a trade," and explore, in the hope of gain, farther and quicker into the heart of a country, no matter what the hardships and

obstacles to be contended against, than any
other; not even his Anglo-Saxon cousins excepted.

Civilization follows more briskly in his wake
than with any other nation; he has scarcely " set
up" in the wilderness, before he finds materials
for a newspaper arriving, and a " spick span"
editor heralding the events of the hour, and that
on a spot where the red man dances and the
wild animals of the forest are still to be seen.

However, to our portage : after proceeding nearly a mile, the canoes were again laid
on the water, and our oars plashed away with
feathered spray towards—where we knew not,
nearer than the mountains. We seemed
hemmed in by mountains, and we positively
talked of nothing but the mountains and the
probability of our making " big strikes," as we
drew nearer them. At dusk, feeling hot and
tired, we drew up in a small natural cove on
the right bank of the river, partly overhung by
a species of water-willow, which for beauty of
position might have had the advantages and
labour of art and cultivation devoted to its
planting and bestowed upon its growth. We

stepped ashore with the feelings of pioneers, and the reliant self-confidence which steals upon us when alone in the wilderness and far away from the haunts of civilization. We felt morally armed, and sledged against danger and foreign foes. We expected to meet with unaccustomed things, and hardships we had hitherto escaped; but fortitude gives strength, and we stood up each as a pillar to brave and to defy.

It is under such circumstances as these that men unite in one common and solid friendship, and are ever ready to join together in the cause of self-defence, and mutual protection, and well-being. All conventionalism is quickly banished or thrown aside, and generosity and the better feelings of the human heart preside and unite men in one honest brotherhood.

The singing of a bird, shrill, long, and musical, and the half-seething murmuring of the flowing waters of the river, alone disturbed the solitude of the seemingly primeval wilderness into which we had plunged, and which the rustling sound gently wafted from the giant forest, only tended to enhance and to render our loneliness the more impressive. But for us solemnity of scene had fewer charms than for those who, fresh from the lap of luxury, may contemplate Nature's beauties in idle peace, and smoke a nargileh beneath a fig-tree, or wander by the rivers of Damascus; for us there was the excitement of danger and uncertainty, the hope of gold and the risk of starvation. True all these were powerful incentives to hard work and enterprise; but they, in their sharpening influence, tended to disturb that calm and happy contemplation of the beautiful which, under less adventurous circumstances, could not have failed to soothe and to inspire. We were eager, impatient, and restless; and, as a matter of necessity, our thoughts were more engrossed by the consideration of where our camping-ground should be, and where and when we might be able to renew our stock of provisions, than by the scenery which met our gaze, and which promised soon to be shrouded in the embrace of night, setting aside the anxiety of the miners as to the " yield" and " big strikes" which were to accrue to them in return for their enterprise and toil; however, I must say, in justice to my own good taste, that, in spite of hope and danger, I dwelt with something like rhapsody on the picturesque region of mountain and forest which delighted my admiring, not to say astonished, gaze. No doubt the brilliant and changing hues of the sky, which were reflected upon the landscape, and threw out the irregular outline and undulations of the mountains, contributed greatly to the fascination of the view; but still I became enamoured of it, and I thought it the loveliest clime it had ever been my changeful lot to wander in.

Not an Indian was to be seen, the woodland was deserted. We began, of course, with our usual avidity, to explore and prospect, from the instant of our mooring the canoe, while our native pilot collected faggots for a fire. I soon saw that the country was not so thickly wooded as at first sight I had been led to suppose; a belt of trees merely flanked the water-side, beyond which deeply-grassed rich prairie land stretched for several miles, bounded to the westward by lofty forest trees, and to the north by the overtowering mountains, but open to the south, and reaching further than the eye could carry. We returned to our camping-ground near the beach, and a few yards only from the canoe, before darkness set in, and very soon the crackling of the pile of leaves and branches which our Indian pilot had collected, was heard amid the lively flames of an al fresco fire.   The weather was warm, so that we would have readily dispensed with such, had it not been for the sake of cooking some dried salmon, and making a decoction of tea—glorious beverage— it reminded me of Australia, where we cannot do without it.   The " Bushman" has his tea three times a day; and although the Chinese only favour him with the big-leaved quality of the commodity, it makes, nevertheless, a plea- sant, cheering beverage, and with a cake of damper, is highly comforting, both " now and hereafter," which is more than can be said of alcohol, or the more complex and sophisticated food and cookery of Paris and of New York; as for London, it need not be mentioned, the orthodox sole, and roast beef of the hotels, with variations of fresh mustard, and a steak for a year together, being too harmless for com- plaint.

The fire crackled as if rejoicing; merrily,

laughingly curled the flames, and the pleasant
smoke wriggling out of their embrace, sailed up
peacefully over our heads and wasted itself away
in the pure atmosphere of the forest.   We
sat ourselves down on the cool turf and partook
of the repast prepared with all the gusto of a
healthy appetite and relish, and then sat round
the cheering fire, which we plied with faggots
from time to time, talking of our hopes and
fears, but chiefly of the successes that awaited
us,—for the miner is constitutionally sanguine,
—and hard, indeed, must have been his luck
when *he* is bowed down and despairing.

Each man had blankets with him, and for
myself I had an opossum rug in addition, which
I found highly serviceable ; it was one that had
served me during a " bush" excursion in Australia, and was now doubly prized by me on
that account.   I spread it at the base of a large
tree not far from the fire, and there I prostrated
myself, the rest of the party following my ex-
ample, one by one, within a radius of twenty
yards.   As the night fell in, the stars shone out
like jets of fire, and the moon again, with steady
light, silvered the landscape : once through an

opening in the forest above me I caught a
glimpse of her radiant face, and felt glad in the
contemplation of such heavenly beauty, which,
although a common sight, was nevertheless to
me, under the circumstances in which I then
lay, peculiarly grateful and soothing; for I am
an admirer of the great and beautiful, and a
sunny clime to me is earthly paradise.

The howling of a wolf and the cries of other
animals of the wilderness were heard from time
to time coming faintly from the distance, but
did not excite our fears; at any rate, our revolvers were ready, and our Indian pilot was as
quick of hearing, whether asleep or awake, as
Paddy might say, as he was sure and composed
as to our safety and his own.

We were up and "hard at it" soon after
daybreak on the following morning. We found
gold everywhere; and my only surprise was, that
a region so palpably auriferous should have
remained so long unproclaimed and hidden from
the gaze of civilization. I found a very choice
quartz " specimen," six ounces in weight, half
jutting out of the sand on the river's bank,
which contained at least four ounces of the

precious metal,—in fact, the larger half of the piece was solid gold, and could have been broken off from the quartz to which it was attached; this was a sure sign to us that large masses of gold must lie somewhere higher up the river than we had yet proceeded, most probably in the recesses, and at the foot of the mountains themselves, and that the gold found on the banks, and which is no doubt equally abundant in the bed of the river, was merely the off-scouring and broken fragments of the great gold region lying further inland. During this day's work seven "nuggets," varying from about half an ounce to five ounces in weight, were picked up, while the average yield of "dust" was no less than four ounces each man, equal to about sixty-four dollars (£12 16s.), besides the nuggets. This was glorious; but still the Yankees were anything but satisfied; it seemed as if the more they got the more they expected to get; and if they could only find out and reach this "source," of which we talked so much, they would have nothing to do but use their picks and shovels in gathering as much gold as they could get horses and canoes to carry. We

appeared to be the first who had tried this
"spot;" but it was known that another party of
six had ascended the river higher than we were,
but they were reported to have diverged into
the interior, and found diggings at the foot of
the Cascade Mountains, many miles in a south-
westernly direction, and away from the river altogether. We therefore entertained strong hopes
of being ourselves the sole discoverers of this
prime mine of wealth, and leaving the rich
diggings behind us, pushed on for richer diggings and "bigger strikes" still, on the very
day following the yield last quoted, assured in
our own minds, and moreover with experience
in our favour, that we could not but be gainers
by the movement, and perhaps—as, indeed, we
sanguinely hoped, and I as reliantly as any of
them—solve the grand problem as to where the
gold came from. So with this hope impelling
us, and this achievement strongly before us, we
moved away from the newly-baptized Willow
Bank, which, by-the-bye, had been and still
promised, if we could do no better elsewhere, to
be a very good bank for us; and while the
word "Excelsior" rang out from the lips of one

on board, rowed swiftly along a somewhat rapid and now shoaly river, the navigation of which was both intricate and dangerous, towards—the mountains now transformed into — visionary gold.

CHAPTER XIX.

OUR BIVOUAC BEYOND THE " FORKS."

As we advanced, low, umbrageous shrubs met
our view from time to time, skirting the river,
amongst which rank weeds and grasses grew up
luxuriantly, and where startled water-fowl rose
in the air or flew half-paddling along the surface of the water before us.   I made ready
my revolver, determined to bring down one of
these birds of the Upper Frazer, but it was some
time before I could find one sufficiently near for
a certain shot ; moreover they were the wildest
birds I had ever seen, and scudded with flurried
and rapid flight into the scrub, or far out of reach,
the instant the canoe was seen approaching along
the various bends of the river.

However one rash bird suddenly flew from under cover of the weeds, a few yards only a-head of us; I had my revolver levelled in a second, when flash—bang—the bullet whizzed forward, and down for an instant went the duck, which lay disabled on the water when we came up to it; the bullet had pierced the back, and the bird died as we lifted it into the canoe.   This was legitimate sport, and moreover very welcome provision, as of the latter our stock was becoming very attenuated, owing to the absence of natives; we, however, expected to meet with them every hour, when we should be able to negociate for the purchase of bears' flesh, wild vegetables, and fresh salmon, which we were too much disinclined to catch in sufficient quantities ourselves, owing to the loss of time which it entailed.   I watched along the right bank of the river with the view of having a shot at one near the surface, but nothing presented itself, so I was baffled in this my endeavour after destruction.   We had to make another portage at about four o'clock in the afternoon, in order to keep clear of the rapids, and proceeded in the same order as on the last similar occasion, carrying our own "kit," while

L

the Indian walked along with the canoe on his back ; he was a fine, intelligent fellow, about six feet in height, and as kind-hearted a guide as I ever had the pleasure of being associated with in any enterprize. We only gave him four dollars a-day for his services, as he had the advantage of making a " pile " on the journey, if luck threw it in his way—a pile being, in digger parlance, a small fortune in " dust " or " nuggets." We had scarcely got the canoe into water again on the other side the rapids, when I caught sight of an ordinary-sized brown bear, standing with one paw bent forward on a shelving part of the river's bank, about twenty yards a-head.   His eye was fixed in evident curiosity, and I saw by his unde-cided position that his movements were uncertain. I directed the attention of the Indian and my companions to him, and quietly levelling my revolver, while the others did likewise, fired straight into his skull before he had time to move.   He uttered a loud hoarse yell and rolled, struggling, down the bank into the water, tearing the ground heavily with his paws.   We did not advance upon him instantly, well knowing that this kind of bear, and in fact all bears, the polar excepted, will instinctively feign death till the near approach of his assailant, when he will spring upon and gnaw and crush him horribly to death. However, in order to ascertain the extent of his liveliness, and to dispatch him the quicker, one of our party sent another bullet into his carcass; this seemed effectually to send the remaining life out of him, for he gave a kick and stretched himself immediately on its receipt, remaining there without further movement flat on his side, his face fronting the river.   We then drew up and examined him; he was quite dead, and in ten minutes afterwards our Indian had successfully "hided" him, and amputated his fore hams and some steaks from off the hind-quarter—cut the tongue out of his mouth and otherwise mangled him. In the course of an hour from the time of his being shot, he was unconsciously undergoing the process of digestion in our respective stomachs, the Red Indian's included.   Such is life.

Still no natives — we were surprized.   Our guide, however, assured us, in a torrent of Chinook, with the smallest perplexing admixture of broken English, which he had acquired from association with the Hudson's Bay traders, that

we should meet with plenty of them shortly;—
it appeared that their encampments lay at some
miles' distance from the shores of the river,
generally near a creek or lagoon.   Gold was just
as abundant here as at Willow Bank, but still
the grand object of our wild expectations remained unrealized—the mountain of gold was not
yet reached.   We had very little time to dig before nightfall, but what labour was expended was
well repaid in the shape of sundry "specimens"
and large grains of the shining metal which we
noticed at this place; it wore a brown, crusty
look, which was attributed to the action of the
soil, air, and water upon particles long separated
from the chief mass.   However, it was gold, and
that was enough for us; we gathered it, and only
wished we had more of it, for the digger is never
satisfied; and if he could make a fortune in a
day, his next wish would be to make one in five
minutes.

We camped beneath the shadow of trees
within sight of the river, in the same manner as
on the previous night, having previously regaled
ourselves with tea and a quantum of brandy, good
neutralizers of the effect of bear's-flesh and dried

salmon ; we also tore the duck, before spoken of, after a cannibal fashion, and devoured it with all the rude appetite of explorers.

The weather had been throughout beautiful ; but a little after dusk it began to rain heavily, accompanied with thunder and with lightning, but it only lasted about two hours, and after that all was calm ; while the coolness which it produced was refreshing, after the heat of the previous few days. I noticed, however, that flies and other insects seemed to spring into life immediately after the storm, for they flew about in great numbers, and were almost as annoying as the mosquitoes in Australia ; but of course in this respect the Frazer River country was no worse than any other, and not half so bad as by an English road-side, where the gnats sting and whirl round, biting poison into every passer-by— the pestilence of ditches. I have always found myself as free from mosquito-bites as from sea-sickness—a happy deliverance for me I own— but I candidly say, that I would sooner take my chance amongst all the mosquitoes in Asia, and all their varieties in British Columbia, than I would amongst a swarm of British gnats.

I was delighted with the country, and this sudden abundance of harmless insect-life did not mar my first feeling and enjoyment of it. The trees sheltered us almost completely from the rain; the upper foliage being dense, and the branches in some places interlaced. The reader has been already led to understand that the river freshets which occur between June and August are not caused by rains, but by the melting of the snow high up on the Rocky Mountains, which pours down through all the streams and rivers leading from them; thus the Thompson, the Harrison, and the Chilcotin rush into the Frazer, and the same is repeated, but to a lesser extent, along the Columbia.

A little after breakfast, and at about eight o'clock on the following morning, we were suddenly startled by the appearance of Indians, who came down to the river-side in a bevy of about a hundred, the number consisting chiefly of men wearing an aspect at once fierce and warlike: these were rapidly followed by about twenty on horseback, evidently men of the same tribe, who came galloping furiously along, and pranced about us in the most humorously despotic style, the whole moving multitude uttering vociferous yells, and brandishing their arms in authoritative delight and savage glee.   Here was revelry.   What was to be done?   I at once ascertained from our native pilot, unpoetically called by us Jack, that although Carriers, they were not of his tribe; this I had anticipated, as we had advanced into other Indian territory since picking him up.   Courage is a grand thing in first confronting the savage; it inspires immediate respect, whereas the slightest faltering or manifestation of fear leaves the traveller at the mercy of those who can entertain contempt, and detect a want of bravery as readily as any vassal of civilisation, and who hold as valueless that which they are not awed by.   The best way therefore is to meet the aborigine with a bold, fearless front, a steady eye and a defiant look and posture; such self-possession is the white man's only moral defence against the hostility of the Indian, and the safest line of procedure he can adopt when friendly, and especially at a first meeting.   With such a look and such a front did I face the rampant Red Indians of the as yet untraversed wilderness of British Columbia.   I made signs of friendship to them in the best way

I could, and put forward our Indian guide to
make proclamations of peace and good will, and
advancing myself to one more gaily caparisoned
than the rest, who sat on a pawing steed, and
whom I rightly judged to be a chief, I held out
my hand in token of friendship, and remember-
ing that I had a knife in my pocket, drew it
forth and gave it to him with every gesture of
delight at our meeting. The Indian received
the gift, and after scrutinising it with evident
pleasure, thanked me, and shook my proffered
hand; a ceremony that he had no doubt witnessed and experienced before amongst the
whites at the stations of the Hudson's Bay
Company, with whom all the Indians had long
been in the habit of trading. During these
movements the crowd assembled round us and
looked on in silence and evident admiration. I
saw that the knife had turned out a talisman, and
that we need apprehend no danger at their hands.
After this they indicated their intention of trading
with us in provisions; which we gladly acceded
to, a detachment of the younger men and
squaws being sent off to their villages for the
necessary produce; in the meantime they dis-

played a curiosity quite unsatisfiable, ransacking everything belonging to us, eating up the remains of Bruin's carcase with evident satisfaction, and making temporary use of everything not actually in hand or on our backs, and all this in the most perfect good humour and friendship. The chief in particular seemed highly fascinated by my opossum skin rug, and wound it round his body and across his shoulders, and in various other ways, as if to see how it would look and suit him, strutting about meanwhile to excite the admiration of his people, who loudly applauded and violently gesticulated on each occasion of his altering the mode of wearing it. Our blankets were simultaneously doing similar service on the backs of half-a-dozen others, and my shirts — two red flannel ones — I had only three in all, and quite enough too—were to be seen dancing about like drunken soldiers in the midst of a street fight. Of course this was very well to look at, and the fun of the thing was worth more than the shirts ; but still—well, perhaps my " particular" friend, Sir Buckram Starch, will say whether he would have liked it.

But—tut—all these things are well in their way, and I congratulated myself on my successful diplomacy, and had a hearty laugh at these wild appropriators of my travelling wardrobe.

CHAPTER XX.

THE EL DORADO.

THE detachment returned with provisions, the opossum rug and the shirts were restored, the natives sat down and fed, and we filled our pouches with gold. Such is the summary of events—the striking incidents of an hour. Excitement with us was at a high pitch, for the banks of the river were literally strewed with gold; the natives rooted it up with sticks, and the heart of the El Dorado seemed already reached; we had only to expend a larger amount of labour in the gathering of that wealth which we had looked forward to in our most sanguine

moments. All was riant as the noonday sun,
and festive as the morn.

Away we dug; it was a day of eager expectation and success. One of our party made
twenty-two ounces, and the others followed
deeply in his wake. I, myself, with the assistance of my geological shovel, turned up sixteen
small nuggets, some of them mixed with quartz,
worth about two hundred and fifty dollars, and
this with an amount of labour which could only
be called an amusement.

The Indians were rooting up the ground for
a mile on either side of us along the beach,
working, to quote popular phraseology, by
fits and starts, and not caring to pick up more
than would purchase for them some unprohibited
luxuries—spirits being very properly disallowed
to them. Night at length set in, to afford rest
to our exhausted frames, bringing with it a
batch of canoes from the lower river, each laden
with its half-dozen hardy, enterprising miners,
who landed immediately in the vicinity of our
canoe. We all hailed the arrival; there was no
envy, no rivalry; we knew there was plenty of
gold for us all, and we were glad to find our

numbers swelled, and a community of men having affinity with ourselves, springing up around us. All was riot and revelry until a late hour on that night, as we became convivial under the influence of some excellent brandy, which the new arrivals had brought with them, and which they dealt out with a liberal hand, *pro bono publico*.

The natives had, before this, retired to their own encampment, and the silent night alone witnessed our corrobberri. We were now, at a guessing calculation, about two hundred and eighty miles from the river's mouth, and one hundred and forty from the mountains.

Early on the succeeding morning we were disturbed by a fleet of canoes coming down river, and manned, judging at a bird's-eye view, by about two hundred Indian warriors, all armed ; we, however, rightly supposed them to belong to the same tribe as those with whom we had made acquaintance on the previous day, and who had so unceremoniously paraded my shirts before the admiring gaze of the multitude. They greeted us with a wild and flexible whooping,—a thrilling chorus of shouts and

ringing cries, and landed immediately in the
vicinity of our encampment.   We soon saw
that their intentions were pacific, notwithstanding their boisterous display of feeling, and the
overwhelming manner in which they gathered
or rather rushed round us after leaving their
canoes.   Their inquisitiveness was just as great
as that which had been manifested by their
brethren of yesterday ; and once more every rag
and implement we possessed was being paraded
and hustled about.   They were, however, more
respectful towards our provisions than had been
their brethren of the previous day, probably on
account of there being no novelty attached to
them; but in all probability had there been
anything in our " pantry" with which they were
unacquainted—roast pig, for instance—it would
have been just as promptly seized upon, and
passed from hand to hand, as were my companion shirts, and that unlucky opossum skin
rug, the evident delight of all.   I suspect the
fascination lay in its great size, square shape,
and the stitching which held the skins together.
However, whatever the cause might have been, it
did not alter the fact of their being in love with
it, and moreover, by the grimaces and signs of

invitation which they made for me to give it them, I very much despaired of being able to claim it for another night's covering. My only chance of preserving it as my own was by the exercise of moral force, and the law of kindness, which is everything, however, with the savage, for our numbers did not permit of the thought of physical resistance of their spirit of caprice; and if it had, I should have been the last in the universe to contend physically against a peaceful and aboriginal people, on whose empire we had encroached, impelled by the hope of gain, and on whose golden territory we stood as sheer usurpers, the forerunners of a civilization, which, alas! cannot fail to blast and eventually to exterminate their valiant race from off the face of the earth.

I knew that this was not the theory entertained by my brethren of the white skin, half of whom, by their own confession, were murderers and assassins, and that too, of a more diabolical type than were the conspirators of Paris, because they inflicted death upon the helpless and defenceless Indian, whose dwindling race bore out too melancholy an attestation of the moral wrongs

which civilization had hurled relentlessly upon
him; whereas the others were secretly, but hazard-
ously, contending against a mightier power than
their own, and by which they were deservedly
vanquished on the scaffold, when the heads of
the guillotined fell dissevered into the basket of
the executioner.

I allude to the reckless and indiscriminate
slaughter of the Indians in California, which
took place from the time of the first rush
there in 1849, and which cold-blooded and
heartless sport is even now persisted in where
the red man is not altogether swept away and
extinct.   It is only the superior numbers of the
Indian over the rude outpourings of civilization
in these regions, which at present deters the
Californian—but will not always—from as cruel
and reckless a use of his revolver as stained
the early annals of the country of the Sacramento with the direst bloodshed of modern
times.   True, the same, to some extent, may
be said of the early squatters of Australia in
their intercourse with the aborigines as well as
the early settlers and conquerors of most other
countries; but it does not tend to mitigate the

crime of indiscriminate murder, merely showing that inhumanity and infamy hold more rampant and ignoble dominion in the breast of the too often morally-debased scion of so-called civilization and enlightenment, than ever loomed on the mental horizon—the unsophisticated mind of primitive man.

Adventurers from out the pale of society never look upon themselves as the real usurpers and invaders, nor pause to consider that every encroachment of theirs is but hurrying destruction the more swiftly to the savage, ousting him of his birthright, and strewing with thorns and calamity the remaining length of his short passage to the grave.

To return to the banks of the Frazer. The river was no longer navigable, save after a portage of some half mile in length, being choked up with rocks; and the waters whirling heavily as they rushed past with all the force of a torrent. The natives, however, indicated that higher up the river was smooth and deep. As yet we had only ascended, as the reader is aware, bout two hundred and eighty miles from the river's mouth; we should have had to travel hun-

dreds of miles further up, following the river's
course, before reaching its source in the Rocky
Mountains. Gold, however, will allure as far as
man can travel or human hopes can reach, and
ere long I have every expectation of hearing a report of "dry diggings," "hill diggings," and monster nuggets having been found at the base and in
the ravines of the Rocky Mountains themselves.

We were a sun-burnt, motley group, as,
camped together by the banks of the noisy river,
we talked on many a diverse thing; of gold, of
home, of murder, of love and enterprise; of
bygone dangers braved, of fallen comrades and
defiant foes. There was something, I thought,
of the hungry beast of prey in the eager, yearning flash of each other's restless eyes, in which
the fire of hardened desperation and unflinching
physical bravery ever glowed, and which seemed
to feed upon continual excitement. There was
something embodying all the wildness of the
savage and all the ghastliness of civilization in
the hair-grown swarthy faces of the men, as now
and again the flickering blaze of the fire round
which we sat was reflected upon them, giving a
look of ferocity even to repose ; while the

boundless waste of universal space—the void
of night—

> Hung o'er and round in solemn silent reign,
> Obscuring deep the mountain and the plain,
> The sea-like prairie rolling in the breeze,
> The giant forms of yonder rustling trees;
> The rocky river's rugged, winding way,
> The bird, the blossom, all that deck'd the day.

Occasionally the hoarse laughter of the whole
party disturbed the natural solitude,—the half-
startling tones of jocose revelry rose up in the
virgin air, and were wafted on the breeze over a
landscape which had hitherto reposed primeval.
We were all merry on the strength of nuggets
found and "dust" gathered, for the yield of to-
day had been with some of us considerably
in excess of the previous day's average, one man
of the new comers having realized, with the
assistance of a rocker, nearly five hundred dollars in dust and nuggets. His "belt" was full
of the former, and two leather bags had grown
pleasingly bulky under the latter. For myself,
I made about ten ounces in nuggets alone—I
did not dig for dust—my geological shovel and
pan being my only artificial machinery employed.

The five hundred-dollar man was a hard, gaunt, stringy, dried-up looking Kentuckian, with a gutta-percha-coloured face, sunk into which, on either side of his nose, twinkled two all alive and piercing grey eyes. His hair was long and light, and crisped up with the dry heat of the weather, so much so that it gave me the idea of extreme fragility and brittleness. He carried a couple of revolvers, and a bowie knife, with the point of which he took the opportunity of picking his teeth immediately after supper, following which he gave us a long yarn about an old " claim " of his at Hangtown,* which yielded sixteen hundred dollars the first day, and about an Indian whom he shot " in the white of the eye " the next day afterwards for stealing his blanket. He seemed to glory in his crime, and was, on the whole, as brutalised a specimen of humanity and the digger, California and the world had ever presented to my individual inspection. However, his dollars were as good as any one else's, and that is the

* In California, so called from an execution which took place there at the instance of Judge Lynch; hence Lynch law.

grand criterion in a new gold country. We were all more or less leathery-looking, but this wretch was, to quote popular phraseology, regularly tanned and dried, and such, that if it came to a matter of casting lots at sea, and he turned out to be the victim, the unfortunate crew would have something very like a mummy to carve. Then there were four long, slop-built, semi-civilized-looking Western States men, with heavy rifles nearly as long as themselves. High shouldered, narrow-chested, sleek-haired gentiles, with hunger seemingly personified in each other's countenances, with a paucity of pale wiry beard and moustache, they moved awkwardly about, the rifle always in the way, and bore evidence of their being better adapted to the felling of trees, and the building of log cabins, than even gold digging.

These men had respectively journeyed overland from Missouri to California, and, moreover, had done the same thing from that again through Oregon, since the Frazer River fever set in; and were clever enough to "shirk the license" on the way. They were exactly the men for such laborious and hazardous undertakings, having always dwelt on, or beyond, the borders of civilisation in their own country ; never having seen half-a-dozen houses together till after they came to California, and being trained to rough it in every sense of the term. They were each provided with an axe, with which they promised to do severe execution in chopping down trees, and building up log huts on the next day, so that we looked forward to a village at once.

For the rest, our party was composed of an English " old chaw," as he once humorously called himself ; a Jack tar, and consequently a Jack of all trades, let loose among the mountains. He gave us his history ; miners are very free and candid in that respect, as indeed in every thing else, for there is less humbug both about them and their profession than is the case with any other class extant.

This history was a long, round-about affair, the most prominent parts of which appeared to be his running away to sea from his grandmother at Bristol ; his subsequent loves and disasters, both by sea and land. On the latter he was thrown off various horses on five distinct occasions during his perilous career, all of which took place in California, the country in which he first made acquaintance with horse-flesh, and that, after clearing out of, or rather deserting, his ship, which was subsequently turned into a boarding-house, in which capacity she gained more money than she could have made in voyaging. After this he had experienced a succession of "good strikes" at various diggings, which, however, were just as often followed by what he termed "a jolly spree," and so the money went. He had travelled by steamer from California, as indeed all of us had done, the party of Missouri men excepted.

Then we had three Frenchmen, partners; as also two Germans; after which the balance was made up of thorough bred, long, straight, black-haired Yankees; a surgeon, a lawyer, a conjuror, and a photographic artist; all, of course, divested of their tools, and shorn of "practice," being amongst their wide-awake number.

The reader may perhaps feel interested in learning the fate of my opossum skin rug and vermilion shirts; know then, that, failing to be-

stow them on the native rulers of the soil, the
former still constituted my bed, and the latter
my pillow, for they were faithfully replaced by
the Indians after they had fully satisfied their
curiosity.   I attributed this to their amiability,
and not to any dread of punishment they might
have entertained, as their numbers were altogether overpowering, and I judged truly ; although I should have considered them quite
justified in appropriating them as rightful spoil
had they chosen to have done so ; for I am
egotist enough to believe that I had sufficient
magnanimity of mind and character to know and
to feel that I stood up in the, till now, almost
primeval territory of aboriginal dominion an
usurper, and was, together with the motley crew
by which I was surrounded, but too painfully
emblematic, in my own mind, of the coming
misery and eventual, yea, rapid extermination
of the race of the Red Man—the valiant children
of the riant wilderness.

The natives had quitted the neighbourhood
of our encampment before dusk, and we were
thus left alone to beguile the flying hours of
night as best we could.   Our fire well fed with

faggots burn gaily, and every crackle was a sound of welcome companionship. There is nothing like a good log fire for making a man feel at home in the woods.

Although the day had been agreeably hot, we felt the warmth which our "log burner" emitted very comforting, and knowing its effect in scaring off grizzly and other bears, we sunk into the unconscious embrace of slumber with our boots, our revolvers—and with me, my vermilion shirts—under our heads, in the happy confidence of safety. And this was two hundred and eighty miles up the shelving banks of the Frazer River, and adjoining a camp of reported warlike Indians. As for the latter, I would thus as readily trust myself into their power as I would to humanity of the white skin; it is only when the savage becomes morally vitiated by his intercourse with civilisation that his unsophisticated honesty and generosity become obscured or perverted; and when he is driven relentlessly to the brink of death by force of vice and starvation engendered by his association with the white man.

It is a preposterous thing for ignorant con-

M

ventional old women, and domesticated men to
match, who have never wandered beyond the
regions of lamp posts, rant about savages, and
pray for the conversion of the heathen, and look
down upon them as degraded beings, lost in
the darkness of sin and iniquity ; when the fact
is, that they themselves are the sinful and ini-
quitous, compared with which the rover of the
woods is very often a personification of magnanimity and virtue, while he is never degraded
till he has succumbed to the blasting, withering
power of a perverted and vicious civilisation,
when his valiant courage and sovereign heroism
forsakes him, and very soon he is no more.
Ashes to ashes.

How much more noble was he than those
vassals of civilisation by whom he was overrun,
who would cringe into servility, and lick the
dust of a petty despotism equally contemptible
with themselves.

Give me a free, wild, boundless solitude,

rises to my lips as I write, for I enjoy about
as supreme a contempt for anything like ser-

vility and social snobbism as any man that ever
sniffed the desert air, or ever tasted the sweets
of triumphant liberty remote from the haunts
of civilized man.

CHAPTER XXI.

A COLD CHOP AND A HOT STEAK.

WE were up and moving soon after day-break ;
several went off prospecting up river, and for
a mile or two inland, if the term may be used
to denote an opposite direction to the river.
The five-hundred dollar Kentuckian went "hard
at it" on a small "bar" of the river, about
five hundred yards higher up than where stood
the tree under whose shelter he had been delighted with happy dreams, full of delicious
prospects, and, to judge by his own vulgar
account, perfectly heavenly and inspiring. The
Western men set to work cutting down pine

trees, and for the first time in that primitive region
the sound of the axe was heard resounding
through the forest, and the work of aboriginal
destruction had commenced. I compared it
with the foundation stone laying of some new
building in the old world, with the difference of
an augmented feeling of its being a great event,
and instead of its being a mere solitary edifice,
here was, perhaps, the foundation of a mighty city
destined to flourish into a rapid existence, and
live when those of Europe and to-day have
crumbled into a second Pompeii, an Herculaneum,
or a Bagdad. So much for my feelings on the
subject of what one of the Yankees called " a
cold chop "—an old joke — saying, that he
should much prefer " a hot steak," or stake,
it does not matter which, in accordance with
which he gashed away with his bowie knife at
some of the bear's flesh which we had purchased
from the Indians, and throwing it gridiron
fashion across a burning faggot, soon had it in
convulsions, blubbering out an amount of bear's
grease sufficient to have anointed the heads of
the whole party. However, no one uses Ma-
cassar, nor yet any substitute therefore at the

mines, so that it did not in its effect cause them
to conjure up the same visions of pomatum pots
and barbers' shops as possibly might have been.

We breakfasted promiscuously between six
and seven o'clock, by which time the Indians were
flocking down to us like so many geese to their
pond.   I enjoyed a refreshing bath in the river
before taking that meal, the best part of which was
the tea; a beverage which I felt almost as necessary
to my existence as the Lascar does to opium.
We also made some damper after the Australian
mode, which was pronounced " fust rate. "
After breakfast the work of trimming the logs
and washing the gold proceeded briskly till noon,
when we assembled to dinner, which, instead of
raw materials, consisted of a savoury dish of stewed
squirrels, a "pan" half full of transmogrified deer's
and bear's flesh, converted into a harricot with the
assistance of wild vegetables, and some yam-like
cereal called potatoes, grown and supplied by the
Indians ; all this had been dished up and ma-
nœuvred by one of the Frenchmen, who, as it
turned out, had been a ranch, or restaurant keeper
near Downieville, in California. We appointed him
forthwith to be inspector and purveyor-general of

our commissariat, and entrusted him with all the duties and responsibilities of the cuisine, at a salary to be made up amongst us of ten dollars a-day, which, strange to say, he agreed to. So much for French enterprize—the fact is, that Frenchmen love the comfortable, and consequently make bad pioneers — they are better adapted for following in the wake of explorers than of constituting such themselves, and more often, like this hero, prefer cooking for them to sharing the risk, and more arduous undertakings which the English and Americans plunge after and rejoice in. I can compare them only, in the wilderness, to so many cats in a storm—they are never happy till they get within doors. To-day I left my shirt and opossum rug tied up for safety from aboriginal touch in a deer skin, and in immediate proximity to the legs of our French cook, who sacré'd the Red men freely, and with all the gesticulations of his country tried to convince them that they were in his way, but in vain; the climax was only reached when they demolished a squirrel fricassée which he had been preparing, when, afraid to use his revolver against them, he sat down and wept desparingly. The

Indians grinned and enjoyed this amazingly well, and just as much as I did myself, for I laughed at him to his face for the space of forty-five seconds without stopping, by the end of which time he looked as foolish as he felt savage. However, in addition to what I have before mentioned, he gave us bear à-la-mode, a newly prepared fricassée of the same animal, and a sort of grill of ditto, with grasshopper sauce, so that it was nearly all bear together, the prairie greens and yam potatoes excepted, as also a pudding stuffed with wild raspberries, and half-a-dozen other wild things which we did not at all expect, but which turned out very well, taking into consideration the Nebuchadnezzar-like quality of the fruit of which it was composed. I believe that if we had been " dead broke," as the term is, for provisions, that this said cook would have dished us up a very palatable pottage of landscape herbage, and made soup out of the few knife handles we were possessed of, or, better still, out of my persecuted opossum-skin rug. However, I am glad to say that we were not driven to any such extremities, so that his utmost skill in making something out of nothing was not called into requisition.

He was an active, but pale, long-faced, emaciated-looking man, of slight frame, with a scanty supply of nearly black hair and a very weak moustache, covering, but not concealing his thin, restless lips, which denoted every passing sensation, and moved as expressively as the small black eyes which peered on either side of his sharp and well-defined nose. He spoke with great rapidity of utterance, and made it his study to anticipate every want of those about him during meal times. He was, moreover, nimble and highly excitable ; in politics, of course, democratic, and on some points entertained such original views, that if he had branched out and suggested the conversion of a Red Indian into a new species of fricassée, or the giving us a feast of squaw à-la-mode, or devilled, I should have considered it quite in keeping with his character, and have laughed accordingly.

After dinner, which occupied about ten minutes, digging, or rather gold seeking, was actively resumed by all, the Missouri men and our French cook excepted, who merely interspersed their other avocations of log-hut building and bear-roasting with an occasional scrape for nuggets.

M 3

All were ardent and impetuous in their eager pursuit of gold, save this our denominated " parley-voo," who displayed no excitement whatever, but went about his work calmly, and as cool as what is commonly called a cucumber ; even the western men worked with almost superhuman energy ; they threw their whole strength into the work of the house-building, in which the newly-cut timber of the forest, and a few nails which they had brought overland, were the only materials employed, and endeavoured by their unceasing toil to dispatch the " business "as quickly as possible.

The yield on this day was equally satisfactory with that of the previous day, but the novelty had died away, so that the men talked less about it, and " realized " their hundreds of dollars without making particular mention of the sum. There was plenty for us all, and tens of thousands beside, so that we had each equally good chances of making a " pile," and moreover a rather bulky one too.   We slept, as usual, in the open air, and recommenced mining one by one, very early ; the five-hundred dollar man whom I have already sketched being up and rousing the whole camp at three o'clock, just after daybreak. I wished him to unmentionable places for breaking my slumber at such an unseasonable hour; but as under cover of the forest, he was in nobody's bedroom in particular, he had the privilege of making as much noise as he chose to trouble himself with. By noon our log house was built, which afforded sleeping room for us all on the *ground floor* that night.

The yield of gold still kept up, with no probability, as far as we could see, of its ever diminishing. The Indians still continued friendly, but we saw less of them than at first; they, however, furnished us with plenty of wild comestibles, which our so-called " parleyvoo " made it his chief study to transmogrify into various unrecognisable substances for the gratification of our universal appetites.

We had plenty of salmon, and a few small fish, so that we were not compelled to confine ourselves to squirrels and bears'-flesh unless our epicurean tastes—query—had induced us to prefer as food the wild animals of the wilderness to the more sober salmon

> " That once did dart and dive,
> But now were split and dried."

I was now becoming rather impatient of this mode of life, and moreover felt a " desperate inclination " to breathe the air of more populous districts.   Here there was just a sufficient amount of civilization to spoil the charm of aboriginalism, and no more.   Besides, I had seen enough of the upper country to satisfy me as to its richness, and now felt a longing to observe life elsewhere.   Accordingly, to be brief, I sold my share in the canoe, and set out alone, with two painted Indians, in a canoe belonging to their tribe, on the second day following the completion of the log-hut.   I wished to reach Victoria as quickly as possible, to see what was to be done ; and being myself of a highly speculative turn of mind, was as much disposed to " invest" a few thousand dollars of the " dust" found, which, indeed, I felt it agreeably oppressive to carry, in anything "likely"—land, for instance—as I was to keep it under my own personal surveillance.   We shot down the river like an arrow, passing by the rugged and the picturesque, and the respective bars of Canoe, La Fontaine, and Foster, and bivouacing for the night on the right bank of the river, where we

made a portage, reached the " Forks," distant
about one hundred and sixty miles from the
river's mouth, and six miles below Mormon Bar,
an hour before noon on the second day out. The
mouth of the Thompson bears every sign of
having been formed by volcanic agency, and
traces of such abound all over the country. The
cactus, also, grows plentifully, a sure sign that
the winters are not severe.   Here the canoe and
I parted, the Indians, according to our figura-
tive understanding, being disinclined to descend
further ; I, however, succeeded in buying one
for a hundred and twenty dollars from a party
of Frenchmen at the Thompson River junction,
in which I proceeded with another Indian down
the river as far as Fort Yale, (which was then
undergoing repairs) making a portage along the
Cascade Mountains on the way, the river here
running very narrow and rocky.   There I had a
bed made up for me of all manner of strange
things, in a square tent-store kept by an Illinois
man, measuring six feet three inches, from the
crown of his Panama hat to the under soles of
his pegged boots, which were stamped with a
pair of flaming red eagles.

   " Eagles again !" I ejaculated to myself,

" they outflap the stars." These boots are
made by steam at large manufactories throughout the States, all of which are stamped with
an impression of the national eagle, and an ace
filled up with stars and stripes, hence their
number; the peculiar distinctive mark being
merely to please the Yankee taste. The yield
here was very high, averaging a hundred, and
in some cases two hundred dollars to the man
per day, but rockers were required.

Tents were numerous, and wooden houses
and stores were going up every day. The " dry
diggings" being worked on a creek parallel with
Hunter's Bar, a few miles further down on
this side Fort Hope, were turning out very rich.
I set out the next morning on my journey down
river as far as Fort Hope, passing hundreds of
boats and canoes on the way. This is a splendid
site for a town, being at the head of steam
navigation; and a land trail stretches direct from
it to Thompson's River and the Forks, so avoid-
ing the canon two miles above Fort Yale as well
as the other dangers of the upper river navigation. Here I sold my canoe for a little more than
half the amount I had given for it, which was

nevertheless profitable enough in its way, seeing that it had carried me down from the Forks, which was all that I had bought it for.   Here human life was more dense, and habitations more abundant than at Fort Yale.   I paid twenty dollars, passage money, and left on the same day that I had arrived there, by the steamer.

Twelve miles below the fort we passed the steamer Sea-bird grounded on a bar.   She had been there a couple of days, and consequently all her passengers had been landed.   She looked very forsaken, and her captain, who " showed up," as we passed, looked just as extremely disgusted.   He was calculating, no doubt, upon the awful loss of her services.   When I left Victoria she was reported to be still in the same place, but as her stern was in deep water she was expected to be got off on the next day. We had very few passengers on board, so that things were a little better than I had found them during the up-trip by the Surprise.   We stopped at Fort Langley, and took in two or three passengers, and passing by two or three heavily timbered islets, on the next day, at noon, rounded the straits of Juan De Fuca, and came to an anchor in the placid and baylike harbour of Esquimault, surrounded by a panorama of rocks and pine trees.

" 'Squimalt at last, I guess," exclaimed an Oregon man.

" Yes," said I.

We all took boat together for Victoria.

" Let's liquor," he ejaculated, as he made a plunge into the first store we came to.

We were bound in politeness to agree, and we did " liquor"—a batch of thirty or so—our Oregon friend standing treat all round. And so ran the custom of the country, while all around was bustle and excitement.

CHAPTER XXII.

BACK TO THE ISLAND.

On reaching Victoria, which is situated on beautiful level ground, on a narrow arm of the Sound, stretching about two miles inland, and gradually sloping towards the water, which at once saves all grading, and affords a splendid natural drainage, I found the now augmented multitude in a wilder state of excitement than on my first arrival there, in the early part of the month. The first sign of the rapid progress going forward on the island that met my eye, was a large store and wharf, both made of logs, at the landing-place of Esquimault, which latter ought decidedly to be included in the town of Victoria; as from the depth and extent of the bar at the mouth of the latter harbour, as well as its general inferiority in point of size and shape to that of Esquimault, a beautifully formed natural granite basin, very much resembling Acapulco harbour save in its superior size, and distant about three miles on water and two on land, it can never be ranked the port proper of the Vancouver metropolis. The harbour,— Esquimault—which, picturesquely rock-bound, is from six to eight fathoms deep to the shore, and about a mile in length by the same in breadth, was crowded with gracefully peaked canoes and boats of all shapes and sizes, scudding from the various vessels in shore, and vice versâ. Some of the canoes were guided by girls, sometimes one, sometimes two, and occasionally a family of four or five would be seen hovering about. They were all more or less striped with vermilion clay —the women having a line drawn down the centre of the head where the hair parted, and from which it fell gracefully over the shoulders. They were all sufficiently clothed ; the men who are tall, broad-shouldered, and full-chested, wearing a mushroom-shaped hat of twisted cedar bark, and a deep girdle ; the women a short petticoat made of strips of cedar bark, bordered with seaweed; in addition to which they had sashes of cotton or woollen material bartered to them by the Hudson's Bay Company, as also various bracelets, while in some cases both men and women were clothed *à la Anglais*, in which, however, they, with their tawny, coppery complexion, looked anything but picturesque. There were also Italian fishermen from San Francisco acting as boatmen here.   Niggers, Chinese, and Sandwich Islanders, I found had been added to the population of Europeans and Yankees.

There was a government, that is to say, a Company's land sale going on at the office at Victoria Fort, on the day of my arrival; the scramble for lots was of course tremendous, one hundred dollars being the fixed price per lot, but lucky indeed were the purchasers, for they were subsequently, in most cases, passed from hand to hand at an advanced price of thousands of dollars.   Judge of the case of a man that I saw in a liquor store at Victoria : " Ye—es, sir," said he, " six thousand nine hundred and fifty dollars I calculate to be the profit of that ar fifty-dollar lot."   This he had invested in when he first arrived from San Francisco, two months previously, when the fixed price of land was a hundred per cent. lower than at present, and which lot he had sold on this very day for seven thousand dollars. This sort of speculation just hit my taste, so I hurried off to the land office, but found it so difficult of approach, owing to the eager crowd of intending purchasers, that' the sale was over before I reached it. I had never been in such a crowd since the year 'fifty-five, when I waited my turn for letters in front of the San Francisco post-office after the arrival of the United States mail. However, I resolved to renew the attack on the morning following, when I succeeded in purchasing three lots already located, and that at the standard price of one hundred dollars, and of the standard dimensions of sixty feet by a hundred and twenty.

My money was taken by a sandy-haired Scotchman, who handed me a voucher in return, with a barren and cautious composure, which struck me as contrasting remarkably with the excited, clamorous crowd who were contending for the first purchase of " City allotments." " You may depend upon it he's had porridge for breakface," remarked an Englishman who had been struggling next behind me, and with whom I made a sort of crushing acquaintance, which resulted in the exchange of sundry " drinks." " I guess he has," was all the reply I made ; for while amongst the Yankees, I sometimes adopt their phraseology, and can guess and calculate as readily as the smartest of them. I thought myself very lucky in having been able to enter thus cheaply into a landed proprietorship, which promised to be about the best paying thing even in a gold country.

I resolved to renew the attack on the land office on the morning following, and in fact to continue buying as far as my purse and *pushing* powers would allow me. In the meantime I revelled away in riotous disorder, together with a floating population of about fifty, in a wo den boarding house, built for the present proprietor during the early part of the month, and which promised to yield him quite as big a " pile " as any made on this side of Fort Hope ; the charge being five dollars a-day, and the supply of provision, as well as its quality being anything but satisfactory to either palate or appeti e. However, matters will improve, as the Americans say,

and therefore it is to be hoped that by this time
either the said proprietor has been *improved out*
of the house, or that he has improved his table *in*
the house, for it was anything but good for the
money when I was there. Here I met a láte
companion of the unfortunate fellow who was
shot by an Indian during the affray near Fort
Hope, when a native chief was killed. He gave
me a narrative of the whole affair, and spoke
with much feeling of the deceased man, as well
as his own narrow escape, as he termed it, from
a similar fate. However, I did not fail to tell
him it was all and deservedly brought upon them
by the ruthless conduct of their barbarous coun-
tryman, who fired the first shot, and in the most
rash and uncalled-for manner, hurried death
upon the unsophisticated chieftain.

" We left Fort Langley," said he, " on the
2nd of June, and took two Indians in our canoe
to pilot us up. We got along as well as any,
until the fourth day out from Fort Langley.
We were then within four miles of Fort Hope.
There was a canoe ahead of us, about thirty or
forty yards, with which we had kept company
for several days. This canoe stopped on shore,

and we saw an Indian speaking with them. We thought they were waiting for us to come up, but when we got within fifteen yards of them, they got into a difficulty with the Indians. The Indian wanted a shovel, which they would not give to him. He (the Indian) then made a grab at the shovel, and wrenched it from the man in the canoe, and struck the man several times over the head with it. The men in the canoe all got up to defend themselves, and the Indians came rushing out of the bushes with long knives and clubs, and some had muskets. One of the men in their canoe fired his pistol at the Indian with the shovel, and shot him through the heart. The Indian made two more strokes, and then fell down. The men next got in their canoe and fled across the river. None of them were killed, but one was badly hurt on the head. They now laid hold of our canoe, and pulled it close to the shore. I told the Indian who had hold of the canoe to let go, that we were not in the fight and didn't want to fight. He drew a big knife, and was about to run it into me, but his squaw, who stood behind him, drew him back, and at the same moment a

shot was fired from the bushes, which hit Henry
Wedeken in the side.   He fell out of the canoe
into the water.   I got hold of his arm and
raised him up and tried to get him in the canoe
again, but I could not.   He tried to speak, but
he could not.   He then made a motion with his
hands that he was dying, and he closed his eyes
and fell back dead. Oh, how I felt at this moment
I cannot tell! Not that I had to die, for I did not
expect to live five minutes longer."

"Pleasant," said I, "happy idea."

My companion stared wondrously as if he
doubted it, but after seemingly satisfying himself that I could not mean it, went ahead with
his narrative.

"I expected a ball would pierce me through
at every moment—but to see him shot who
never raised a hand against them! But an
Indian is bound to have the life of a white man
if one of them gets killed—no matter whether
he is guilty or innocent.   We could not then do
even as much for him as to make him a grave,
for when he fell, the current caught the canoe,
and I could not hold on to him.

"After much difficulty we got across the river,

where we met the other canoe. We then held council, and decided to go to Fort Hope by land, and leave our canoes; but we failed in this attempt, for the rocks were too steep, and several thousand feet high." At this point my eyebrows rose up as if instinctively. "We then went back to our canoes. Our only chance of escape was now to make a desperate effort. It was about five o'clock in the afternoon, but when we counted our number, we missed three of our party. We called for them; but got no answer, and we had not a moment to lose, the danger was increasing every moment—the Indians were giving their war-whoop up and down the river. We then got into the canoe which belonged to the other party, for ours had drifted a little ways down. We threw the most part of the provisions overboard, and then darted like an arrow down the river. This surprised the Indians, and they did not give chase as we expected, for the Indian that had been shot was their chief, and as they had no commander, they didn't know how to act. This circumstance alone saved our lives. Night soon covered us, and we paddled as hard as we could, hungry, wet, and

N

tired as we were, until next morning, when
about five o'clock we reached the mouth of the
river, and here we were out of danger."

"And a lucky thing for you, too," said I.
"My greatest regret is, that the assassin was
not the recipient of the bullet instead of your
unfortunate friend.   However, such is life."

"Yes," said he, "it is ;" and in the gravest
possible manner he breathed forth in solemn
accents, sad and slow, those momentous words,
"Let's liquor."   The effect was magical; we
were off in an instant to a bar-room, not twenty
yards from our boarding-house.   "Will you
liquor ?" asked he, of a group of half-a-dozen
standing in the bar-room, to whom he introduced
me one by one, and with whom, after the custom
of the country, I exchanged a shake of the hand.

Nobody refuses to " liquor" in America, that
is, among the Yankees, unless immediately after
dinner, so of course the half-dozen responded,
when, after drinking our glasses together, and
giving each a nod of the head, we swallowed
our respective "drinks" slick, and after that
proceeded, one by one, to return the compliment
and stand drinks all round likewise, the treater

saying, " My respects," as he nodded his head and at one quaff sent his julep out of sight. Thus, a flash of lightning was no sooner seen than it was gone, and so with the thunderbolts and hailstones, other favourite drinks of my slivery friends. They were all bound for the up-river diggings, and had taken passage by the morrow's steamer. In the course of conversation I was made acquainted with the unhappy fate of Captain Frazer, the employé of the Hudson's Bay Company, from whom the river derived its name.

" Some half-dozen years ago," said a weatherbeaten old julep drinker, " they were excavating in San Francisco, down there in Commercial Street, and they turned up a coffin—it was pretty much the worse for wear, and had a tin label with Captain Frazer on it; and this, gentlemen, was the coffin of the identical Frazer who committed suicide in that city fourteen years before, and I guess warn't considered any the better for't.—Let's liquor," were his next words, and so we liquored.

Our party was just then augmented by a rough, stalwart, and amphibious-looking per-

sonage, who came up with a buoyant swagger,
and was greeted with applause as he went.   He
was evidently being lionised a little, so I began
to wonder what it was all about.   This man
was introduced to me as " Mr. Reuben Davis,"
and I did not fail to shake the hard, rusty hand
of the said Mr. Reuben Davis, in recognition of
such introduction.

" This, sir," spoke the introducer, whose
eloquence waxed high, " is the gentleman who,
in conjunction with his partner, saved the lives
of twenty-three of his fellow men and women,
who had been precipitated, together with eleven
others, who, I regret to say, were drowned, into
the water, in consequence of the capsizing of
the sloop Alcatraz, while rounding McCauley's
Point on her way with passengers," — very
redundant, thought I,—" from the steamship
Panama, in Esquimault Harbour ; and, gentlemen, who on being offered a bag of dollars
by them in gratitude, refused to receive it."
(Cheers.)   " This is the gentleman, gentlemen ;
he's a true-born Yankee, and, I guess, as transcendant a hero as ever swilled a cocktail.   We'll
liquor :" laughter, and a perfect enthusiasm of

applause, during which everybody invited him to drink.

Here, again, we were regaled with juleps, brandy pawnees, and neck-twisters, mixed by a real live Yankee, got up between a pair of shiny collars, and set off with a flaming crimson silk sash, quite in keeping, however, with a retailer of flashes of lightning and thunderbolts.

The accident alluded to had taken place two days previous to my return, and was supposed to have been caused by the carelessness of the helmsman jibbing the sail, and not taking the precaution of hauling the sheet up in doing so. There was a heavy sea running at the time, so that the bodies of three only of the drowned were recovered; these had been brought to Victoria, and after some inquisitorial examination, were buried.

On the morning following I repaired to the fort at an early hour, that is, between three and four o'clock, and took up my place, post-office fashion, to await the opening of the land-office at ten.

The excitement which swayed the multitude was even more frantic than on the previous day. Lots in private hands were resold several times

at enormous advances amongst the crowd before
the office opened. I succeeded in buying three
additional lots, making six in all, such being
the number limited to each individual; but these
were unspecified,—in fact, not yet surveyed or
denoted, and were just as likely to turn up at
Esquimault as at any part of Victoria. However, I had purchased, as per voucher, those lots
of 60 by 120, lying somewhere, and with this
vague knowledge I was satisfied, and concluded
that I had already made twenty thousand dollars by my speculation and investment.

The town of Victoria is very picturesquely
situated on high sloping ground. Its harbour,
although perplexingly crooked in the eyes of
navigators, and high barred, is nevertheless very
prettily located, and forms a beautiful granite
basin like that of Esquimault.

There is a bridge, erected by the Hudson's
Bay Company at a cost of one thousand pounds,
which spans the harbour from the town site on
the Victoria side to the opposite or north side,
and leading to the trunk road to the interior,
which passes by the Company's extensive farm,
(the Esquimault,) the settlement at Herbert Head,

at Metchosen, and at Sooke, all thriving agricultural districts.

At the present time Victoria consisted of about one hundred and fifty houses and stores, one-third of which had been recently erected. Almost every house or shanty in the town proper was a restaurant or coffee stand, fitted up in the most primitive manner. They were all, however, "doing a good business," in spite of a scarcity of everything necessary for the comfort and well being of man. Mutton chops and the bread formed the only palatable food; as for cutlery and crockery there was a scantier proportionate allowance per dozen men than the Frenchmen brought with them, including our cook, beyond the " Forks," and that we had at our joint disposal there, far beyond the pale of civilised society, although that indeed was sorry enough. However, things were improving every day. Besides these, there were numerous tents scattered about the outskirts, some choking up ravines with their number; others spread out on the broad open plain that surrounds the town, and further off their fleecy summits were to be seen along the shores of the bay, while through

the woods, still further from the dust and
clamour of the streets, here and there an iso-
lated specimen tenanted by some individual
enamoured of " a lodge in the wilderness " was
to be seen.   These temporary habitations varied
considerably in size and construction.   In fixing
them a ground space was cleared and cleaned ;
two uprights were then fixed in the ground, their
tops being joined by a ridge pole, over which the
regular canvas covering, or a substitute of
blankets was hung, and the tent was then made,
leaving the interior to be fitted up according to
the taste and resources of the occupant. Outside
was arranged a simple fire-place.   From some
of these after nightfall the sound of music, vocal
and instrumental, broke forth in cheering reso-
nance ; while by the fires, and at the doors of
others, groups of men, pipe in mouth, were
collected, each discussing the chances of the
golden future, or recalling memories of the
golden past.   Order was the ruling feature.of
these communities, and of riot and unseemly
noise there was an utter but agreeable absence.
Such are the suburbs of Victoria in 1858. Who
or what will be their occupants in 1859 imagi-

nation may picture, but how truthfully time can alone tell. There was also a small wooden palisaded encampment of Indians standing aloof not far from the town.

The Company have two chief stations on the island, besides Victoria, viz.: at Nanaimo, where they have been working, in an imperfect manner, however, extensive coal-mines, which there extend over two thousand acres, the surface seams being from one to three feet thick; the other station is Fort Rupert, situated at the extreme north end of the island.

It was here rumoured, and I have since heard it verified, that the Company had made an offer of their entire property, stations, and stock, situated in the territory of the United States, of course, to the Government of that country, through Lord Napier, our ambassador at Washington, for the sum of six hundred thousand dollars, which was correctly considered to be very cheap.

Property lots in central parts of the town were readily sold at from two thousand to seven thousand dollars, although originally sold for fifty dollars, and that but a few weeks before.

All the land bordering on the harbour of Esquimault, and from thence to Victoria, was selling
at the same extravagantly high prices. Rents for
wooden buildings were higher than they were for
brick ones at San Francisco. In spite, however, of
the difficulty of getting carpenters and such like
to work, wooden houses were to be seen rising
up everywhere and every day, and the sound of
the hammer might have been heard amid the
clamour of the busy and excited multitude—the
din of daily life on all sides—the wages of the
workmen ranging from ten to fifteen dollars a
day. There is an abundance of various kinds
of fish, including salmon, in the bay, and both
large and small I have seen caught from the
bridge. There are numerous pleasant—I may
say delightful—walks in the neighbourhood of
the town site. I strolled out as far as the
Sound Shore, distant about six miles. It is a
curious beach, covered over with millions of
tons of pebbles, varying in size from that of an
egg to that of a small bean. These pebbles are
used largely in Victoria for the streets and in
road-making, as also garden walks, and wherever
there is much traffic.

The more I experienced of the climate and the country, the more I liked them. The temperature was equable and deliciously warm, and day by day there came a gentle breeze, which, wafted from Mount Olympus and the coast range that loomed far away through the circumambient space, was at once balmy and refreshing. Within two minutes' walk of Fort Victoria, miles of fields, rich in clover, are presented to the eye, bordered or intersected by bushes of the blackberry and wild rose. Strawberry plants also flourish there, and I had the pleasure of gathering a little of the unlimited quantity of the fruit which ripened there in uncultivated luxuriance. These berries, as also oranges, are sold by the Indians about the streets. Groves of oak, aspen, and pine-trees grew up, stretching far as the eye could reach, and forming regions of delicious shade, through which it was delightful to walk. However, the tens of thousands of keen gold-hunting Californians, flocking over the island, were already making a visible impression upon its timbered coast, alike with the forests and the adjacent mainland.

These rapidly-growing towns, some of which dated their existence by *marks*, even now claim the designation of cities. The rise and progress of California from the eventful year of forty-nine, was without a parallel in the world's history; but I felt that I saw going on around me what is destined to eclipse even the glorious national career of that richly-endowed land.

Hundreds of brick and stone buildings were being projected, and all this in spite of a popular feeling of uncertainty as to which place would turn out *the city* of the gold regions, upon which subject a perfect babel of confusion prevailed. Each favourite selected locality was announced as certain to be the San Francisco of Puget Sound; so that a new comer, wide awake though he might be, would soon have been bewildered had he believed half of what was told him. Whatcom and Séhome were prominently put forward for public favour equally with Victoria, and each had numberless advocates who would undertake to prove to anybody and everybody, that his or their favourite was THE PLACE.

An ordinary mortal would suppose that these three would have afforded a sufficiently ample

field for the speculators. But no. A party
had just set off in frantic haste to Point Roberts,
on Semiamoo Bay, for the purpose of laying out
another city. Thus merchants seeking a "location " for business, and others seeking an investment, had, and still have, a wide and fertile field
to choose from—to say nothing of the weaker
rivals, Seattle and Steilacoom, which think " awful strong " of themselves. Victoria controls
the trade of the main river, but not entirely, as
a large number of canoes and boats were being
fitted out at Bellingham Bay, and took their way
up Frazer River from that point. The main
hopes of Sehome and Whatcom were based upon
their trail to Thompson River, which report said
had just been completed beyond the Lake. So
confident were those concerned as to its success
that a large ferry boat was being built for the
purpose of plying across it, a distance of two
miles.

After reaching the summit of the trail, the
remaining road to be traversed before reaching
Thompson River is through an open country.
Those who had tried the trail spoke favourably
of it, and some had gone to California to procure

mules to pack on it.   If their expectations are
realized, and the trail is practicable, they will inevitably, to a great extent, monopolise the trade
of Thompson River, so that there appeared to be
good chances for each of these places becoming
flourishing townships ; as there is no doubt
but that there are thousands of square miles of
British Columbian territory, not to speak of treasures beyond the boundary line, incalculably rich
in as yet undiscovered gold.

Already " dry diggings " were announced,
miles away from the rivers, in various places,
while along the ravines and gulches of the country, wherever found, quartz specimens of astonishing richness, evident signs of large beds,
were as frequently met with as nuggets.   The
field open to gold mining enterprise will be
limitless, so that all the world — at least all
who come—may dig and feast, and at length
abandon the gold field heavily laden with its
spoils.

Then, again, there is the group of Queen
Charlotte's Islands, also indisputably rich in
gold as well as copper and other minerals, and,
like all gold countries, just as bountifully en-

dowed with the gifts of Ceres and of Flora, as
they are beautiful to look upon, and as their
clime is balmy. These islands, of which there
are three, lying close together, although popularly
confounded as one, possess an area but little less
than Vancouver, and are furnished with excellent
harbours; of these, Port Estrada on the north
coast, and Croft's Sound, a little to the westward
of it; Skitekis and Cummashawon on the north,
and Port Sturges farther south; Magee's Sound,
on the west or Pacific coast, and Port Ingram
on the north-west coast, are the principal. However, the light of British Columbia must needs
be dimmed before these islands can be seen to
shine.

Still the rush of civilisation to these hitherto but scarce or thinly-trodden lands will
develope resources hitherto unknown—will extend the empire of British domination, and the
spread of the Anglo-Saxon tongue, over regions
where the Indian is still a mighty family—over
territories hitherto unfrequented and scarce
known to civilisation and the world, but where
a motley yet a mighty throng now contend and
yearn for gold. It is the giant infancy of a na-

tion which has risen in a day, over which the
British banner proudly floats, the symbol of
strength and safety, of progress and enlightenment borne on the flying wings of time, and
which nation will one day,—and that not far
removed—glitter in the wealth and splendour
meet for the sovereign cities of the North Pacific.
The extensive gold fields which in all probability
will be found within the neighbouring American
territory, will, in their influence, both tend to
swell their triumph and enhance their greatness
by augmented wealth.

CHAPTER XXII.

PRODIGIOUS DOINGS.

I REALLY felt it quite worth the passage-money from New York, to see the rampant excitement, and to watch the eager speculation going on amongst the disordered community assembled together at Victoria. There were individuals who but two weeks previously had been plodding their way in San Francisco, tolerably well satisfied with the profits of a small and legitimate business, who now looked upon themselves, and were looked upon by others, as *millionaires*. They would tell you that they owned a thousand or twelve hundred lots in the town of Esquimault—or Squimalt as it was pronounced—

which cost them but five dollars an acre but a
few days since — and which they now sold at as
many thousands per acre; and had any doubt
been expressed as to their being able to " realize"
as much for the remainder, they would favour you
with a smile of pity at your ignorance and want of
foresight. This sort of thing was highly amusing,
and afforded me considerable entertainment.

When I awoke on the fourth morning after
my return, I found an *ex habitué* of St. James's,
who slept in the same room with me, very busily
occupied at the table in drawing the plan of a
house which he proposed to erect forthwith on
one of the lots in whose ownership he rejoiced.
I asked him how much his lots had advanced
since he bought. " Two hundred and fifty
thousand," was the prompt reply, meaning so
many dollars—fifty thousand pounds. I thought
him luckier than I had been, and began to
regret " most awfully" my absence up river
during the best buying times.

However, I had six lots, three of which were
first class,—that is, well situated and worth any
amount of money, and the other three, yet to
be surveyed, might turn out equally well. I

did not hope for much beyond, as land in private hands was held at too high a price to speculate in. The time for getting it cheap, as I have already mentioned, had gone by, the half-dozen lots, at a hundred dollars each, allowed per man by the Company excepted. The real estate panic was, however, higher than it had ever been, and promised to become still more mad and desperate with each succeeding week. The individual who occupied the next bed to me was " raising a brick windmill on the hill," and considered himself to be, taking into consideration that and other " specs," the richest man in Victoria, and worth about a million and a half of dollars.

I observed that the coloured people, *i. e.* " niggers," collected here, many of whom were " real estate " owners, conducted themselves in a manner rather bellicose than otherwise, which of course excited derision ; and one of their number I heard attempted to take his seat with white people at a boarding-house table in town, but was expelled in a manner as prompt and merciless as the style of doing the thing was ludicrous. The newly ap-

pointed police of the place were negroes, and
consequently heartily despised by the Americans.

Some enterprising individual opened a
butcher's shop in a canvas house on the open
space in front of the fort, and, as a reasonable
consequence, several others followed his ex-
ample,—some, even, building houses, and the
whole space was very soon staked off into
claims. One morning, however, a notice made
its appearance on the gate-post of the Fort,
warning, or rather calling upon these appropriators of the land to quit it by noon on the
day following, by which time most of the tenements had disappeared, having been removed to
the outskirts.

I heard but little inquiry made as to the
richness of the "mines," as everybody took it
for granted that they were the richest ever
heard of; and that being a settled fact, they
were too much whirled in the maze of their
own exciting speculations to dwell long at a
time on the subject of the diggings. But diggers from California, who intended to become
diggers on the Frazer, arrived in half frantic
haste to ascend that river, and were only the

more madly impelled by the almost bewildering reports of their prodigious yields and extent, which came from every quarter. The news of the dry diggings, discovered up a small stream near Hunter's Bar, seven miles below Fort Yale, as also of the Thompson and its tributaries, having been "prospected" for a distance of a hundred miles from its mouth, and found to be highly auriferous, seemed to fill them, even these veterans of California, with the wildest hopes of anticipated gain, and on they rushed, pell mell, and eager after gold, by the first vessel that had room for them.

It is not, however, as the reader is aware, alone on Frazer River that gold exists, but throughout the entire Cascade Mountains—a fact demonstrated by actual discovery. Captain McClelland, in 1853, while surveying the military road from Fort Walla Walla, on the Columbia River, to Fort Steilacoom, on Puget Sound, through the Nachess Pass, found gold in considerable quantities, his men making two dollars a day, sometimes, with a pan. Still later, gold was found in the vicinity of Mount St. Helens, south of the Nachess Pass, by a small prospecting party from Oregon, but, from some cause or other, nothing resulted from the discovery. As early as 1850, information was received from Indians that there was plenty of gold on the Catlapoodle River, which reaches the Columbia River some fifteen or twenty miles below Fort Vancouver. In 1853, the story was heard from the same Indians, that there were three white men then on the river making " hiyu" (much gold). About the same time, there was a man who occasionally "dropped in" at Fort Vancouver for a mule load of provisions, mysteriously arriving and departing in the night time, and so effectually concealing his trail that it was impossible to follow him. He might have been a trapper, engaged in his pursuit; but he always had gold-dust with which to pay for his supplies. There was also at the town of Seattle, on Puget Sound, well up twards Bellingham Bay, an old dissipated mountaineer, who used to talk confidentially to his immediate acquaintances of a place near by, where he could get gold by the pound. Nobody paid any attention to his yarns; but that man used to make occasional hunting

excursions with his squaw—and he always returned with gold enough to pay for a " big
drunk"—a spree that would last for months.
So much for the country and the man.

In many respects British Columbia is not
unlike Northern California; and but little more
than a year since, auriferous deposits found in
pretty large quantities made the resemblance
still more marked, and created the wildest excitement among all the adventurers on the western
slope of the mountains from San Diego to the
mouth of the Columbia.   The richest placers
seemed to lie in the table land between the
Frazer and Columbia Rivers.   For nearly two
centuries, as the reader is aware, the navigation
of these rivers, together with their tributaries,
and the bays, straits, or sounds into which they
flow, has been monopolised by the Hudson's
Bay Company ; in addition to this, the company holds, under a tripartite tenure, all the
territory extending from the northern American
frontier to the Arctic Sea.   Firstly, they hold
under license from the Crown the island of
Vancouver ; secondly, the magnificent territory
extending from the Pacific to the Rocky Moun-

tains, now called British Columbia ; and thirdly, under their original Charles the Second's charter, the vast territories extending from the Rocky Mountains to Hudson's Bay. The Crown, of course, will resume occupation of the land held under license expiring in May '59, but the charter is a rather more difficult matter. Mr. Roebuck, as one of the deputation to the premier on the subject, represented that such a policy should be pursued as would develop the British possessions, and make a continuous line of populated and improved country from the Atlantic to the Pacific as a counterpoise to the rapidly-increasing preponderance of the United States on the American continent. While, he said, the Americans had increased from thirteen to thirty-six independent states, and from a population of three millions to one of thirty millions, the English had achieved nothing on that continent ; and while the border states, Minnesota and Iowa, were filling up to the frontier, the British had, on the other side, nothing but a little colony on the Red River. This primitive state of things he with justice attributed to the monopoly of the Hudson's Bay Company. He proposed that they should be dismissed at once. If it was decided that they had a legal right to remain, they should be paid for relinquishing their right; if not, they should be dispossessed without compensation.

Certain it is that the Hudson's Bay Company have exercised an anti-civilizing influence in the countries over which they presided. They have also manifested, with regard to the enlightenment of the Indians, an apathy rarely to be met with in this age of the world. I do not blame them for this, as the result has been good. Still it cannot be attributed to philanthropy on their part, although unconsciously, in thus leaving the aborigines to themselves, they were treating them as well as was compatible with their own presence amongst them. I ascertained at Victoria that no school, or means of instruction and civilization, had ever been devised on the island, and that even the chaplain of the island cannot speak the native language. The result, however, is, that a Roman Catholic bishopric has been there established, and that three or four priests are actively engaged in puzzling these primitive people into what they call a conversion

o

to their faith.   There are two schoolmasters on
the island, whose salaries are paid out of the
fund arising from the sale of land; but what,
and who, and where these gentlemen taught, I
was unable to ascertain during my short stay.
Still, at the present time, the Hudson's Bay
Company have proved themselves, although expensive, very useful agents in the establishment
both of the colonies of Vancouver and British
Columbia.   They have, however, since the date
of their charter, reaped a harvest quite sufficient
to amply repay them for any service they may
have done the crown; and if, as appears to be
the case, according to law and license, the vast
proceeds of the present land sales at Victoria
are to entirely accrue to them, they will certainly
be rewarded beyond complaint at having to surrender those colonies, on the expiration of their
license in the month of May next.

On the 21st of the month, the day of the
boat accident, the first number of the *Victoria
Gazette* had been issued, the first newspaper
printed on the island. It is a Government organ,
and temporarily edited by the proprietor of the
San Francisco News Letter, who has been ap-

pointed printer, "by authority," to the Imperial Government of her Majesty Queen Victoria in Vancouver's Island, and who had already put proclamations into type for the edification of the Yankees, with the orthodox "God save the Queen!" like a flourish of trumpets at the end. In an edition of this paper, the first regular one, published on the 25th, a return of the number of miners' licenses issued up to that date was given, viz. 1,000 at Victoria, and 300 at Fort Langley; a remarkably small number, when compared with the number of immigrants.

The issue of the *Gazette* woke up many of the old Vancouver fogies, some of whom had not seen a printing press in operation for years, and others had never witnessed its performances even on the limited scale of the journal in question. They could not be expected, however, to take in all the features of the new system in a day; consequently, all the government announcements and many private business notions of the attachés thereof were still only given to the public in the shape of written placards on the Fort's doors.

The trade of Victoria, if such it could be

called, was in a very curious condition, as perplexing as it was unsettled and disordered.
Sometimes the Company's prices were slightly
above those of the few traders in the place, but
more often far below them.   When, for instance,
flour was selling at thirty-five and forty dollars
per barrel, large loaves of bread were furnished
at the Company's bakery at twenty-five cents
each.   I may observe that, although trade with
the interior of British Columbia was prohibited
by them, that no restriction upon such existed
on the island.   The company, however, being
out of supplies at the Frazer River Forts, and
nearly out of flour here, it was expected that
they would be compelled to throw open the trade
very shortly, by sheer force of a pending famine
and consequent clamour amongst the miners. Two
hundred pounds' weight only was now allowed to
be taken by each man going up river, and this included *everything*, so that miners were precluded
from taking a supply of more than two months'
provision with them.   In purchasing from the
company the buyers formed in a line, as at the
land sale, only presenting a more composed aspect, in front of one of the whitewashed buildings

of the Fort, which I have described in an earlier
portion of the work ; while in an office at the
upper end of it, an order was written by one of
the clerks, with a slow and serious certainty,
authorizing the store-keeper to deliver the required amount of pork or beans, sugar or tea, as
the case might be.   On receiving this, the
favoured recipient rushed off to another building of the Fort, of the same size and shape as
the other, having a door and two windows on
the ground floor, and there took up his place
in the line, as at the first building.   At length
the door would be reached.   The party would
then present his order to a ruminating-look-
ing individual, opening it to the extent of
five inches, after which he would quietly shut
it again.   After time had elapsed sufficient to
discharge a schooner, the desired articles would
be as quietly handed out through one of the
windows appointed for that purpose, and so the
methodical door opening would be repeated till
four o'clock, when the company's stores and
offices were closed, to be opened at ten A.M. on
the ensuing morning.

It was now the 27th of the month, and

June was in her pride, for more delicious weather
I had never experienced in any country. The
San Francisco steamer Republic had just arrived,
and the town was thronged with an additional thirteen hundred Californians. Most of them walked
across from Esquimault in preference to waiting
for boats to bring them round. I had a sight
of them on the road, and a curious and exciting
sight it was. The entire length of the road was
lined with them. They were all "packed," that is,
they all carried more or less baggage across
their shoulders, and were all equipped with the
universal revolver, many of them carrying a
brace of such, as well as a bowie-knife. One
of the many curious sights visible in town after
the arrival was the spectacle of the Danish con-
sul at San Francisco marching wearily up one
of the streets—Johnson Street—under the burthen of his blankets, and followed by a batch of
Chinese; but as to whether their efforts were to
be devoted to the washing of gold or of shirts,
I could not ascertain. I also recognised the
arrival of some notorious San Francisco "sharps,"
whose coming was by no means grateful to the
well-disposed. Bellingham Bay had hitherto

been the point of destination for these gentry, and, but for the uncharitableness of the wish, I might have desired that it should have remained so.   I am afraid some of them will be almost a " poser " for the worthy governor.

By the way, I heard a good story told of him and a noted steamboat man of San Francisco, who recently paid this region a visit.   The latter had been purchasing coal for his vessel of the Company for eight dollars a ton,and was about proceeding to Nanaimo to obtain a supply.   Just before his departure, Governor Douglas placed a letter in his hands requesting him to see as a particular favour that it be delivered to the superintendent of the coal depot immediately on the arrival of the steamer.   The steamboat man courteously agreed, and promptly delivered the document.   The contents turned out to be an order to increase the price of coal to eleven dollars a ton, and as it was delivered before the steamer coaled, the Governor had the steamboat man " in the door."   Rather a sharp trick that !

This was the first occasion of the entire " cargo" of San Francisco passengers landing here, and seemed to act as fuel to the burning fire

of popular excitement. Moreover, the steamer
Surprize had also just arrived from Fort Hope,
bringing reports of the most dazzling description.
The river was rapidly falling, and the yield was,
as a natural consequence, increasing, and was
expected to be prodigious; the present average
in some places being fifty dollars to the man
per day, and in others double that amount.
There was a Vancouver Indian, a passenger by
her, who had brought twenty-seven pounds'
weight of " dust" and nuggets, slung round his
body in bags and belts, the produce of his own
digging, and there were several Americans and
Frenchmen also by her with even larger amounts
in their possession. The Surprize was to leave
again for Fort Hope on the day following—
people lived as much in a day here as they do
in a month elsewhere—and would take about
four hundred passengers, the balance of the number by the Republic having either to wait for the
steamer following, or to take boats and canoes,
that is, as many as could get them.

There was a popular impression afloat, that
it was unsafe for miners to leave this port in
their own boats, (some of which were punty,

awkward-looking things of their own building,
and about as good imitations of coffins as of anything else), for the diggings, owing to the risk of
their being attacked by the Indians at points
where they might require to stop on the way, but
I rather think that the report originally ema-
nated from the steamboat owners, who had perhaps looked forward to a paucity of traffic ; men
were even reported to have been murdered at
these points; but I must say that, in spite of my
endeavours to refute or establish the veracity
of such, I was still left in doubt.   I heard now
for the first time that the Surprize was boarded
off Point Roberts, near Fort Hunter, on her last
uptrip, by an armed boat's crew from the Satellite
stationed there, the vessel, however, being now
at Esquimault ; when each passenger was compelled to show or to purchase a license, on
pain of being put ashore.   This brought-to
the recusants, of whom there were many on
board, with something like a jerk ; those who
had not the money accepted the loan of such,
for the miners will never see a man " dead
broke " without offering him assistance; the
others paid and went ahead, with five dollars

less in their respective pockets than on first confronting the " Man-o'war's-men."

The Republic was unexpectedly announced to
leave the next morning for Bellingham Bay,
just opposite the southern extremity of the island,
on American territory, from thence to proceed to
San Francisco, without returning as usual to
Victoria.   At the latter place there were no
gambling houses; but on the American territory
at Bellingham Bay, Whatcom, and Sehome, gam-
blers and monte tables were in full play, and as
publicly as at San Francisco during the glorious
days of 'forty-nine, and until their nefarious
traffic was forbidden.

Now the real estate panic was at a high pitch,
and I was just as impatient to get to Europe as
the majority of the people were to get to the diggings, for I had a certain defined speculative
object in view, which I was anxious to realize.   I
therefore resolved "instanter " to put my three
first lots into market and sell, and sell them I did
within three hours;   one, a corner allotment, for
five thousand eight hundred dollars, the other
two, adjoining, to another party, a speculator,
for eight thousand dollars, who put them into

the market at seven thousand dollars a lot immediately afterwards. The other three not being yet located, I could not have sold save at a great disadvantage. I therefore decided, and no doubt wisely, to hold them over till after my return from Europe, *en route* for which I now intended proceeding by the Republic.

Accordingly, between eight and nine o'clock on the following morning, I took boat for the steamer lying at Esquimault, with a single valise, and my opossum skin rug; the former I had left at a liquor store on my first arrival, where it had remained till my return from the mines; it was now heavy with gold dust and "big chunks" of ditto, in making room for which I had to "fling away" a pair of boots and sundry other things appertaining to my *travelling* wardrobe. Ten minutes after I had boarded her, the Republic was off with half-a-dozen cabin passengers only, and these composed of San Francisco merchants and miners returning for supplies.

The scenery around was highly picturesque. Far away in the distance, and within the Washington territory, loomed loftily the giant forms of Mount Baker and Mount Rainer; while

nearer, the beautiful cluster of the San Juan
islands diversified the straits which rippled in the
glare of the noon-day sun, beneath the bold and
declivious shores of both Vancouver and the
main land.

On reaching Bellingham Bay, the steamer
dropped anchor opposite Séhome, with Whatcom lying a mile and a half to the right. They
both wore a miserable, God-forsaken look. As
a particular favour, I procured a place in the
purser's boat, and went ashore, landing beneath
the frown of an almost perpendicular hill, which
rising from the water, reaches to a considerable
altitude, being nearly as high as the well-known
Telegraph Hill, San Francisco. A jutting
wharf had been recently built, at the extremity of which, there is a water depth of
fifteen feet at low tide. There were a dozen or
twenty wooden shanties only, on the site of the
proposed city, and I must say that the prospects
of the place appeared to be anything but bright.
In fact, to use the phraseology of the land
speculators, this place had " gone in " alike
with Whatcom and several other " sound "
ports, which had been puffed by Bogus (i.e.

sham) News into a momentary blaze, and then died out.

I went up on a waggon as far as Whatcom, which I found to present a much more animated appearance than at a bird's eye view I had been led to suppose; the entire population, however, wore an idle, drunken, and dissolute aspect, and were as noisy and expectant of good things as any set of eagle-topped boot wearers I had ever seen. They all appeared to be waiting for something; it was for the city to grow up, and with it to swell their fortunes. I am afraid, however, that they have since become wearied of the result. Whatcom lies under a bluff fifty feet in height. From this bluff there stretches a sand-flat for the distance of about two miles before reaching deep water. This flat is dry at low water, and on it they propose to build a city. There will be an immense amount of piling to do, and it will take years to improve the place. The town consisted of about a hundred houses, chiefly wooden, and mostly occupied as stores, restaurants, and gambling houses. There is a lake and river adjoining; the river perpetually pouring a sheet of clear, soft water, into the bay, within the limits of the town. This water is said to be cool and fresh during the whole year. Millions of speckled and mountain trout dart to and fro in the waters of both lake and river, some of them weighing eight, but in general from one to four pounds. The river or stream, which is the outlet of the lake, is about five miles in length; the lake being twelve miles long by a width of a mile and a half. From the latter to the bay, there is a fall of about a hundred and fifty feet, one hundred feet of which consists of perpendicular cascades, and the other fifty of rapids. Forty-two feet of this fall is within one-fourth of a mile of the town; and within half a mile from the latter, sufficient fall can be obtained to water the whole district. The scenery surrounding the lake is highly picturesque and varied. To the northward is seen a mountain rising abruptly from the water, something like the hill at Sehome, and presenting a series of indentations and irregularities which contrast pleasantly with the gentle sloping country to the westward, leading towards the bay, and the diversified hills and valleys which extend east and south, far as the eye can carry, here and there sprinkled with cedar, fir, and pine trees, which in giant form stand with extended arms the seeming guardians of the wilderness, and but to enhance its beauty.

There was a saw-mill, with two saws in operation, near the town, driven by the "fall" current of the river, which will furnish water power sufficient to drive any amount of machinery which may be planted along its course.

"Yes, sir," spoke a Yankee, addressing me between two stray shots of "juice"—I speak regardfully—and evidently in one of his most transcendant moments of cocktail and julep inspiration. "The time is not remote when the hum of machinery and the buzz of active business life will resound along the river's length, and awake the startled echoes which now slumber in the solitudes of Whatcom lake."

"You speak like a book, Mr. ————," observed some one standing by. The orator did not deign to reply ; he had achieved a success, and placing his back against the bar-room wall, near which he stood, turned over his quid with a solemn look of majesty. He felt that he had

uttered an oracle, and that was enough for him;
—he had triumphed over language and imagination; and it was not until after he had un-
bound himself in a prodigious jet of—the reader
knows what—that he consented to " liquor."

I could write a volume about this one man,
but I must return to Sehome and the steamer. I
ascertained here that the report which I had heard
at Victoria, as to the trail to the Thompson River
being completed, was false—a little more of the
bogus news. But it is no less likely that it will be
made practicable in the course of time, although
perhaps not to be much used. I returned with
some fellow passengers and the purser, by waggon
again to Sehome, within two hours of my having
landed there, and soon after getting aboard again,
the steamer drew anchor and was off.

From Bellingham Bay we took up half-a-
dozen more cabin and two steerage passengers; there were fourteen in all. After this,
we went ahead as fast as we could, hugging the
broken, rugged, and pine-clad shores, past the
eighteen beautiful headlands from Cape Flattery
to Point Reyes, towards the Golden Gate of
San Francisco Bay, reaching the wharf at that

city at seven o'clock on the evening of the 3rd of July.

The city of people were of course half-mad for news ; and when they heard the news, were still more mad that no steamer was leaving that night that would take them to the El Dorado. Extras were at once issued from the newspaper offices, and the whole place was in even a greater ferment than when I had left it, more than a month before—all was bustle, tumult, and disorder, even greater and more frantic than that which characterised Victoria. There was some slight murmur expressed when the amount of treasure brought by the steamer was found to be so small, twenty-five thousand dollars only, but this was easily accounted for. In the first place the miners had mostly carried with them from San Francisco supplies of provisions and other necessaries sufficient to last from three to six months. Consequently they would have no immediate occasion to barter their dust for supplies — and should they require to make small purchases, would naturally prefer using the coin which they took with them. In the next place the business of the country being exclusively in the hands

of the Hudson's Bay Company, all the gold
dust that was sold was purchased by that rich
monopoly, giving in exchange therefore goods,
which if bought in the San Francisco market,
were paid for *not by gold dust*, but by bills
drawn on London.

These bills are more convenient to the San
Francisco merchants than gold-dust, and in
the meantime the company quietly store up
the metal at Fort Victoria, shipping it from
time to time to England. Witness the arrival
in London, since my return, of the Princess
Royal, on the ninth of June, with an unspecified
amount of the company's gold from Victoria.
Thus it was that the newly dug gold had been
kept out of circulation. In this respect the
British Columbian mines differ from those of
California, where everybody was unprovided with
" stock," and where everything bought was paid
for in dust. Still, as the New El Dorado, in
spite of thus having, to use a scriptural simile,
its candle hid under a bushel, has blazed out so
vividly upon the world, it augurs well of its
surpassing richness and permanent wealth, for
gold, like merit, will, sooner or later, make itself

known, and both are sufficiently rich in their
own resources to emerge from and shine forth
as luminaries through any depth of cloud that
may for a time be heaped upon and obscure
them, for worth is but seldom left unappreciated.
The one is base, and " of the earth—earthy;"
the other is divine; for gold is a bauble, but the
spirit of intellect is sublime, and looketh down
upon Mammon and the children of Mammon
with an eye of pity—soaring beyond. Nevertheless, as the respective possessors of intellect
are living creatures, eating, drinking, and
sleeping, they have to invoke the aid of their
butchers and their grocers in the provision of
sustenance; and as these said butchers and
grocers have a due regard for money—witness
Jones's landlady—why, then it becomes a matter
of great convenience, — Experience whispers
absolute necessity—to have a little of the other
worth besides and beyond the intellectual. Consequently it is the happiest thing in the world,
next to love, when there is no mistake about it,
—and matrimony, when it is merely the seal of
such,—for a needy man suddenly to feel his
pockets full of money, and to know that there

is plenty more coming.   How he can laugh and
enjoy himself, to be sure.   All this has been
said to show that the two worths, gold and
genius, go much better together than alone, and
that it is much better and healthier for them to
shine in unison, than it is for the man of genius
to scorn gold, and the man of gold to mock
at the evils of disdainful genius.

I am becoming discursive; the chink of gold
brings me back again to San Francisco.

The next day being the anniversary of the
disunion of the United States from England,—
Independence Day, as it is familiarly called,
— there was much talking, feasting, and
rejoicing.   Speeches were as plentiful as strawberries, but still all these things were subordinate to, and swallowed up by, the gold excitement.   In the midst of everything, everybody
was dealing in Frazer River, either for goods
or passage; and so the Yankees delighted
themselves.   On the next day I embarked on
board the steamer, Golden Gate, for Panama,
after renewing acquaintance with which dila-
pidated city I was jolted across the isthmus by
railway, and took steamer from Colon, or As-

pinwall, as the Americans call it, to the island
of St. Thomas ; after undergoing a transhipment at which place, and escaping the yellow
fever—let this not be confounded with the other
yellow fever—I was again

" O'er ocean onward borne,"

towards Southampton, at which port, to quote
commercial phraseology, I duly arrived in the
month of August.

I may here make allusion to the subject of
communication with our El Dorado. The Canadians, it is gratifying to observe, are already
alive to the necessity of direct communication
with the new gold regions. They have a regular line of steamships from Toronto to
Fort William on the north-west coast of Lake
Superior, and a bill has been introduced in the
Canadian legislature for the construction of a
route from Fort William to the settlement at
Red River. This route will be nearly all by
water, and will avoid the round-about way by
St. Paul, thus saving eight hundred miles of
distance. Again; to another route. England
has but one secure harbour accessible at all

seasons of the year, on the Atlantic seaboard
of British North America, and that is Halifax
in Nova Scotia.   But its natural resources and
advantages cannot be too highly estimated.
It is situated nearer to the British Isles by 400
miles than any other port on the continent, and,
whereas our Canadian harbours are blocked up
by ice during half the year, it is always open,
and moreover is the finest along the entire coast.
From Halifax to Quebec, through British territory, the distance is about 600 miles.   There is
a railway, now making, over 170 miles of the
extent.   From the latter place there is a direct
line of railway, stretching over five hundred
miles of Canadian territory to the shores of
Lake Huron.   A short ship canal there connects Lake Huron with Lake Superior, and from
the railway terminus on the former lake to the
head of Lake Superior it is 500 miles distance.
From that on, via the Red River Settlement and
the valley of the Saskatchewan, which is navigable for a considerable length, to the head waters
of the Columbia River, in our new colony, is
about 1,200 miles further, and thence to the
mouth of the Frazer an additional 300 miles,

making in all, from Halifax to the heart of our
El Dorado, a little more than 3,100 miles, and
allowing 2,466 miles, the distance from Liverpool to Halifax, makes the entire journey about
5,600 miles. This, as the reader may judge
from the foregoing facts, appears to be a very
desirable line of route, being shorter even than
that by way of Panama ; but whether, till the
construction of an overland railway across the
Rocky Mountains, it will take precedence of the
route from Canada direct, depends upon which
offers the earliest and best facilities for the conveyance of passengers. As for the regular
mails, it is likely that they will be sent by way of
Panama, *viâ* the West India steamers, for some
time to come, although a large number of the
letters will no doubt be specially directed by their
respective writers to be sent by the other routes,
so that every steamer leaving for North America
will be likely to take British Columbia and Vancouver letters, as well as the vessels sailing direct
to those places.

As the reader is aware, Sir Edward Bulwer
Lytton announced that an offer had been made
by Messrs. Cunard to convey the mails, toge-

ther with goods and passengers, from Liverpool,
through to Vancouver Island, within the space
of thirty-five days; most probably this was
meant to be *viâ* New York. Now the only
great line of ocean way unoccupied by British
mail steamers is that between New York and Aspinwall and Panama and San Francisco. This
route the Americans considered as peculiarly
their own, there being no British settlements
along its entire length. The discoveries of gold
in British Columbia, however, and the consequent rush that is taking place in that direction,
have entirely altered the aspect of the case in our
favour. It is not, therefore, likely that English
mails will be conveyed to British Columbia
in American bottoms. Mail packets must
be put on between Panama and Vancouver,
and as a matter of course other British packets
may run between New York and Aspinwall to
meet those packets. Glancing at another line
of route, from Southampton to Aspinwall, the
distance is 4,400 miles. As everybody knows,
it is only a forty-mile railway ride from the
latter to Panama, across the isthmus. From
thence to Frazer River is 3,800 miles, so that

the entire distance from Southampton to British
Columbia is but a little more than 8,200 miles.
Now the distance of Panama from New York is
2,300 miles, so that the latter city is 6,100
miles from the new colony.

If the steamers of the West India Company
were to proceed direct to Aspinwall instead of to
St. Thomas', and thence by inter-colonial steamer,
the voyage would be performed in sixteen instead of twenty-two days, as at present. The
whole of the mails along the south-western
coast of America, as a consequence, would be
accelerated. British steamers might run from
Panama to Vancouver in conjunction with
them, calling at Acapulco, Mazanilla, and San
Francisco on the way. The speculation would
certainly be remunerative. Two hundred thousand passengers, and forty millions of pounds
sterling in gold dust, were conveyed by the
American mail steamers between California and
Panama in nine years. This will give the un-
initiated an idea of the enormous traffic between
these places, and which is now undergoing considerable augmentation.

The great trunk mail packet line between

P

England and Aspinwall has become one of great
and increasing importance, and no means should
be neglected to improve it. Not only is it our
only medium of communication from England
with the silver-mining districts of Chili and
Peru, but now with the great gold regions of
British Columbia. In all probability it will
very soon carry the monster Australian mails;
thus, with the line of British steamers already
traversing three thousand miles of coast as far
down as Valparaiso, it will have three immense
feeders.

This one to the left, the other to Vancouver
to the right, and the third straight ahead, will
extend nearly eight thousand miles to Tahiti,
New Zealand, and the ports of Australia.

Submarine cables will ensure to us instanta-
neous communication with the cities at the Anti-
podes, and, for that matter, with the other great
places of the earth, as readily as now exists
between England and New England, thus comparatively annihilating the effect of distance.
How elevating and sublime is this victory of
man over the obstacles of Nature! We live
in an age of revolution; the things of our in-

fancy are being superseded by the superior inventions, discoveries, and improvements of our manhood; and ere the nightfall of age shall have clouded our maturity, the giant Progress will have entered upon a new and surpassing era of enlightenment and civilization! Truly man is but of the dust; but how great are his conceptions and achievements! how massive his handiwork! and how bold and courageous his undertakings! In his hands lieth the destiny of the world!

The greater the march of discovery and improvement, the higher shall we ascend in the scale of civilization and refinement. Superior tastes will supersede our present ones; and the squalid barbarism, vice, and infamy which now lurk, revolting in their sin and hideousness, in the hearts of our cities, will be swept away by the purer morals, better organization, and higher intelligence and refinement of the masses. Then, also, will self-respect scorn hypocrisy, and our social institutions and conventional barriers become more suited to our mutual welfare. The time is not far off for all this; the trumpet-call has been already heard, and the march is just begun. Let us on!

Having thus spoken, my task is ended ; and British Columbia shines out upon the world— another gem in the British crown—a land of gold, and still more dazzling promise.

APPENDIX.

No. I.

AN ACT TO PROVIDE FOR THE GOVERNMENT OF BRITISH COLUMBIA. 2d August, 1858.

WHEREAS divers of her Majesty's subjects and others have, by the licence and consent of her Majesty, resorted to and settled on certain wild and unoccupied territories on the north-west coast of North America, commonly known by the designation of New Caledonia, and from and after the passing of this Act to be named British Columbia, and the islands adjacent, for mining and other purposes; and it is desirable to make some temporary provision for the civil government of such territories, until permanent settlements shall be thereupon established, and the number of colonists increased: be it therefore enacted by the Queen's most excellent Majesty, by and with the advice and consent of the Lords spiritual and temporal, and Commons, in this present parliament assembled and by the authority of the same, as follows:

Boundaries of British Columbia.

I. British Columbia shall, for the purposes of this act, be held to comprise all such territories within the dominions of her Majesty as are bounded to the south by the frontier of the United States of America, to the east by the main chain of the Rocky Mountains, to the north by Simpson's River and the Finlay branch of the Peace River, and to the west by the Pacific Ocean, and shall include Queen Charlotte's Island, and all other islands adjacent to the said territories, except as herein-after excepted.

Her Majesty by order in council may make or provide for the making of Laws for the government of her Majesty's subjects and others in British Columbia.

II. It shall be lawful for her Majesty, by any order or orders to be by her from time to time made, with the advice of her privy council, to make, ordain and establish, and (subject to such conditions or restrictions as to her shall seem meet) to authorize and empower such officer as she may from time to time appoint as Governor of British Columbia, to make provision for the administration of justice therein, and generally to make, ordain, and establish all such laws, institutions, and ordinances as may be necessary for the peace, order, and good government of her Majesty's subjects and others therein ; provided that all such orders in council, and all laws and ordinances so to be made as aforesaid, shall be laid before both Houses of Parliament as soon as conveniently may be after the making and enactment thereof respectively.

Her Majesty may establish a local legislature in British Columbia.

III. Provided always, That it shall be lawful for her Majesty, so soon as she may deem it convenient, by any such order in council as aforesaid, to constitute or to authorize and empower such officer to constitute a legislature to make laws for the peace, order, and good government of British Columbia, such legislature to consist of the Governor and a Council, or Council and Assembly, to be composed of such and so many persons, and to be appointed or elected in such manner and in for such periods, and subject to such regulations, as to her Majesty may seem expedient.

Certain provisions of 40 *G.* 3, *c.* 138, *and* 1 *and* 2 *G.* 4,
  c. 66, *as regards British Columbia repealed.*

IV. And whereas an Act was passed in the forty-third
year of King George the Third, intituled " An Act for
extending the Jurisdiction of the Courts of Justice in the
provinces of Lower and Upper Canada to the trial and
punishment of persons guilty of crimes and offences
within certain parts of North America adjoining to the
said provinces :" and whereas by an Act passed in the
second year of King George the Fourth, intituled " An
Act for regulating the Fur trade, and establishing a Criminal and Civil Jurisdiction within certain parts of
North America," it was enacted, that from and after the
passing of that Act the Courts of Judicature then existing
or which might be thereafter established in the province
of Upper Canada should have the same civil jurisdiction,
power, and authority, within the Indian territories and
other parts of America not within the limits of either of
the provinces of Lower or Upper Canada or of any civil
government of the United States, as the said courts had
or were invested with within the limits of the said provinces of Lower or Upper Canada respectively, and that
every contract, agreement, debt, liability, and demand
made, entered into, incurred, or arising within the said
Indian territories and other parts of America, and every
wrong and injury to the person or to the property committed or done within the same should be and be deemed
to be of the same nature, and be cognizable and be tried
in the same manner, and subject to the same consequences
in all respects, as if the same had been made, entered
into, incurred, arisen, committed, or done within the said
province of Upper Canada ; and in the same Act are contained provisions for giving force, authority, and effect
within the said Indian territories and other parts of
America to the process and Acts of the said Courts of
Upper Canada ; and it was thereby also enacted, that it
should be lawful for his Majesty, if he should deem it
convenient so to do, to issue a commission or commissions to any person or persons to be and act as justices

o the peace within such parts of America as aforesaid, as well within any territories thereto granted to the company of adventurers of England trading to Hudson's Bay as within the Indian territories of such other parts of America as aforesaid ; and it was further enacted, that it should be lawful for his Majesty from time to time by any commission under the great seal to authorize and empower any such persons so appointed justices of the peace as aforesaid to sit and hold courts of record for the trial of criminal offences and misdemeanours, and also of civil causes, and it should be lawful for his Majesty to order, direct, and authorize the appointment of proper officers to act in aid of such courts and justices within the jurisdiction assigned to such courts and justices in any such commission, provided that such courts should not try any offender upon any charge or indictment for any felony made the subject of capital punishment, or for any offence or passing sentence affecting the life of any offender, or adjudge or cause any offender to suffer capital punishment or transportation, or take cognizance of or try any civil action or suit in which the cause of such suit or action should exceed in value the amount or sum of two hundred pounds, in every case of any offence subjecting the person committing the same to capital punishment or transportation, the court, or any judge of any such court, or any justice or justices of the peace before whom any such offender should be brought, should commit such offender to safe custody, and cause such offender to be sent in such custody for trial in the court of the province of Upper Canada.

From and after the proclamation of this Act in British Columbia the said Act of the forty-third year of King George the Third, and the said recited provisions of the said Act of the second year of King George the Fourth, and the provisions contained in such Act for giving force, authority, and effect within the Indian territories and other parts of America to the process and Acts of the said courts of Upper Canada, shall cease to have force in and to be applicable to British Columbia.

Appeals from judgments in Civil Suits to the Privy Council.

V. Provided always, that all judgments given in any civil suit in British Columbia shall be subject to appeal to her Majesty in council, in the manner and subject to the regulations in and subject to which appeals are now brought from the civil courts of Canada, and to such further or other regulations as her Majesty, with the advice of her Privy Council, shall from time to time appoint.

Vancouver's Island, as at present established, not to be included in British Columbia.

VI. No part of the colony of Vancouver's Island, as at present established, shall be comprised within British Columbia for the purpose of this Act; but it shall be lawful for her Majesty, her heirs and successors, on receiving at any time during the continuance of this Act a joint address from the two houses of legislature of Vancouver's Island, praying for the incorporation of that island with British Columbia, by order to be made as aforesaid, with the advice of her privy council, to annex the said island to British Columbia, subject to such conditions and regulations as to her Majesty shall seem expedient; and thereupon and from the date of the publication of such order in the said island, or such other date as may be fixed in such order, the provisions of this Act shall be held to apply to Vancouver's Island.

Governor.

VII. In the construction of this Act the term " Governor," shall mean the person for the time being lawfully administering the government of British Columbia.

Act to continue in force until Dec. 31, 1862. *Expiration of Act not to affect boundaries, &c.*

VIII. This Act shall continue in force until the thirty-first day of December, one thousand eight hundred and sixty-two, and thenceforth to the end of the then next Session of Parliament : Provided always, that the expiration of this Act shall not affect the boundaries hereby defined, or the right of appeal hereby given, or any act done or right or title acquired under or by virtue of this Act, nor shall the expiration of this Act revive the Acts or parts of Acts hereby repealed.

No. II.

LETTER FROM GOV. STEVENS, CONGRESSIONAL DELEGATE FROM WASHINGTON, TO MR. CASS—PROTEST AGAINST THE TAX ON MINERS—HISTORY OF THE AFFAIR—THE FORM OF LICENSE—EXTORTIONS OF THE HUDSON'S BAY COMPANY— THE LEGAL ASPECT OF THE QUESTIONS INVOLVED.

WASHINGTON CITY, JULY 21, 1858.

HON. LEWIS CASS, Secretary of State :

SIR,—I had the honour to inform you by my communication of May 18 and June 29, of the extensive immigration of American citizens into the British possessions of New Caledonia, in consequence of the discoveries of "gold placers" on Frazer and Thompson Rivers, and of the obstructions which had been placed upon this immigration by Governor Douglas, acting as chief factor of the Hudson's Bay Company, and as Governor of Vancouver's Island and its dependencies, and assuming authority over the region in which the new "placers" have been found.

The object of the present communication is to exhibit to the government of the United States the enormity and absolute illegality of the impositions placed upon the citizens of the United States by the British authorities assuming to exercise jurisdiction over the whole territory in which the late gold discoveries have been made, and to ask the interposition of the government in behalf of our citizens seeking to enter that territory.

On the 28th of December, 1857, his Excellency James Douglas, styling himself Governor of Vancouver's Island and its dependencies, issued a proclamation declaring that all mines of gold in its natural place of deposit within the districts of Frazer River and of Thompson

River, belong to the crown of Great Britain, and that no person will be permitted to dig, search for, or remove gold on or from any lands, public or private (within said district), without first taking out and paying for a license in the form annexed.

The form of license annexed is as follows:

The bearer having paid to me the sum of twenty-one shillings on account of the territorial revenue, I hereby license him to dig, search for, and remove gold on and from any such crown land within the —— of —— as I shall assign to him for that purpose during the month of ——, 185—.

This license must be produced whenever demanded by me or any other person acting under the authority of the government.

A. B., Commissioner.

On the 8th of May, 1858, Governor Douglas issued the following proclamation:

PROCLAMATION.

By his Excellency James Douglas, Governor and Commander-in-Chief of the colony of Vancouver's Island and its dependencies, and Vice Admiral of the same, &c. &c.

Whereas it is commonly reported that certain boats and other vessels have entered Frazer River for trade; and whereas, there is reason to apprehend that other persons are preparing and fitting out boats and vessels for the same purpose.

Now, therefore, I have issued this my proclamation, warning all persons that such acts are contrary to law, and infringements upon the rights of the Hudson's Bay Company, who are legally entitled to trade with the Indians in the British possessions on the north-west coast of America, to the exclusion of all other persons, whether British or foreign.

And also that after fourteen days from the date of this, my proclamation, all ships, boats, and vessels, together with the goods laden on board found in Frazer River, or in any of the bays, rivers, or creeks of the said British possessions on the north-west coast of America, not having a license from the Hudson's Bay Company, and a sufferance from the proper officer of the Customs at Victoria, shall be liable to forfeiture, and will be seized and condemned according to law.

Given under my hand and seal at Government House, Victoria, this eighth day of May, in the year of our Lord one thousand eight hundred and fifty-eight, and in the twenty-first of her Majesty's reign.

JAMES DOUGLAS, Governor.

By his excellency's command, RICHARD GOLLEDGE, Secretary.

God save the Queen.

A copy of the sufferance referred to in the Governor's proclamation follows :

GENERAL SUFFERANCE.

PORT VICTORIA, Vancouver's Island.

These are to certify, to all whom it doth concern, that the sufferance for the present voyage is granted on the condition annexed to ——, master of the ——, burthen ——, mounted with —— guns, navigated with —— men, to proceed on a voyage to Fort Langley with passengers, their luggage, provisions, and mining tools. The above mentioned —— register being deposited in the Custom House at Victoria, hath here entered and cleared his said —— according to law

RODK. FINLAYSON.

Pro Hudson's Bay Company.

CONDITIONS OF SUFFERANCE.

1. That the owner of the boat does bind himself to receive no other goods but such goods as belong to the Hudson's Bay Company.

2. That the said owner also binds himself not to convey or import gunpowder, ammunition, or utensils of war except from the United Kingdom.

3. That he also binds himself to receive no passengers, except the said passengers do produce a gold mining

license and permit from the government at Vancouver's Island.

4. That the said owner also binds himself not to trade with Indians.*

The first consideration presented is the effect of these proclamations, provided they should be submitted to, upon the enterprise of the citizens of the United States.

It is estimated by the most intelligent gentlemen of the Pacific coast that not less than forty thousand persons will enter the "gold placers" of New Caledonia within the present year. Nearly all these persons will be citizens of the United States. The tax of twenty-one shillings (say five dollars) per month upon these forty thousand persons will amount in one year to two millions four hundred thousand dollars. The consumption of provisions, clothing, &c. of these men cannot be estimated at less than thirty dollars per month, at the fair cost of the supplies. If the Hudson's Bay Company should have the exclusive right of furnishing supplies, they will receive from these miners the sum of fourteen millions four hundred thousand dollars. But it is shown by evidence taken before the British Parliament, that this company has been in the habit of charging for supplies furnished to persons outside the company a profit of from two hundred to three hundred per cent. These supplies cannot be drawn from the present resources of the Hudson's Bay Company, but must be obtained from the state of California and the territories of Oregon and Washington. So that in fact these states are compelled to make the Hudson's Bay Company their factor for the

* The sufferance costs twelve dollars for a decked vessel, and six dollars for an open boat. All vessels of every nationality must take out this permit and pay these fees. No exceptions of any kind are made in favour of British bottoms. The British man-of-war, Satellite, is stationed to enforce the conditions of the sufferance, the instructions to her commander, Captain Prevost, being " to stop all vessels or boats of any description from entering (Frazer's River) without a permit."

sale of their produce, and allow them all the profit from the sale of goods to their own citizens.

This simple statement is sufficient to show that a state of things exists in the newly-discovered gold regions which cannot be submitted to by American citizens, unless imposed by positive and imperative law.

I have no hesitation in declaring this opinion, that these proclamations have been made without any legal or binding authority which should be respected by the citizens or government of the United States.

The two important questions presented are, the authority of the Governor of Vancouver's Island to impose a tax of twenty-one shillings per month upon every person searching for gold on Frazer or Thompson Rivers, and the right to compel all persons in those territories to purchase their supplies from the Hudson's Bay Company. The first question which I propose to consider is the right to impose the tax, and demand a license.

It is well known that the right of the British crown to all those mines which are properly royal, namely, those of gold and silver, was anciently claimed as one of its prerogatives. This had its origin, as Blackstone says, "from the king's prerogative of coinage, in order to supply him with materials." The reason for this prerogative mentioned by Blackstone is sufficient to show that it can no longer exist. The materials for coinage have not for centuries, and probably never will be furnished by the working of mines by the crown. The foundation for the prerogative no longer exists, " *cessante ratione cessat lex.*" This prerogative has been obsolete from non use. It has never been exercised in the United Kingdom. It has not been called in force in Ireland, although considerable " placer washings" have been worked there of late years. It has never been applied on this continent.

The late discoveries in Siberia, California, and Australia, have shown that the most extensive deposits of gold are not in mines proper, but are diffused through the soil. Mines proper, in which it was anciently supposed gold was to be found, being entered by simple shafts, and developed by adits and levels beneath the ground, could be worked without disturbing the superficial soil. The enjoyment of the ancient prerogative of the crown in the "gold placers" would be totally inconsistent with private rights in the soil, and from consideration of public policy cannot be exercised in such "placers."

The crown undoubtedly possesses the right to prohibit or regulate by law the digging for gold in its possessions, just as it might prohibit or regulate by law the cutting of timber or using the soil; but in the absence of positive law prohibiting such occupation and use, it is believed to be the natural right of every man who enters a totally unoccupied country, to cut timber and wood, to consume the fruits of the earth, and gather all the products of the soil, which have not before been appropriated. It is believed that, while the jurisdiction simply of the British crown over the territory of Frazer and Thompson Rivers is not questioned, the crown has made no appropriation of that territory by law, and has exercised no acts restricting the natural rights of man in a wild and unoccupied country. Until the passage of such positive laws by proper authority, every man possesses the right to dig gold in that country, just as much as he has the right to cut timber or appropriate the fruits of the earth.

It is further believed that the acts of Governor Douglas, before referred to, in no respect constitute a legal and authorized prohibition to enter the gold-bearing country of New Caledonia, and that his demand of payment of money for a license to dig gold is a high-handed usurpation of power.

Vancouver's Island belongs to a class of colonies called Provincial Establishments. As Blackstone says : — "Their constitution depend upon the respective commissions issued by the crown to the governors, and the instructions which usually accompany those commissions, under the authority of which provincial assemblies are constituted with the power of making local ordinances, not repugnant to the crown of England." I have been unable to obtain a copy of the commission of Governor

Douglas, or the instructions to the first governor. It is
clear that he could exercise no power which was not
conferred upon him by his commission and instructions.
But it is hardly conceivable that his commission and instructions should authorize him to regulate or license
the digging of gold in New Caledonia, a region far distant from his own territory, and especially when the
existence of gold in that country was not even suspected.
It is not pretended that any law regulating the gold-
digging of New Caledonia had ever been passed by the
General Assembly of the colony. Indeed, that assembly
had a mere nominal existence, so that the power to issue
these proclamations was not derived from them. Governor Douglas, it seems, had formerly claimed, under
his commission, the power, with the advice of his council
only, to pass such laws as he considered required by the
exigency of the time. I have before me a copy of a
despatch from the Right Honourable H. Labouchere,
Secretary of State of the imperial government, to Governor Douglas, in which the Secretary says:—"It has
been doubted by authorities conversant in the principles
of colonial law, whether the crown can legally convey
authority to make laws, in a settlement founded by
Englishmen, even for a temporary and special purpose,
to any legislature not elected wholly or in part by the
settlers themselves. If this be the case, the clause in
your commission, on which you relied, would appear to
be unwarranted and invalid."

Granting the authority of Governor Douglas over
Vancouver's Island proper, there are strong reasons for
believing that his authority does not extend to the regions where the "gold placers" are situated. As I
stated to you in a former communication, he has always
declined to exercise authority over Indians on the main
land in British territory in his capacity of governor,
while he has consented to treat with them as chief factor
of the Hudson's Bay Company. A further reason for
believing that his authority does not extend to the main
land is the fact that the committee appointed by Parliament to consider the state of the British possessions in

North America which are under the administration of
the Hudson's Bay Company, recommended that means
should be provided for the ultimate extension of the
colony of Vancouver's Island over any portion of the
adjoining country to the west of the Rocky Mountains
on which permanent settlement may be found practicable.

Assuming that the governor in his position as general
agent of the crown had the right to prohibit trespass
upon the property of the crown, it cannot for a moment
be pretended that, without express authority, he had the
right to demand money for licenses to appropriate the
crown's property.

The declaration of his proclamation is, that all mines
of gold belong to the crown. But the law upon which
he founds that doctrine states that they belong to the
crown, not for general purposes of revenue, but for the
specific purpose of furnishing materials for coinage. No
agent of the crown has a right to authorize the diversion
of gold, the material of coinage, from the specific purpose to which the law appropriates it. In receiving
money for licenses to dig gold, he sells that which is not
his, and the crown, if it be the owner of the gold, as the
governor alleges, may legally confiscate every ounce of
gold dug under the governor's license.

The most aggravating circumstance connected with
this extortion is the fact, that the name and authority of
the crown are invoked, not for its benefit, but to fill the
coffers of the Hudson's Bay Company. The form of
license above quoted declares that the license-fee is paid
on account of territorial revenue. Governor Douglas is
not only the territorial governor of Vancouver's Island,
but the chief factor of the Hudson's Bay Company.

In 1848, Vancouver's Island was granted to the Hudson's Bay Company, and that company assumed the
expenses of the possession of the island, and appropiated
all the revenues of the island. The territorial revenue
enters into the treasury of the company. The tax imposed upon our mines goes not to the crown, as is pre-

tended, but to the company, who have not the shadow of a claim to the territory where the gold is situated.

The next question which I propose to consider is the more important one, of the right of the British authorities to compel our miners and citizens entering the gold regions in New Caledonia, to purchase their supplies solely of the Hudson's Bay Company, and to prohibit the passage of vessels except upon certain onerous conditions.

The right to enter a foreign territory for lawful purposes is claimed by all civilized nations. As Chancellor Kent says:—" Every nation is bound to grant a passage for lawful purposes over their lands, rivers, and seas, to the people of other states, whenever it can be permitted without inconvenience, and burthensome conditions ought not to be annexed to the transit of persons and property." He also says:—" As the end of the law of nations is the happiness and perfection of the general society of mankind, it enjoins upon every nation the punctual observance of benevolence and good will as well as justice towards its neighbours. This is equally the policy and duty of nations. They ought to cultivate a free intercourse for commercial purposes in order to supply each other's wants and promote each other's prosperity. The variety of climates and productions on the surface of the globe, and the facility of communication by means of rivers, lakes, and oceans, invite to a liberal commerce as agreeable to the law of nature, and extremely conducive to national amity, industry, and happiness." I need not point out to you how utterly inconsistent with these principles are the vexatious restrictions imposed by the proclamations above referred to.

The right of trade with and entry into a foreign country, is called by lawyers one of imperfect obligation, and is subject to the discretion of the government which tolerates it. But it exists until forbidden or restrained by positive and binding law.

I maintain that no positive law exists of binding authority which forbids the free entry of persons and goods into the British possessions on the north-west coast.

Very vague and inaccurate notions popularly prevail with respect to the rights of the Hudson's Bay Company on the north-west coast. The company itself has given currency to the opinion that it possesses by charter absolute territorial rights over the whole British possessions on the north-west coast. Nothing can be farther from the fact.

In 1670, a royal charter was granted by Charles II., for incorporating the Hudson's Bay Company. The grant to the company was of "the whole trade and commerce of all those seas, straits, bays, rivers, lakes, creeks, and sounds, in whatsoever latitude they shall be, that lie within the entrance of the straits, commonly called Hudson's Straits, together with all the lands and territories upon the countries, coasts, and confines of the seas, bays, lakes, rivers, creeks, and sounds aforesaid, that are not already actually possessed by or granted to any of our subjects, or possessed by the subjects of any other Christian prince or state, with the fishing of all sorts of fish, whales, sturgeons, and all other royal fishes in the seas, bays, inlets, and rivers within the premises; and the fish therein taken, together with the royalty of the sea upon the coasts within the limits aforesaid, and all mines royal, as well discovered and not discovered, of gold, silver, gems, and precious stones, to be found or discovered within the territories, limits, and places aforesaid;" and the charter declares that "the said lands be from henceforth reckoned as one of our plantations or colonies in America, called Rupert's Land."

By reference to the best maps it will be seen that "Rupert's Land" extends on the west only to the eastern base of the Rocky Mountains. It includes none of the North-west Pacific possessions.

The validity, even, of this charter has been seriously questioned. Eminent lawyers have asserted that the sovereign in the exercise of the prerogatives of the crown may grant a charter, but that it has always been held that no sovereign can grant to any of his subjects exclusive rights and privileges without the consent of Parliament; and this charter having been so granted, the powers and privileges sought to be exercised under it are illegal.

This was evidently the opinion of the Hudson's Bay Company themselves as early as 1690, viz. twenty years after the date of this charter. At that period they petitioned for an act to be passed for the confirmation of those rights and privileges which had been sought to be granted to them by charter. The act of the first of William and Mary did legalize and confirm them, but only for the period of seven years, and no longer. That act of Parliament has never been renewed since it expired in 1697; consequently the charter is left where it originally stood, and wholly unaffected by any conformity act of Parliament.

The very foundation for the charter is a grant of territory presumed to have been made in the year 1670. It has been maintained that as Charles the Second could not grant away what the crown of England did not possess, much less could he grant away the possessions of another power, the very words of the charter excluding from the operation of the grant those identical territories which the Hudson's Bay Company now claim. For at the date of the charter, these territories were then actually in possession of the crown of France, and held and occupied by the Company of New France, under a charter granted by Louis the Thirteenth of France, bearing date 1626.

These facts are presented not as bearing directly upon the questions I have in view, otherwise than as showing a characteristic feature of the company in its illegal and unwarranted assumption of privilege and power.

A controversy having arisen between the North-west Company and the Hudson's Bay Company, and the difficulties having been adjusted, the former company was merged in the latter, and on the 30th day of May, 1838, the crown issued a grant or license to the Hudson's Bay Company of the exclusive trade with the Indians in certain parts of North America for the term of twenty-one years; the terms of the grant being as follows:—" We do grant and give our license under the hand and seal of one of our principal Secretaries of State, to the said Governor and Company, the Hudson's Bay Company, and their successors, for the exclusive privilege of trading with the Indians in all such parts to the northward and westward of the lands and territories belonging to the United States of America as shall not form part of any of our provinces in North America, or of any lands or territories belonging to the said United States of America, or to any European government, State or Power, but subject nevertheless as hereinafter mentioned; and we do by these presents give, grant, and secure to the said Governor and company and their successors, the sole and exclusive privilege for the full period of twenty-one years from the date of this our grant of trading with the Indians in all such parts of North America as aforesaid.

On the 5th day of February, 1857, a select committee was appointed by the British Parliament " to consider the state of those British possessions in North America which are under the administration of the Hudson's Bay Company, or over which they have a license to trade."

This committee having taken voluminous evidence, reported on the 31st of July, 1857. In their report they carefully waive all considerations as to the validity of the charter, or the right to the monopoly of trade, and confine themselves to the declaration of an opinion as to the expediency of allowing the Hudson's Bay Company the privileges of exclusive trade which they now possess.

The question as to the rights of the Hudson's Bay Company, before the British Parliament, resolved itself, as I have said, into one purely of expediency. That is a question with which the American government has no concern. But when the pretended rights of the Hudson's Bay Company are set up against American citizens, the government of the United States has solely to consider the validity and legality of these pretended rights.

Upon examination it will be seen that the only colour of right of the Hudson's Bay Company in the Pacific British possessions is that of exclusive trade with the Indians. It is evident that the possibility of this country being opened to colonization or the enterprize of civilized settlers was never contemplated by the British government. The report of the committee of Parliament declares this. They say, " that as to those extensive regions, whether in Rupert's Land or in the Indian territory, for the present, at least, there can be no prospect of permanent settlement to any extent by the European race for the purpose of colonization. The granting of the license had regard to such a supposed state of things. There is nothing in the letter or spirit of the license for exclusive trade with the Indians which justifies the exclusion of goods for the supply of European or American miners and settlers.

It may, however, be urged that the free admission of goods may indirectly interfere with the monopoly of the Hudson's Bay Company.

It becomes, therefore, an important question to determine whether, by the laws of the British realm, such a monopoly as has been granted to the Hudson's Bay Company can legally exist.

This question, it seems to me, has been absolutely determined by the famous statutes of monopolies passed in the 21st of James First.

The provisions of this statute are mainly as follow :—

Be it declared and enacted by authority of this present Parliament, That all monopolies and all commissions, grants, licenses, charters, and letters patent heretofore made and granted or hereafter to be made and granted to any person or persons, bodies politic or corporate whatsoever, or for the sole buying, selling, making, working, or using of anything within this realm, &c., are altogether contrary to the laws of this realm, and, &c., are and shall be utterly void and of no effect, &c.

Sec. 3. And be it further enacted, that all person and persons, bodies politic and corporate whatsoever, which now are, or hereafter shall be, shall stand and be disabled and incapable to have, use, exercise, or put in use, any monopoly or any such commission, grant, license, charter, letters patent, proclamation, &c., or any liberty, power or faculty, grounded or pretended to be grounded upon them or any of them.

This statute has never been repealed or annulled. It stands as a part of the common law of England, and there can be no question that it renders totally void and inoperative the license for exclusive trade granted to the Hudson's Bay Company. This question would have been undoubtedly determined by the courts of law if individuals had been found powerful enough to contend with this wealthy company.

Chief Justice Draper, of Canada, in his evidence before the committee of Parliament, says : — " With regard to the exclusive license to trade (perhaps with the prejudice which lawyers have in favour of their particular views), I never could understand how it could be contended for in a court of law for an instant. The exclusive license to trade appears to me to be diametrically contrary to the statute of James the First." (Referring undoubtedly to the statute before quoted, although he does not cite it.) " The only question, I think, which could arise upon it, speaking always individually, would be whether or not that statute applied to a colony, or was confined to a monopoly within the mother country. Assuming that it was confined to a monopoly within the mother country, it still, I think, would be open to a very fair argument that it did apply to this company, because their charter makes the seat of their government in England."

He further says, in answer to a question from Lord John Russell—"I understand you to give a decided opinion as to the monopoly of trade ?" " Upon that point I have never entertained a doubt."

The simple question presented to the Department of State, in view of the facts above presented, is this :— Will the government of the United States suffer the natural rights of its citizens to labour and trade to be controlled and restrained by a company of merchants, the legal existence of whose rights is hardly recognised by the British government, and only so far upheld as they are, from considerations of political expediency, but not of law.

I beg leave to submit to the Department of State that this is a question of no trifling importance to the Pacific States and Territories of the United States. One quarter part of the labouring element of the State of California and the Territories of Oregon and Washington will be diverted to these new regions. The product of gold in California and the agricultural produce of Oregon and Washington Territories will be materially diminished. If the present restrictions are allowed, the gold of the new regions, after paying enormous profits to the British monopolists, will pass through their hands to England without benefitting our own country or people, The countries of California, Oregon, and Washington, although furnishing all the supplies for the new gold region, will be impoverished by the abstraction of their own labourers, while the profits from the sale of supplies produced in these American territories will be absorbed by foreign monopolists.

The government of the United States must determine whether it is consistent with its own self-respect and its duty to its citizens, that this state of things should continue.

In behalf of the citizens of Washington Territory, whom I immediately represent, and further in behalf of the citizens of our whole Pacific coast, I would request that the government of the United States should interpose with the British authorities for the removal of the restrictions above referred to. And I further request that this government demand the repayment of all sums collected by the Governor of Vancouver's Island for licenses to dig gold, and that it make reclamation for the value of all vessels and cargoes confiscated in consequence of the proclamations of Governor Douglas, before referred to.

In conclusion, I would say that I have no hesitation in expressing my opinion upon the legal questions involved in this paper, as I have been aided in their investigation by the professional advice of my friend, John L. Hayes, Esq., counsellor at law of this city, to whom I am happy to express my obligation.

I have the honour to be,

Very respectfully, &c.

ISAAC J. STEVENS,

Delegate to Congress from Washington Territory.

TREATY MADE BETWEEN THE UNITED STATES AND GREAT BRITAIN IN REGARD TO LIMITS WESTWARD OF THE ROCKY MOUNTAINS, JUNE 15, 1846.

Art. 1. From the point on the forty-ninth parallel of north latitude, where the boundary laid down in existing treaties and conventions between the United States and Great Britain terminates the line of boundary between the territories of the United States and those of her Britannic Majesty shall be continued westward along the said forty-ninth parallel of north latitude to the middle of the channel which separates the continent from Vancouver's Island, and thence southerly through the middle of the said channel, and of Fuca's Straits, to the Pacific ocean: Provided, however, that the navigation of the whole of the said channel and straits, south of the forty-ninth parallel of north latitude, remain free and open to both parties.

Art. 2. From the point at which the forty-ninth parallel of north latitude shall be found to intersect the great northern branch of the Columbia river, the navigation of the said branch shall be free and open to the Hudson's Bay Company, and to all British subjects trading with the same, to the point where the said branch meets the main stream of the Columbia, and thence down the said main stream to the ocean, with free access into and through the said river or rivers, it being understood that all the usual portages along the line thus described shall, in like manner, be free and open. In navigating the said river or rivers, British subjects, with their goods and produce, shall be treated on the same footing as citizens of the United States; it being, however, always

Q

understood that nothing in this article shall be construed
as preventing, or intended to prevent, the government
of the United States from making any regulations respecting the navigation of the said river or rivers not inconsistent with the present treaty.

Art. 3. In the future appropriation of the territory
south of the forty-ninth parallel of north latitude, as provided in the first article of this treaty, the possessory
rights of the Hudson's Bay Company, and of all British
subjects who may be already in the occupation of land or
other property lawfully acquired within the said territory,
shall be respected.

Art. 4. The farms, lands, and other property of every
description belonging to the Puget's Sound Agricultural
Company, on the north side of the Columbia River, shall
be confirmed to the said company. In case, however,
the situation of those farms and lands should be considered
by the United States to be of public and political importance, and the United States government should signify
a desire to obtain possession of the whole or of any part
thereof, the property so required shall be transferred to
the said government, at a proper valuation, to be settled
upon between the parties.

No. III.

DESPATCH FROM WASHINGTON.

The "New York Times" has the following despatch
from Washington :—

The Government is perfectly satisfied that the steps
taken by Great Britain will prevent any collision or
misunderstanding between the miners and the Government authorities at the newly-discovered gold-diggings
in New Caledonia. It is an interesting fact, never yet
made public, that the Hudson's Bay Company have for
some time been anxious to sell to the United States all
their rights and interests under the treaty of 1845.

Under the provisions of this treaty this company own and hold a number of forts, posts, and trading-houses situated in the territory of the United States ; also large stocks of horses, sheep, and cattle. Lord Napier, the British Minister, was authorized by the company to sell them to the United States for the sum of six hundred thousand dollars. Several meetings were held at the State Department on the subject, but without a sale being effected. According to the testimony of General Lane and Governor Stevens, the sum named was very low for the property proposed to be transferred. The stock alone, they stated, would bring at auction one-half the price named. The Secretary of State was favourable to the purchase, but he much doubted the disposition of Congress to make the necessary appropriation. As things now stand, in order to avoid a complication of our matters with the Hudson's Bay Company, the Secretary of State may close the contract, provided the offer is still open, and provided, further, Congress wil make the appropriation to meet the payment. It is essential to the peace and good understanding of the two Governments that this interest of the Hudson's Bay Company on our side of the line be extinguished. The popular impression, however, that this company is unfriendly in its feelings towards our people is entirely erroneous. In 1855, when the people of Oregon were engaged in a bloody Indian war, and could not obtain supplies from any other quarter, this company furnished them with provisions and ammunition at a low price and on time. They have always endeavoured to keep down Indian disturbances, and have frequently furnished important information to the Government authorities.

Another Washington correspondent writes :—

At the instance of Governor Stevens, of Washington Territory, our country, through Mr. Dallas, called the attention of the British Government to the apprehended difficulties with the Governor of Vancouver's Island in arresting the passage of our citizens into the gold regions. The British Secretary of State for Foreign

Affairs, Lord Malmesbury, promptly responded, and I am permitted to lay his lordship's reply before the readers of the "Times:"—

"Foreign Office, June 17, 1858.

"The undersigned, her Majesty's Principal Secretary of State for Foreign Affairs, has the honour to acknowledge the receipt of the note which Mr. Dallas, Envoy Extraordinary and Minister Plenipotentiary of the United States of America, addressed to him on the 13th inst., calling the attention of her Majesty's Government to the obstructions which it is apprehended may be offered by the Governor of Vancouver's Island to the passage of citizens of the United States to the districts of British Oregon, where gold is reported to have been found.

"The undersigned begs leave to assure Mr. Dallas that the subject of his note shall receive immediate attention, and that her Majesty's Government are, on their part, disposed, as far as they can properly do so, to deal liberally with any citizens of the United States who may desire to proceed to that quarter of the British possessions. But her Majesty's Government must necessarily ascertain, in the first place, how far the charter of the Hudson's Bay Company bears upon the question, and then generally from the law officers of the crown whether any legal considerations require attention on the part of her Majesty's Government in connection with this question.

"The undersigned has the honour to renew to Mr. Dallas the assurances of his highest consideration.

"MALMESBURY.

"G. M. Dallas, Esq., &c."

No. IV.

No. 1.

Copy of a Despatch from Governor Douglas to the Right Hon. Henry Labouchere, M.P.

(No. 10.) Victoria, Vancouver's Island,
April 16, 1856.
(Received June 30, 1856.)
(Answered. No. 14, August 4, 1856.)

SIR,

I hasten to communicate for the information of her Majesty's Government a discovery of much importance, made known to me by Mr. Angus McDonald, clerk in charge of Fort Colville, one of the Hudson's Bay Company's trading posts on the Upper Caledonian District.

That gentleman reports, in a letter dated on the 1st of March last, that gold had been found in considerable quantities within the British territory, on the Upper Columbia, and that he is moreover of opinion that valuable deposits of gold will be found in many other parts of that country; he also states that the *daily earnings* of persons then employed in digging gold were ranging from 2*l.* to 8*l.* for each man. Such is the substance of his report on that subject, and I have requested him to continue his communications in respect to any further discoveries made.

I do not know if her Majesty's Government will consider it expedient to raise a revenue in that quarter, by taxing all persons engaged in gold digging, but I may remark, that it will be impossible to levy such a tax without the aid of a military force, and the expense in that case would probably exceed the income derived from the mines.

I will not fail to keep you well informed in respect

to the extent and value of the gold discoveries made; and circumstances will probably be the best indication of the course which it may be expedient to take, that is, in respect to imposing a tax, or leaving the field free and open to any persons who may choose to dig for gold.

Several interesting experiments in gold-washing have been lately made in this colony, with a degree of success that will no doubt lead to further attempts for the discovery of the precious metal. The quantity of gold found is sufficient to prove the existence of the metal, and the parties engaged in the enterprise entertain sanguine hopes of discovering rich and productive beds.

I have, &c.

(Signed)   JAMES DOUGLAS,
The Right Hon. Hen.   Governor.
Labouchere, &c. &c.

No. 2.

Copy of a Despatch from the Right Hon. Henry Labouchere to Governor Douglas.

(No. 14.)

Sir,   Downing Street, August 4, 1856.
        I have to acknowledge the receipt of your Despatch, No. 10, of the 16th April last, reporting the discovery of gold within the British territory on the Upper Columbia River district.

In the absence of all effective machinery of Government, I conceive that it would be quite abortive to attempt to raise a revenue from licences to dig for gold in that region. Indeed, as her Majesty's Government do not at present look for a revenue from this distant quarter of the British dominions, so neither are they prepared to incur any expense on account of it. I must, therefore, leave it to your discretion to determine the best means of preserving order in the event of any considerable increase of population flocking into this new gold district; and I shall rely on your furnishing me

with full and regular accounts of any event of interest
or importance which may occur in consequence of this
discovery.

I have, &c.

(Signed)   H. LABOUCHERE.

To Governor Douglas,
&c. &c.

No. 3.

*Copy of a Despatch from Governor Douglas to the Right
Hon. Henry Labouchere, M.P.*

(No. 28.)   Victoria, Vancouver's Island,
Oct. 19, 1856.

(Received January 14, 1857.)

(Answered, No. 5, January 24, 1857.)

SIR,

1. I have the honour to acknowledge the receipt
of your Despatch, No. 14, of the 4th of August, communicating the arrival of my Despatch, No. 10, of the
16th April last, in which was reported the discovery of
gold within the British territory in the Upper Columbia
River district.

2. I have, since the date of that letter, received several
other communications from my correspondent in that
part of the country, who, however, scarcely makes any
allusion to the subject of the gold discovery; but I have
heard through other almost equally reliable sources of
information, that the number of persons engaged in gold
digging is yet extremely limited, in consequence of the
threatening attitude of the native tribes, who being hostile to the Americans, have uniformly opposed the entrance of American citizens into their country.

3. The people from American Oregon are therefore
excluded from the gold district, except such as, resorting
to the artifice of denying their country, succeed in passing for British subjects. The persons at present engaged
in the search of gold are chiefly of British origin and
retired servants of the Hudson's Bay Company, who,
being well acquainted with the natives, and connected
by old acquaintanceship and the ties of friendship, are

more disposed to aid and assist each other in their common pursuits than to commit injuries against persons or property.

4. They appear to pursue their toilsome occupation in peace, and without molestation from the natives, and there is no reason to suppose that any criminal act has lately taken place in that part of the country.

* * * * * *

5. It is reported that gold is found in considerable quantities, and that several persons have accumulated large sums by their labour and traffic, but I cannot vouch for the accuracy of those reports ; though, on the other hand, there is no reason to discredit them, as about 220 ounces of gold-dust have been brought to Vancouver's Island direct from the Upper Columbia, a proof that the country is at least auriferous.

From the successful result of experiments made in washing gold from the sands of the tributary streams of Fraser's River, there is reason to suppose that the gold region is extensive, and I entertain sanguine hopes that future researches will develop stores of wealth, perhaps equal to the gold fields of California. The geological formations observed in the "Sierra Nevada" of California being similar in character to the structure of the corresponding range of mountains in this latitude, it is not unreasonable to suppose that the resemblance will be found to include auriferous deposits.

6. I shall not fail to furnish you with full and regular accounts of every event of interest connected with the gold district, which may from time to time occur.

I have, &c.
(Signed)   JAMES DOUGLAS, Governor.
The Right Hon. H. Labouchere, &c.

No. 4.

Copy of a Despatch from the Right Hon Henry Labouchere to Governor Douglas.

(No. 5.)
SIR,   Downing Street, January 24, 1857.
    I have to acknowledge your despatch (No. 28) of

the 29th October, 1856, relative to the discovery of gold in the Upper Columbia River district.

I have, &c.

(Signed)   H. LABOUCHERE.

Governor Douglas, &c.

No. 5.

Copy of a Despatch from Governor Douglas to the Right Hon. Henry Labouchere, M.P.

(No. 21.)

Victoria, Vancouver's Island, July 15, 1857.

(Received, September 18, 1857.)

SIR,

1. I have the honour of communicating for your information the substance of advices which I have lately received from the interior of the continent, north of the 49th parallel of latitude, corroborating the former accounts from that quarter respecting the auriferous character of certain districts of the country on the right bank of the Columbia River, and of the extensive table land which divides it from Frazer's River.

2. There is, however, as yet a degree of uncertainty respecting the productiveness of those gold fields, for reports vary so much on that point, some parties representing the deposits as exceedingly rich, while others are of opinion that they will not repay the labour and outlay of working, that I feel it would be premature for me to give a decided opinion on the subject.

3. It is, however, certain that gold has been found in many places by washing the soil of the river beds and also of the mountain sides ; but on the other hand, the quantities hitherto collected are inconsiderable, and do not lend much support to the opinion entertained of the richness of those deposits; so that the question as to their ultimate value remains thus undetermined, and will probably not be decided until more extensive researches are made.

4. A new element of difficulty in exploring the gold country has been interposed through the opposition of

the native Indian tribes of Thompson's River, who have lately taken the high-handed, though probably not unwise course, of expelling all the parties of gold diggers, composed chiefly of persons from the American territories, who had forced an entrance into their country. They have also openly expressed a determination to resist all attempts at working gold in any of the streams flowing into Thompson's River, both from a desire to monopolize the precious metal for their own benefit, and from a well-founded impression that the shoals of salmon which annually ascend those rivers and furnish the principal food of the inhabitants, will be driven off, and prevented from making their annual migrations from the sea.

5. The officers in command of the Hudson's Bay Company's posts in that quarter, have received orders carefully to respect the feelings of the natives in that matter, and not to employ any of the company's servants in washing out gold, without their full approbation and consent. There is, therefore, nothing to apprehend on the part of the Hudson's Bay Company's servants, but there is much reason to fear that serious affrays may take place between the natives and the motley adventurers who will be attracted by the reputed wealth of the country, from the United States' possessions in Oregon, and may probably attempt to overpower the opposition of the natives by force of arms, and thus endanger the peace of the country.

6. I beg to submit, if in that case it may not become a question whether the natives are not entitled to the protection of her Majesty's Government, and if an officer invested with the requisite authority should not, without delay, be appointed for that purpose.

I have, &c.

(Signed)　　JAMES DOUGLAS, Governor.
The Right Hon. H. Labouchere. &c.

No. 6.

Extract of a Despatch from Governor Douglas to the Right Hon. Henry Labouchere, M.P., dated Victoria, Vancouver's Island, December 29, 1857. (Received March 2, 1858.)

(No. 35.)

Since I had the honour of addressing you on the 15th of July last, concerning the gold fields in the interior of the country north of the 49th parallel of latitude, which, for the sake of brevity, I will hereafter speak of as the " Couteau mines " (so named after the tribe of Indians who inhabit the country), I have received further intelligence from my correspondents in that quarter.

It appears from their reports that the auriferous character of the country is becoming daily more extensively developed, through the exertions of the native Indian tribes, who, having tasted the sweets of gold finding, are devoting much of their time and attention to that pursuit.

They are, however, at present almost destitute of tools for moving the soil, and of washing implements for separating the gold from the earthy matrix, and have therefore to pick it out with knives, or to use their fingers for that purpose ; a circumstance which in some measure accounts for the small products of gold up to the present time, the export being only about 300 ounces since the 6th of last October.

The same circumstance will also serve to reconcile the opinion now generally entertained of the richness of the gold deposits by the few experienced miners who have seen the Couteau country, with the present paucity of production.

The reputed wealth of the Couteau mines is causing much excitement among the population of the United States territories of Washington and Oregon, and I have no doubt that a great number of people from those territories will be attracted thither with the return of the fine weather in spring.

In that case, difficulties between the natives and whites will be of frequent occurrence, and unless measures of prevention are taken, the country will soon become the scene of lawless misrule.

In my letter of the 15th of July, I took the liberty of suggesting the appointment of an officer invested with authority to protect the natives from violence, and generally, so far as possible, to maintain the peace of the country.

Presuming that you will approve of that suggestion, I have, as a preparatory step towards the proposed measures for the preservation of peace and order, this day issued a proclamation declaring the rights of the crown in respect to gold found in its natural place of deposit, within the limits of Frazer's River and Thompson's River districts, within which are situated the Couteau mines; and forbidding all persons to dig or disturb the soil in search of gold, until authorized on that behalf by her Majesty's Government.

I herewith forward a copy of that proclamation, and also of the regulations since published, setting forth the terms on which licences will be issued to legalize the search for gold, on payment of a fee of ten shillings a month, payable in advance.

When mining becomes a remunerative employment, and there is a proof of the extent and productiveness of the gold deposits, I would propose that the licence fee be gradually increased, in such a manner, however, as not to be higher than the persons engaged in mining can readily pay.

My authority for issuing that proclamation, seeing that it refers to certain districts of continental America, which are not strictly speaking within the jurisdiction of this Government, may perhaps be called in question; but I trust that the motives which have influenced me on this occasion, and the fact of my being invested with the authority over the premises of the Hudson's Bay Company, and the only authority commissioned by her Majesty within reach, will plead my excuse. Moreover, should her Majesty's Government not deem it advisable to enforce the rights of the Crown, as set forth in the proclamation, it may be allowed to fall to the ground, and to become a mere dead letter.

If you think it expedient that I should visit the Couteau Mines in the course of the coming spring or summer, for the purpose of enquiring into the state of the country, and authorize me to do so, if I can for a time conveniently leave this colony, I freely place my services at the disposal of her Majesty's government.

Enclosure 1 in No. 6.

Proclamation by his Excellency James Douglas, Governor of Vancouver's Island and its Dependencies, &c.

Whereas by law all mines of gold, and all gold in its natural place of deposit, within the districts of Frazer's River and of Thompson's River, commonly known as the " Quââtlan," " Couteau," and " Shuswap " countries, whether on the lands of the Queen or of any of her Majesty's subjects belong to the crown.

And whereas information has been received by the government that gold exists upon and in the soil of the said districts, and that certain persons have commenced, or are about to commence, searching and digging for the same for their own use, without leave or other authority from her Majesty.

Now, I, James Douglas, the Governor aforesaid, on behalf of her Majesty, do hereby publicly notify and declare that all persons who shall take from any lands within the said districts any gold, metal, or ore containing gold, or who shall dig for and disturb the soil in search of gold, metal, or ore, without having been duly anthorized in that behalf by her Majesty's Colonial government, will be prosecuted, both criminally and civilly, as the law allows.

And I further notify and declare that such regulations as may be found expedient will be prepared and published, setting forth the terms on which licenses will be issued for this purpose on the payment of a reasonable fee.

Given under my hand and seal at Government Office, Victoria, this 28th day of December, in the year of our Lord one thousand eight hundred and fifty-seven, and in the twenty-first year of her Majesty's reign.

(Signed)   JAMES DOUGLAS, Governor.

By his Excellency's command,

(Signed)   RICHARD GOLLEDGE, Secretary.

God save the Queen.

Enclosure 2 in No. 6.

Government House, Victoria, December 29, 1857.

With reference to the proclamation issued on the 28th of December, declaring the rights of the crown in respect to gold found in its natural state of deposit within the districts of Frazer's River and of Thompson's River, commonly known as the Quââtlan, Couteau, and Shuswap countries, his Excellency the Governor, has been pleased to establish the following provisional regulations, under which licences may be obtained to dig, search for, and remove the same.

1st. From and after the first day of February next, no person will be permitted to dig, search for, or remove gold, on or from any lands, public or private, without first taking out and paying for a license in the form annexed.

2nd. For the present, and pending further proof of the extent and productiveness of the gold deposits, the licence fee has been fixed at 10s. per month, to be paid in advance; but it is to be understood that the rate is subject to future adjustment, as circumstances may render expedient.

3rd. The licences can be obtained at Victoria, Vancouver's Island, until a Commissioner is appointed by his Excellency the Governor to carry those regulations into effect, and who will be authorized to receive the fee payable thereon.

4th. Rules adjusting the extent and position of land, to be covered by each licence, and for the prevention

of confusion, and the interference of one licence with
another, will be regulated by the said Commissioner.
(Signed)   JAMES DOUGLAS, Governor.
By his Excellency's command,
(Signed)   RICHARD GOLLEDGE, Secretary.

No. 7.

*Copy of a Despatch from the Governor of Vancouver's
Island to the Right Hon. H. Labouchere, M.P.*

(No. 1.)
Victoria, Vancouver's Island, January, 22, 1858.
(Received March 15, 1858.)

SIR,

1. With reference to the Proclamation and Regulations legalizing the search for gold in the districts of
Frazer's River and Thompson's River, transmitted with
my despatch No. 35, of the 29th of December last, I have
now the honour to communicate for your information,
that we have since that date raised the licence fee from
ten shillings to twenty-one shillings a month, payable in
advance, which is the present charge for gold licences.

2. We were induced to make that change through a
desire to place a larger amount of revenue at the disposal
of Government to meet the expense of giving protection
to life and property in those countries, and at the same
time from a well-founded conviction that persons really
bent on visiting the gold district will as readily pay the
increased as the lower rate of charge.

I have, &c.
(Signed)   JAMES DOUGLAS, Governor.
To the Right Hon. Henry Labouchere, &c.

No. 8.

*Copy of a Despatch from Governor Douglas to the Right
Hon. H. Labouchere, M.P.*

(No. 15.)
Victoria, Vancouver's Island, April 6th, 1858.

SIR,

1. Since I had last the honour of addressing you

in my Despatch No. 35, of the 29th of December last, in reference to the discovery of gold in the Couteau, or Thompson's River District, we have had much communication with persons who have since visited that part of the country.

2. The search for gold and "prospecting" of the country, had, up to the last dates from the interior, been carried on almost exclusively by the native Indian population, who have discovered the productive beds, and put out almost all the gold, about eight hundred ounces, which has been hitherto exported from the country, and who are moreover extremely jealous of the whites, and strongly opposed to their digging the soil for gold.

3. The few white men who passed the winter at the diggings, chiefly retired servants of the Hudson's Bay Company, though well acquainted with Indian character, were obstructed by the natives in all their attempts to search for gold. They were on all occasions narrowly watched, and in every instance when they did succeed in removing the surface and excavating to the depth of the auriferous stratum, they were quietly hustled and crowded by the natives, who having by that means obtained possession of the spot, then proceeded to reap the fruits of their labours.

4. Such conduct was unwarrantable and exceedingly trying to the temper of spirited men, but the savages were far too numerous for resistance, and they had to submit to their dictation. It is, however, worthy of remark, and a circumstance highly honourable to the character of those savages, that they have on all occasions scrupulously respected the persons and property of their white visitors, at the same time that they have expressed a determination to reserve the gold for their own benefit.

5. Such being the purpose of the natives, affrays and collisions with the whites will surely follow the accession of numbers, which the latter are now receiving by the influx of adventurers from Vancouver's Island and the United States territories in Oregon; and there is no doubt in my mind that sooner or later the intervention

of her Majesty's government will be required to restore
and maintain the peace.   Up to the present time, however, the country continues quiet, but simply, I believe,
because the whites have not attempted to resist the impositions of the natives.   I will, however, make it a part
of my duty to keep you well informed in respect to the
state of the gold country.

6. The extent of the gold region is yet but imperfectly known, and I have, therefore, not arrived at any
decided opinion as to its ultimate value as a gold-producing country.   The boundaries of the gold district
have been, however, greatly extended since my former
report.

7. In addition to the diggings before known on
Thompson's River and its tributary streams, a valuable
deposit has been recently found by the natives on a
bank of Frazer's River, about five miles beyond its confluence with the Thompson, and gold in small quantities
has been found in the possession of the natives as far as
the Great Falls of Frazer's River, about eighty miles
above the Forks.   The small quantity of gold hitherto
produced,—about eight hundred ounces,—by the large
native population of the country is, however, unac-
countable in a rich gold-producing country, unless we
assume that the want of skill, industry, and proper
mining tools, on the part of the natives, sufficiently
account for the fact.

8. On the contrary, the vein rocks and its other geological features, as described by an experienced gold
miner, encourage the belief that the country is highly
auriferous.

9. The miner in question clearly described the older
slate formations thrown up and pierced by beds of
quartz, granite, porphyry, and other igneous rocks; the
vast accumulations of sand, gravel, and shingle extending from the roots of the mountains to the banks of
Frazer's River and its affluents, which are peculiar characteristics of the gold districts of California and other
countries.   We therefore hope and are preparing for a

rich harvest of trade, which will greatly redound to the advantage of this Colony.

10. I have further to communicate for your information that the Proclamation issued by me, asserting the rights of the Crown to all gold in its natural place of deposit, and forbidding all persons to dig for gold without a licence, have been published in the newspapers of Oregon and Washington territories, and that notwithstanding some seventy or eighty adventurers from the American side have gone by the way of Frazer's River to the Couteau mines without taking out licences.

11. I did not, as I might have done, attempt to enforce those rights by means of a detachment of seamen and marines from the "Satellite," without being assured that such a proceeding would meet with the approval of Her Majesty's Government; but the moment your instructions on the subject are received, I will take measures to carry them into effect.

*   *   *   *   *

I have, &c.

(Signed)   JAMES DOUGLAS, Governor.

The Right Hon. Henry Labouchere, M.P. &c.

[An explanatory sketch of Frazer's River is forwarded with this Report.]

No. 9.

Copy of a Letter from the Governor of the Hudson's Bay Company to the Right Hon. Sir E. Bulwer Lytton, M.P.

Hudson Bay House, June 3, 1858.

SIR,

I have the honour to enclose for your information extracts of two letters received by the last mail from Governor Douglas, dated respectively, Victoria, Vancouver's Island, 22nd and 25th March, giving the latest information from the gold fields recently discovered on the North-west Coast of America.

I have, &c.

(Signed)   JOHN SHEPHERD, Governor.

Sir Edward Bulwer Lytton, Bart., &c.

Enclosure 1 in No. 9.

Extract of Letter from James Douglas, Esq., to W. G. Smith, Esq., dated Victoria, Vancouver's Island, March 22, 1858.

" The winter has been remarkably dry and mild, and the farmers generally report their stock to be in fair condition for the season. Seed time has commenced in earnest, and with the most favourable weather for that important operation of husbandry. There is, however, a great scarcity of labourers, as nearly the whole floating population of the colony have moved off towards the Thompson's River gold mines.

" There will be much suffering in that quarter for want of food, as the country is without resources, and the transport from the sea coast is difficult and expensive.

" I trust Her Majesty's Government will take measures for the prevention of crimes, and the protection of life and property in that quarter, or there will, ere long, be a large array of difficulties to settle.

" A great number of Americans have also gone towards Thompton's River, and others are preparing to follow.

" I have written to Her Majesty's Government on that subject, and shall not fail to communicate with you as soon as I receive their reply."

Enclosure 2 in No. 9.

Extract of a Letter from James Douglas, Esq., to W. G. Smith, Esq., dated Victoria, Vancouver's Island, March 22, 1858.

" I returned from Fort Langley on the 16th instant, having dispatched a party to build Fort Dallas, and another party with a further supply of trade goods for Thompson's River.

" Mr. Simpson's transport party had experienced some difficulty above the Falls, and lost two canoes, which were dashed to pieces on the rocks, but the property was saved, and no lives were lost. We have received no more definite tidings from the gold country than we before possessed.

"An experienced miner whom I met at Fort Langley, assured me that the country was much richer in gold than the Colvile District. The principal diggings are on the banks of Frazer's River, about five miles above the Forks, and the natives beyond that point are said to have found gold. The country is in fact but imperfectly known, and it is hardly possible to give any decided opinion at present in regard to the ultimate yield of gold. The bed rock, and other geological features of the country as described by the miner in question, would, however, lead one to believe that the district will be found productive of gold. He perfectly described the older slate formations thrown up and pierced by quartz, granite, and porphyry beds, and the vast accumulations of gravel and shingle extending from the roots of the mountains to the banks of Frazer's River, and its affluents; which are all characteristics of the gold districts of California and other countries.

No. 10.

Extract of a Despatch from Governor Douglas to the Right Hon. Henry Labouchere, dated Victoria, Vancouver's Island, May 8, 1858.

(No. 19.)

Since I had the honour of addressing you on the 6th of April last, on the subject of the " Couteau " gold mines, they have become more than ever a source of attraction to the people of Washington and Oregon territories, and it is evident from the accounts published in the latest San Francisco papers, that intense excitement prevails among the inhabitants of that stirring city on the same subject.

The " Couteau " country is there represented and supposed to be in point of mineral wealth a second California or Australia, and those impressions are sustained by the false and exaggerated statements of steamboat owners and other interested parties, who

benefit by the current of emigration which is now setting strongly towards this quarter.

Boats, canoes, and every species of small craft, are
continually employed in pouring their cargoes of human
beings into Frazer's River, and it is supposed that not
less than one thousand whites are already at work and
on the way to the gold districts.

Many accidents have happened in the dangerous
rapids of that river; a great number of canoes having
been dashed to pieces and their cargoes swept away by
the impetuous stream, while of the ill-fated adventurers
who accompanied them many have been swept into
eternity.

The others, nothing daunted by the spectacle of ruin,
and buoyed up by the hope of amassing wealth, still
keep pressing onwards towards the coveted goal of their
most ardent wishes.

On the 25th of last month the American steamer
" Commodore " arrived in this port direct from San
Francisco, with 450 passengers on board, the chief part
of whom are gold miners for the " Couteau " country.

Nearly 400 of those men were landed at this place,
and have since left in boats and canoes for Frazer's
River.

I ascertained through inquiries on the subject that
those men are all well provided with mining tools, and
that there was no dearth of capital or intelligence among
them.   About sixty British subjects, with an equal
number of native-born Americans, the rest being chiefly
Germans, with a smaller proportion of Frenchmen and
Italians, composed this body of adventurers.

They are represented as being, with some exceptions,
a specimen of the worst of the population of San Francisco; the very dregs, in fact, of society.   Their conduct
while here would have led me to form a very different
conclusion; as our little town, though crowded to excess
with this sudden influx of people, and though there was
a temporary scarcity of food, and dearth of house ac-
commodation, the police few in number, and many temptations to excess in the way of drink, yet quiet and order

prevailed, and there was not a single committal for rioting, drunkenness, or other offences, during their stay
here.

The merchants and other business classes of Victoria
are rejoicing in the advent of so large a body of people
in the colony, and are strongly in favour of making this
port a stopping point between San Francisco and the
gold mines, converting the latter, as it were, into a
feeder and dependency of this colony.

Victoria would thus become a depôt and centre of
trade for the gold districts, and the natural consequence
would be an immediate increase in the wealth and population of the colony.

To effect that object it will be requisite to facilitate
by every possible means the transport of passengers and
goods to the furthest navigable point on Frazer's River;
and the obvious means of accomplishing that end is
to employ light steamers in plying between, and con-
necting this port (Victoria) with the Falls of Frazer's
River, distant 130 miles from the discharge of that river,
into the Gulf of Georgia; those falls being generally
believed to be at the commencement of the remunerative
gold diggings, and from thence the miners would readily
make their way on foot or after the summer freshets by
the river into the interior of the country.

By that means also the whole trade of the gold regions
would pass through Frazer's River and be retained
within the British territory, forming a valuable outlet
for British manufactured goods, and at once creating a
lucrative trade between the mother country and Vancouver's Island.

Taking a view of the subject, simply in its relations
to trade and commerce, apart from considerations of
national policy, such perhaps would be the course most
likely to promote the interests of this colony; but, on
the contrary, if the country be thrown open to indiscriminate immigration, the interests of the empire may
suffer from the introduction of a foreign population,
whose sympathies may be decidedly anti-British.

Taking that view of the question, it assumes an alarming aspect, and suggests a doubt as to the policy of permitting the free entrance of foreigners into the British territory for residence without in the first place requiring them to take the oath of allegiance, and otherwise to give such security for their conduct as the government of the country may deem it proper and necessary to require at their hands.

The opinion which I have formed on the subject leads me to think that, in the event of the diggings proving remunerative, it will now be found impossible to check the course of immigration, even by closing Frazer's River, as the miners would then force a passage into the gold district by way of the Columbia River, and the valuable trade of the country in that case be driven from its natural course into a foreign channel, and entirely lost to this country.

On the contrary, should the diggings prove to be unremunerative, a question which as yet remains undecided, the existing excitement we may suppose will die away of itself, and the miners having no longer the prospect of large gains, will naturally abandon a country which no longer holds out any inducement for them to remain.

Until the value of the country, as a gold-producing region, be established on clearer evidence than can now be adduced in its favour,—and the point will no doubt be decided before the close of the present year,—I would simply recommend that a small naval or military force should be placed at the disposal of this government, to enable us to maintain the peace, and to enforce obedience to the laws.

The system of granting licenses for digging gold has not yet come into operation.

Perhaps a simpler method of raising a revenue would be to impose a customs' duty on imports, to be levied on all supplies brought into the country, whether by Frazer's or the Columbia River.

The export of gold from the country is still inconsiderable, not exceeding 600 ounces since I last addressed you. The principal diggings are reported to be at present, and will probably continue, flooded for several months to come, so that unless other diggings apart from the river beds are discovered, the production of gold will not increase until the summer freshets are over, which will probably happen about the middle of August next. In the meantime the ill-provided adventurers who have gone thither will consume their stock of provisions, and probably have to retire from the country until a more favourable season.

I shall be most happy to receive your instructions on the subjects in this letter.

No. 11.

COPY OF A LETTER FROM THE GOVERNOR OF THE HUDSON'S BAY COMPANY TO SECRETARY SIR E. BULWER LYTTON.

SIR,   Hudson's Bay House, June 24, 1858.

I have the honour to acknowledge the receipt of the Earl of Carnarvon's letter of the 22nd instant, stating your desire to be furnished with extracts of the letters lately received by the Hudson's Bay Company from Governor Douglas, on the subject of the gold fields on Frazer's River, and I beg, in accordance therewith, to transmit the accompanying copy of a letter from Governor Douglas, dated Victoria, April 27th, and extracts of his letters of the 19th and 30th of the same month.

I have, &c.

(Signed)   JOHN SHEPHERD, Governor.

Sir Edward Bulwer Lytton, Bart.,
        Colonial Office.

Enclosure 1 in No. 11.

Victoria, Vancouver's Island,
April 27, 1858.

(Extract.)

I have to communicate for the information of the Governor and Committee that the steam vessel " Commodore " arrived in this port on the 25th instant, direct from San Francisco, with 450 passengers, chiefly gold miners, who have come here with the intention of working the gold mines of the interior.

About 400 of those men were landed on the same day, and, with the exception of a few who left yesterday for Frazer's River, are now engaged in purchasing canoes and making arrangements for continuing their journey by Frazer's River into the Couteau country.

They all appear to be well provided with mining tools, and there seems to be no want of capital and intelligence among them. About sixty of the number are British subjects, with about an equal number of Americans, and the rest are Germans, Frenchmen, and Italians.

Though our little town was crowded to excess with this sudden influx of people, and there was a temporary scarcity of food and dearth of house-accommodation, the police force small, and many temptations to excess in the way of drink, yet they were remarkably quiet and orderly, and there has not been a single committal for rioting or drunkenness since their arrival here.

The merchants and general dealers of Victoria are rejoicing in the increase of wealth and business produced by the arrival of so large a body of people in the colony, and are strongly in favour of making this place a stopping point between San Francisco and the gold mines, which, so far as respects the prosperity of the colony, is evidently an object of the utmost importance, as both in going and returning, the miners would make purchases, and spend a great deal of money ; the value of property would be vastly enhanced, while the sale of public land

R

and the colonization of the country would be greatly promoted.

The interests of the empire, if I may use the term, may not, however, be improved to the same extent by the accession of a foreign population, whose sympathies are decidedly anti-British.

From that point of view the question assumes an alarming aspect, and leads us to doubt the policy of permitting foreigners to enter the British territory, *ad libitum*, without taking the oath of allegiance, and otherwise giving security to the government of the country.

In the meantime, the people who have gone into the interior will meet with innumerable difficulties of route in their progress towards the mines, both from the nature of the country and the dangerous state of the rivers.

The principal diggings on Frazer's and Thompson's Rivers are also at present, and will continue, flooded for many months to come; there is moreover a great scarcity of food in the gold districts, so that those united causes will, in all probability, compel many of the ill-provided adventurers to beat a retreat, and for the time to relinquish the enterprise.

The licence system has not been yet carried into effect, and it will be difficult to bring it into a general operation. It has since occurred to me, that by levying an import duty on goods, the gold districts might be taxed to any desirable extent, without clamour or exciting discontent among the people, an object which might be effected at a moderate expense, by means of a customs station on Frazer's River, and another at the point where the road from the Columbia strikes the ford of the O'Kanagan River, those being the only two commercial avenues of the Couteau country.

I shall soon address her Majesty's government on the subjects referred to in this communication, and it is also my intention to represent how seriously the peace of the country may be endangered by the presence of so many people wandering over the interior in a vagrant state, especially in the event of the diggings proving unremunerative, and the miners being, as an inevitable consequence, reduced to poverty, and destitute of the common necessaries of life.

We have this moment been informed of the arrival of the Pacific Mail Steamer " Columbia," at Port Townsend, with eighty passengers from San Francisco, who are also bound for the Couteau gold district, and we observe by the latest Francisco papers that several other vessels are advertised for the same destination.

Enclosure 2 in No. 11.

Extract of a Letter from James Douglas, Esq., to William G. Smith, Esq., Secretary of the Hudson's Bay Company, dated Victoria, Vancouver's Island, April 19, 1858.

" Mr. George Simpson was the bearer of despatches from Fort Langley of the 14th, and from Chief Trader M'Lean, dated Forks (Thompson's River), the 4th inst., and arrived here by canoe on the 17th instant.

" The tidings from the gold district are of the most flattering description, but are not supported by a large return of gold dust. Mr. Simpson reports that gold is found in more or less abundance on every part of Frazer's River, from Fort Yale to the Forks, but I presume those diggings cannot be very productive, or there would have been a larger return of gold. Chief Trader Yale reports that parties are proceeding up Frazer's River towards the gold diggings almost every day."

Enclosure 3 in No. 11.

Extract of a Letter from James Douglas, Esq., to W. G. Smith, Esq., Secretary of the Hudson's Bay Company, dated Victoria, Vancouver's Island, April 30, 1858.

" We have received no official intelligence from the gold mining districts since my letter of the 19th instant.

"'Several parties of Americans and Canadians have, however, lately returned from thence disappointed and unsuccessful. They report that the waters of Frazer's River had risen so much, that the auriferous 'bars' were flooded, and they could not consequently employ themselves to advantage. They, however, think that the country is decidedly auriferous, and will yield large returns of gold.

"About one hundred and fifty white miners had already arrived at the Forks of Thompson's River when they left that place, and they met about as many more on the river travelling towards that point."

No. 12.

COPY OF A LETTER FROM THE SECRETARY OF THE ADMIRALTY TO HERMAN MERIVALE, ESQ.

Admiralty, June 26, 1858.

Sir,

I am commanded by my Lords Commissioners of the Admiralty to send you herewith, for the information of Secretary Sir E. Bulwer Lytton, a copy of a letter from Captain Prevost, of H.M. ship "Satellite," dated at Vancouver's Island, 7th May, 1858, respecting the discovery of gold on Frazer's and Thompson's Rivers, near to the fifty-first parallel of north latitude, in North America.

The newspaper and specimen of the gold dust referred to in Captain Prevost's letter are also enclosed.

I am, &c.

(Signed)   H. CORRY.

Herman Merivale, Esq.,
   Colonial Office.

Enclosure in No. 12.

H.M.S. "Satellite," Esquimalt,
Vancouver's Island, May 7, 1858.
(Extract.)

I have the honour to report to you that considerable excitement has been occasioned recently in this neighbourhood by the discovery of gold on Frazer's and Thompson's Rivers, at about the position of the juncture of the latter with the former river, near to the fifty-first parallel of north latitude.

The reports concerning these new gold diggings are so contradictory, that I am unable to furnish you with any information upon which I can depend. That gold exists is certain, and that it will be found in abundance seems to be the opinion of all those who are capable of forming a judgment upon the subject; but it is so obviously to the advantage of the surrounding community to circulate exaggerated, if not altogether false reports, for the purpose of stimulating trade, or creating monopolies, that it is most difficult to arrive at any correct conclusion, or to obtain any reliable information. I have every reason to believe that the Indians have traded some quantity of gold with the officers of the Hudson's Bay Company, and I am satisfied that individuals from this immediate neighbourhood who started off to the diggings upon the first intelligence of their existence, have come back with gold dust in their possession, and which they assert was washed by themselves; but whether such be really the case, or whether it was traded from the Indians, I am unable to determine. These persons all declare that at the present moment, although the yield is good, yet that there is too much water in the rivers to admit of digging and washing to be carried on with facility; but that when the water falls somewhat, as the summer advances, that the yield will be abundant. I am inclined myself to think that this information is not far from the truth; for these persons, after obtaining a fresh stock of provisions, have all returned to the diggings.

The excitement in Vancouver's Island itself is quite insignificant compared to that in Washington and Oregon territories, and in California, and which, of course, is increased by every possible means by interested parties. The result has been that several hundred persons from American territory have already flocked to the newly reported auriferous regions, and by the last accounts fresh steamers, and even sailing vessels, were being chartered to convey passengers to Puget Sound, or to Vancouver's Island, whence they have to find their way to the diggings principally by canoes.

I have heard that all the crews of the ships in Puget Sound have deserted, and have gone to the diggings; I am happy to say that as yet I have not lost a single man from the "Satellite" since the information was received, and I have every reason to hope that I may not be unfortunate in this respect, although, doubtless, soon the temptations to desert will be of no ordinary character.

No. 13.

COPY OF A DESPATCH FROM SECRETARY SIR E. BULWER LYTTON TO GOVERNOR DOUGLAS.

(No. 2.)

Downing Street, July 1, 1858.

SIR,

I have to acknowledge your Despatch No. 19, of the 8th ultimo, in continuation of former despatches, informing the Secretary of State from time to time of the progress of the gold discoveries on Frazer's River, and the measures which you had taken in consequence. I am anxious not to let the opportunity of the present mail pass without informing you that her Majesty's government have under their consideration the pressing necessity for taking some steps to establish public order and government in that locality, and that I hope very soon to be able to communicate to you the result.

In the meantime her Majesty's government approve of the course which you have adopted in asserting both tho dominion of the Crown over this region, and the right of the Crown over the precious metals. They think, however, that you acted judiciously in waiting for further instructions before you endeavoured to compel the taking out of licences, by causing any force to be despatched for that purpose from Vancouver's Island.

They wish you to continue your vigilance, and to apply for instructions on any point on which you may require them. They are, however, in addition, particularly anxious to impress on you that, while her Majesty's government are determined on preserving the rights, both of government and of commerce, which belong to this country, and while they have it in contemplation to furnish you with such a force as they may be able to detach for your assistance and support in the preservation of law and order, it is no part of their policy to exclude Americans and other foreigners from the gold fields. On the contrary, you are distinctly instructed to oppose no obstacle whatever to their resort thither for the purpose of digging in those fields, so long as they submit themselves, in common with the subjects of her Majesty, to the recognition of her authority, and conform to such rules of police as you may have thought proper to establish. The national right to navigate Frazer's River is of course a separate question, and one which her Majesty's government must reserve.

Under the circumstance of so large an immigration of Americans into English territory, I need hardly impress upon you the importance of caution and delicacy in dealing with those manifold cases of international relationship and feeling which are certain to arise, and which but for the exercise of temper and discretion might easily lead to serious complications between two neighbouring and powerful states.

It is impossible by this mail to furnish you with any instructions of a more definite character. Her Majesty's government must leave much to your discretion on this most important subject; and they rely upon your exercising whatever influence and powers you may possess in the manner which from local knowledge and experience you conceive to be best calculated to give development to the new country, and to advance imperial interests.

I have, &c.

(Signed)   E. BULWER LYTTON.

Governor Douglas,
&c.   &c.

Appendix.

Extract of a Letter from James Douglas, Esq., to W. G. Smith, Esq., Secretary of the Hudson's Bay Company, dated Victoria, Vancouver's Island, February 18, 1858.

" They say that the country is as rich as any part of California, though we have as yet no satisfactory evidence of that fact, there being circumstances indeed which rather favour the opposite conclusion. It is, for instance, well known that the export of gold dust from the state of California exceeded 150,000 ounces during the eight months following the discovery of gold in that country, and that the stream of wealth had in that time forced its way into all the neighbouring countries. We had a good share of it at Fort Vancouver, where we purchased at the Company's shops about 8,000 ounces in the course of a few months, and that formed but a small part of the wealth that had been actually brought into the country.

" Now the ascertained export from Thompson's River up to the present time does not much exceed 500 ounces, and admitting, for the sake of comparison, that an equal quantity still remains in the hands of the diggers and at our own establishment in Thompson's River, that would only give a total yield since the discovery of about 1,000 ounces, which, after making due allowance for the disproportion in the number and skill of the mining population in the two countries, is relatively a small return compared with that of the first eight months of the gold miners in California.

" The conclusion is obvious, but still Thompson's River may turn out to be a very valuable gold district."

No. V.

REPORT OF A CANOE EXPEDITION ALONG THE EAST COAST OF VANCOUVER'S ISLAND. COMMUNICATED BY GOVERNOR DOUGLAS TO THE COLONIAL OFFICE.

Fort Victoria, August 27, 1852.

SIR,

Since I had last the honour of addressing you on the 22d instant, I have carried out the project, which I have long entertained, of a canoe expedition through the Canal de Arro, and along the East coast of Vancouver Island, for the purpose of examining the country and of communicating with the native tribes who inhabit that part of the colony; and I will now concisely state the result of my observations in the course of that journey.

2. In our passage through the Canal de Arro, we were struck with the extreme incorrectness of the maps of Vancouver's Island. The line of coast is well delineated, and could be traced upon our maps as far as the promontory named Cowichin Head; but from that point all resemblance to the coast ceases; the multitude of islands forming the Arro Archipelago, which extend as far as, and terminate at Cala Descauso, being laid down as an integral portion of Vancouver Island; whereas the true line of coast runs from fifteen to twenty miles west of its position, as laid down on our maps; the intermediate space being occupied by islands and channels of various breadths, generally navigable, but probably inconvenient for sailing vessels, on account of the strong currents and frequent calms which occur in these narrow waters. A correct survey of these channels will remove the difficulties that would at present be experienced by sailing vessels navigating these straits; and should her Majesty's government at any time direct surveys to be made in this quarter, I think the Arro Archipelago will be found to have peculiar claims to their attention, as there is a prospect of its soon becoming the channel of a very important trade.

R 3

3. On the route through the Channel de Arro, we touched at the Cowichin river, which falls into that canal about twenty miles north of Cowichin Head, and derives its name from the tribe of Indians which inhabit the neighbouring country. They live in several villages, each having a distinct chief, or headsman, who cannot be said to rule the community which acknowledges his supremacy, as there is no code of laws, nor do the chiefs possess the power or means of maintaining a regular government, but their personal influence is nevertheless very great with their followers. The Cowichins are a warlike people, mustering about 500 fighting men among a population of about 2,100 souls. They were extremely friendly and hospitable to our party, and gave us much information of the interior, which, by their report, appears to be well watered, and abounding in extensive tracts of arable land. The Cowichin rises in a lake within a few hours' journey of the salt-water arm of Nitinut (Barclay Sound), on the west coast of Vancouver's Island, and is navigable for canoes to its source. These Indians partially cultivate the alluvial islands near the mouth of the river, where we saw many large and well-kept fields of potatoes in a very flourishing state, and a number of fine cucumbers, which had been raised in the open air without any particular care.

4. About ten miles north of the Cowichin, the Chemanis river enters the Canal de Arro. It is altogether a smaller stream than the former, and is navigable but a short distance from the coast. It is inhabited by a branch of the Cowichin tribe, whom we did not see.

5. As we proceeded north from the Cowichin, a complete change was observed in the physical character of the country; the primitive and transition rocks of the Victoria district being replaced by the sandstone formations, in some places falling with a gentle slope, in others presenting precipitous cliffs towards the sea.

6. The promontory of Cala Descanso is the northern point of the Arro Archipelago, beyond which is the inlet of Wentuhuysen, to which point my attention was particularly attracted through a report of coal having been

seen by the Indians in that vicinity. These people are called Nanaimo, and speak nearly the same language, but have not the reputation of being either so numerous or warlike as the Cowichin tribe. We entered into immediate communication, and found them very friendly, and disposed to give every information we desired in regard to all matters concerning their own affairs and the country which they inhabit. They live chiefly by fishing, and also grow large quantities of potatoes in fields, which they have brought into cultivation near their villages. These are built chiefly on a river, named Nanaimo, which falls into the inlet, and is navigable for canoes to the distance of forty miles from the sea coast. Food is cheap and abundant, and we were plentifully supplied with fresh salmon and excellent potatoes during the stay there.

7. The reports concerning the existence of coal in that place were, I rejoice to say, not unfounded; as the Indians pointed out three beds cropping out in different parts of the inlet; and they also reported that several other beds occurred on the coast and in the interior of the country, which we did not see. One of these beds measured $57\frac{3}{4}$ inches in depth of clean coal; and it was impossible to repress a feeling of exultation in beholding so huge a mass of mineral wealth so singularly brought to light by the hand of nature, as if for the purpose of inviting human enterprise at a time when coal is a great desideratum in the Pacific, and the discovery can hardly fail to be of signal advantage to the colony. The two other seams which we examined were about three-fourths of a mile distant from the former, and measured respectively 3 inches and 20 inches in depth, and are valuable chiefly as indicating the direction of the beds. There is every reason to believe, from the appearance of the country and its geological phenomena, that Vancouver's Island, about Wentuhuysen Inlet, is one vast coal field; and if that conjecture be correct, the progress of the colony will be rapid and prosperous, notwithstanding the many adverse circumstances which have hitherto retarded the development of its resources.

8. That consideration induces me to offer a few remarks on the navigation of the coast between Victoria and Wentuhuysen Inlet. The shortest and most direct route between those points is through the Canal de Arro, a part of the coast of which little is known, and judging from the maps in my possession, has never been correctly surveyed. Merchant vessels are therefore deterred from taking that route, and follow the circuitous channel explored by Vancouver in the year 1795, which greatly prolongs the voyage, making the difference of nearly a week in point of time on a short run of one hundred and forty miles. It is therefore of the very greatest importance to the trade of this colony that the Canal de Arro should be explored, and a correct survey prepared as soon as possible, showing the soundings, shoals, and anchorages where ships may bring-to in calms, or during the continuance of adverse winds; and I beg most earnestly to recommend that measure to your consideration, especially as her Majesty's Government would thereby render an essential service not only to this colony but to the general interests of trade and navigation.

9. Our excursion did not extend beyond the Inlet of Wentuhuysen, from whence we commenced our return to Victoria, after distributing small presents to the chiefs of the various tribes, with which they appeared highly satisfied.

10. In the course of that journey we observed traces of iron-stone on several parts of the coast, and we also procured a rich specimen of copper ore, found in a distant part of Vancouver Island, which will be hereafter examined. The Hudson's Bay Company's schooner Cadborough lately visited the coal district in Wentuhuysen Inlet, and succeeded in procuring, with the assistance of Indians, about fifty tons of coal in one day. The harbour is safe and accessible to vessels of any class, and the coal is within two cables' length of the anchorage, so that every circumstance connected with this valuable discovery is suggestive of success.

11. The Hudson's Bay Company have also sent a

small body of miners to examine the coal-beds and to commence operations there.

12. Her Majesty's ship Thetis arrived at Esquimault on the 22nd instant, direct from Queen Charlotte's Islands, and I believe Captain Kupaı has orders from the commander-in-chief to remain on the coast till the month of January next, chiefly with the view of guarding the ports of Queen Charlotte's Island. The gold diggings in that quarter have not been productive this season, which has not, however, altered the general opinion entertained as to its wealth in the precious metal, the adventurers ascribing their late want of success simply to the circumstance of the true beds not having been discovered. Fine specimens of lead and copper-ore have also been procured on Queen Charlotte's Island, which, in a commercial view, gives it an additional value.*

* The discovery of gold in this part of her Britannic Majesty's dominions was made by Captain Rooney, who commanded the schooner Susan Sturge, belonging to a San Francisco firm, by whom he was instructed to go up to Queen Charlotte's Islands, and explore, and see what business could be done with those islands, that would be advantageous to the trade of San Francisco; and in the early part of the year 1852, he sailed for these northern islands, and on arrival made several discoveries, one of which was, that instead of there being, as laid down on the charts, one large island, a group of three islands existed. He also discovered and named Victoria Island, Elliott Isles, Wantly Isle, and laid down various other places. Having entertained friendly intercourse with the natives, whom he found anxious to trade with him, he returned to San Francisco in the latter part of May, and besides bringing a variety of matters and things relating to the commerce that might be opened with these islands, he had on board two sons of native chiefs, who came with him as a guarantee of good faith to parties wishing to trade with them. A specimen of the gold-bearing quartz from Una Point, Mitchell Harbour, in the middle island of the Queen Charlotte's group was also brought, which, from an assay made in London, yielded 6317 dwts. 4 grs. of gold to the ton of quartz. Some pieces of gold, varying in size from a grain of wheat to a pigeon's egg, fell out of the rock, after blasting. Traces of silver have also been found in the rock. It is a singular circumstance that Captain Rooney had his schooner taken and plundered by the natives of these very islands on the 26th of September, 1852.

No. VI.

Charles the Second, by the Grace of God King of England, Scotland, France, and Ireland, Defender of the Faith, &c. To all to whom these presents shall come greeting: Whereas our dear and entirely beloved cousin Prince Rupert, Count Palatine of the Rhine, Duke of Bavaria and Cumberland, etc.; Christopher Duke of Albemarle, William Earl of Craven, Henry Lord Arlington, Anthony Lord Ashley, Sir John Robinson, and Sir Robert Vyner, Knights and Baronets; Sir Peter Colleton, Baronet; Sir Edward Hungerford, Knight of the Bath; Sir Paul Neele, Knight; Sir John Griffith, and Sir Philip Carteret, Knights; James Hayes, John Kirke, Francis Millington, William Prettyman, John Fenn, Esqrs.; and John Portman, Citizen and Goldsmith of London; have at their own great cost and charges undertaken an expedition for Hudson's Bay, in the north-west part of America, for the discovery of a new passage into the South Sea, and to the finding some trade for furs, minerals, and other considerable commodities, and by such their undertaking, have already made such discoveries as do encourage them to proceed further in pursuance of their said design, by means whereof there may probably arise very great advantage to us and our kingdom: And whereas the said undertakers for their further encouragement in the said design have humbly besought us to incorporate them and grant unto them and their successors the sole trade and commerce of all those seas, straits, bays, rivers, lakes, creeks, and sounds in whatsoever latitude they shall be that lie within the entrance of the straits commonly called Hudson's Straits, together with all the lands, countries, and territories upon the coasts and confines of the seas, straits, bays, rivers, creeks,

and sounds aforesaid, which are not now actually possessed by any of our subjects or by the subjects of any
other Christian prince or State: Now know ye that we,
being desirous to promote all endeavours tending to the
public good of our people, and to encourage the said undertaking, have, of our especial grace, certain knowledge,
and mere motion, given, granted, ratified, and confirmed,
and by these presents for us, our heirs, and successors,
do give, grant, ratify, and confirm unto our said cousin,
Prince Rupert (here the names are repeated), that they
and such others as shall be admitted into the said Society
as is hereafter expressed, shall be one body corporate
and politic in deed and in name, by the name of "The
Governor and Company of Adventurers of England
trading into Hudson's Bay," and thereby the name of
"The Governor and Company of Adventurers of England trading into Hudson's Bay," our body corporate
and politic, in deed and in name really and fully for
ever for us, our heirs and successors, we do make, ordain,
constitute, establish, confirm, and declare by these presents, and that by the same name of Governor and Company of Adventurers of England trading into Hudson's
Bay, they shall have perpetual succession, and that
they and their successors, by the name of the Governor
and Company of Adventurers of England trading into
Hudson's Bay, be and at all times hereafter shall be
personable and capable in law to have, purchase, receive, possess, enjoy, and retain lands, rents, privileges,
liberties, jurisdictions, franchises, and hereditaments of
what kind, nature, or quality soever they be to them
and their successors; and also to give, grant, demise,
alien, assign, and dispose lands, tenements, and hereditaments, and to do and execute all and singular other
things by the same name that to them shall or may ap-
pertain to do; and that they and their successors by the
name of "The Governor and Company of Adventurers
of England trading into Hudson's Bay," may plead and
be impleaded, answer and be answered, defend and be defended in whatsoever courts and places, before whatsoever judges and justices and other persons and officers

in all and singular actions, pleas, suits, quarrels, causes, and demands whatsoever, of whatsoever kind, nature, or sort, in such manner and form as any other our liege people of this our realm of England, being persons able and capable in law, may or can have, purchase, receive, possess, enjoy, retain, give, grant, demise, alien, assign, dispose, plead, defend and be defended, do permit and execute; and that the said Governor and Company of Adventurers of England trading into Hudson's Bay and their successors may have a common seal to serve for all the causes and businesses of them and their successors, and that it shall and may be lawful to the said Governor and Company and their successors, the same seal from time to time at their will and pleasure to break, change, make anew or alter as to them shall seem expedient. And further, we will and by these presents for us, our heirs and successors, we do ordain that there shall be from henceforth one of the same company to be elected and appointed in such form as hereafter in these presents is expressed, which shall be called the Governor of the Company; and that the said Governor and Company shall or may elect seven of their number in such form as hereafter in these presents is expressed, which shall be called the Committee of the said Company, which committee of seven or any three of them, together with the Governor or Deputy Governor of the said Company for the time being, shall have the direction of the voyages of and for the said Company, and the provision of the shipping and merchandizes thereunto belonging, and also the sale of all merchandizes, goods, and other things returned in all or any the voyages or ships for the said Company, and the managing and handling of all other business, affairs, and things belonging to the said Company: And we will, ordain, and grant by these presents for us our heirs and successors, unto the said Governor and Company and their successors, shall from henceforth for ever be ruled, ordered, and governed according to such manner and form as is hereafter in these presents expressed, and not otherwise; and that they shall have, hold, retain, and enjoy the grants, liberties,

privileges, jurisdictions, and immunities only hereafter
in these presents granted and expressed, and no other ;
And for the better execution of our will and grant in
this behalf, we have assigned, nominated, constituted,
and made, and by these presents for us, our heirs and
successors, we do assign, nominate, constitute, and make
our said cousin Prince Rupert to be the first and present
Governor of the said Company, and to continue in the
said office from the date of these presents until the 10th
November the next following, if the said Prince Rupert
shall so long live, and so until a new Governor be chosen
by the said Company in form hereafter expressed : And
further, we will and grant by these presents, for us, our
heirs and successors, unto the said Governor and Company and their successors, that it shall and may be lawful to and for the said Governor and Company for the
time being or the greater part of them present at any
public assembly commonly called the Court General, to
be holden for the said Company, the Governor of the
said Company being always one, from time to time, to
elect, nominate, and appoint one of the said Company to
be Deputy to the said Governor, which Deputy shall take
a corporal oath before the Governor and three or more of
the Committee of the said Company for the time being,
well, truly, and faithfully to execute his said office of Deputy to the Governor of the said Company; and after his
oath so taken shall and may from time to time in the absence of the said Governor exercise and execute the office
of Governor of the said Company in such sort as the said
Governor ought to do : and further, we will and grant
by these presents for us, our heirs, and successors, unto
the said Governor and Company of the Adventurers of
England trading into Hudson's Bay and their successors,
that they, or the greater part of them, whereof the Governor for the time being or his Deputy to be one from
time to time and at all times hereafter, shall and may
have authority and power, yearly and every year, between the first and last day of November, to assemble
and meet together in some convenient place to be appointed from time to time by the Governor, or in his

absence by the deputy of the said Governor for the time
being, and that they being so assembled, it shall and
may be lawful to and for the said Governor or deputy of
the said Governor and the said Company for the time
being, or the greater part of them which then shall
happen to be present, whereof the Governor of the said
Company or his Deputy for the time being to be one, to
elect and nominate one of the said Company which shall
be Governor of the said Company for one whole year then
next following, which person being so elected and nominated to be Governor of the said Company as is aforesaid before he be admitted to the execution of the said
office, shall take a corporal oath before the last Governor being his predecessor or his Deputy, and any
three or more of the Committee of the said Company for
the time being, that he shall from time to time well and
truly execute the office of Governor of the said Company for the time being, that he shall from time to time
well and truly execute the office of Governor of the said
Company in all things concerning the same; and that
immediately after the same oath so taken, he shall and
may execute and use the said office of Governor of the
said Company for one whole year from thence next following : And in like sort we will and grant that as well
every one of the above-named to be of the said Company
or fellowship as all others hereafter to be admitted are
free of the said Company, shall take a corporal oath before the Governor of the said Company or his Deputy
for the time being, to such effect as by the said Governor
and Company or the greater part of them in any public
court to be held for the said Company, shall be in reasonable or legal manner set down and devised, before they
shall be allowed or admitted to trade or traffic as free-
men of the said Company : And further, we will and
grant by these presents for us, our heirs and successors,
unto the said Governor and Company and their successors, that the said Governor or Deputy Governor and
the rest of the said Company and their successors for the
time being or the greater part of them, whereof the
Governor or Deputy Governor from time to time to be

one shall and may from time to time and at all times
hereafter have power and authority, yearly and every
year between the first and last day of November, to
assemble and meet together in some convenient place,
and that they being so assembled, it shall and may be
lawful to and for the said Governor or his Deputy and
the Company for the time being, or the greater part of
them, which then shall happen to be present, whereof
the Governor of the said Company or his Deputy, to
elect and nominate seven of the said Company, which
shall be a Committee of the said Company for one whole
year from then next ensuing, which persons being so
elected and nominated before they be admitted to the
execution of their office shall take a corporal oath before
the Governor or his Deputy, and any three or more of
the said Committee, being their last predecessors, that
they and every of them shall well and faithfully perform
their said office of Committee in all things concerning
the same, and that immediately after the said oath so
taken, they shall and may execute and use their said
office of Committees of the said Company for one whole
year from thence next following.

[*Subordinate matter for the regulation of Committees
omitted.*]

And, that the said Governor and Company, or the
greater part of them, whereof the Governor for the time
being, or his Deputy, to be one, being then and there
present, shall and may, before their departure from the
said place, elect and nominate one or more of the said
Company to be of the Committee of the said Company,
in the place and stead of him or them that so die, or
were or was so removed, which person or persons so
nominated and elected to the office of Committee of the
said Company, in the place and stead of him or them
that so died, or were or was so removed, which person
or persons so nominated and elected to the office of Committee of the said Company shall have and exercise the
said office for and during the residue of the said year,
taking first a corporal oath, as is aforesaid, for the due
execution thereof, and this to be done from time to time,

so often as the case shall require. And to the end the
said Governor and Company of Adventurers of England,
trading into Hudson's Bay, may be encouraged to undertake and effectually to prosecute the said design, of our
especial grace, certain knowledge, and mere motion, we
have given, granted, and confirmed, and by these presents for us, our heirs, and successors, do give, grant,
and confirm unto the said Governors and Company, and
their successors, the sole trade and commerce of all those
seas, straits, bays, rivers, lakes, creeks, and sounds, in
whatsoever latitude they shall be, that lie within the
entrance of the straits, commonly called Hudson's Straits,
together with all the lands and territories upon the
countries, coasts, and confines of the seas, bays, lakes,
rivers, creeks, and sounds aforesaid, that are not already
actually possessed by, or granted to, any of our subjects,
or possessed by the subjects of any other Christian Prince
or State, with the fishing of all sorts of fish, whales,
sturgeons, and all other royal fishes in the seas, bays,
inlets, and rivers within the premises, and the fish
therein taken, together with the royalty of the sea upon
the coasts within the limits aforesaid, and all mines
royal, as well discovered as not discovered, of gold, silver, gems, and precious stones, to be found or discovered
within the territories, limits, and places aforesaid ; and
that the said land be from henceforth reckoned and reputed as one of our plantations or colonies in America,
called 'Rupert's Land.' And, further, we do, by these
presents, for us, our heirs, and successors, make, create,
and constitute the said Governor and Company for the
time being and their successors the true and absolute
lords and proprietors of the same territory, limits, and
places aforesaid, and of all other the premises, saving
always the faith, allegiance, and sovereign dominion due
to us, our heirs, and successors, for the same to have,
hold, possess, and enjoy the said territory, limits, and
places, and all and singular other the premises hereby
granted, as aforesaid, with their and every of their rights,
members, jurisdictions, prerogatives, royalties, and appurtenances whatsoever to them, the said Governor and

Company, and their successors for ever—to be holden of us, our heirs, and successors, as of our manor of East Greenwich, in our county of Kent, in free and common soccage, and not *in capite*, or by knight's service; yielding and paying yearly to us, our heirs, and successors for the same two elks and two black beavers, whensoever and as often as we, our heirs, and successors shall happen to enter into the said countries, territories, and regions hereby granted.—And, further, our will and pleasure is, and by these presents, for us, our heirs, and successors, we do grant unto the said Governor and Company, and to their successors, that it shall and may be lawful to and for the said Governor and Company, and their successors, from time to time to assemble themselves for or about any the matters, causes, affairs, or businesses of the said trade in any place or places for the same convenient, within our dominions or elsewhere, and there to hold court for the said Company and the affairs thereof; and that also it shall and may be lawful to and for them and the greater part of them, being so assembled, and that shall then and there be present, in any such place or places, whereof the Governor, or his Deputy for the time being, to be one, to make, ordain, and constitute such and so many reasonable laws, constitutions, orders, and ordinances as to them, or the greater part of them, being then and there present, shall seem necessary and convenient for the good government of the said Company, and of all governors and colonies, forts and plantations, factors, masters, mariners, and other officers employed, or to be employed, in any of the territories and lands aforesaid, and in any of their voyages, and for the better advancement and continuance of the said trade, or traffic, and plantations, and the same laws, constitutions, orders, and ordinances so made, to put in use and execute accordingly, and at their pleasure to revoke and alter the same, or any of them, as the occasion shall require. And that the said Governor and Company, so often as they shall make, ordain, or establish any such laws, constitutions, orders, and ordinances, in such form as aforesaid, shall and may lawfully impose, ordain, limit, and provide such pains, penalties, and punishments upon all offenders, contrary to such laws, constitutions, orders, and ordinances, or any of them, as to the said Governor and Company for the time being, or the greater part of them, then and there present, the said Governor, or his Deputy, being always one, shall seem necessary, requisite, or convenient for the observation of the same laws, constitutions, orders, and ordinances; and the same fines and amerciaments shall and may. by their officers and servants, from time to time to be appointed for that purpose, levy, take, and have to the use of the said Governor and Company and their successors, without the impediment of us, our heirs, or successors, and without any account, therefore, to us, our heirs, or successors to be made. All and singular which laws, constitutions, orders, and ordinances so as aforesaid to be made, we will to be duly observed and kept under the pains and penalties therein to be contained; so always as the said laws, constitutions, orders, and ordinances, fines, and amerciaments be reasonable, and not contrary or repugnant, but as near as may be agreeable to the laws, statutes, or customs of this our realm. And, furthermore, of our ample and abundant grace we have granted, and by these presents for us, our heirs, and successors do grant unto the said Governor and Company, and their successors, that they and their successors, and their factors, servants, and agents for them, and on their behalf, and not otherwise, shall for ever hereafter have, use, and enjoy not only the whole, entire, and only trade and traffic, and the whole, entire, and only liberty, use, and privilege of trading and trafficking to and from the territory, limits, and places aforesaid, but also the whole and entire trade and traffic to and from all havens, bays, creeks, rivers, lakes, and seas into which they shall find entrance or passage by water or land out of the territories, limits, or places aforesaid; and to and with all the natives and people inhabiting, or which shall inhabit within the territories, limits, and places aforesaid; and to and with all other nations inhabiting any the coasts adjacent to the said territories, limits, and places which are not already possessed, as aforesaid, or whereof the sole liberty or privilege of trade and traffic is not granted to any other of our subjects. And we, of our further royal favour, and of our most especial grace, certain knowledge, and mere motion, have granted, and by these presents, for us, our heirs, and successors, do grant to the said Governor and Company, and to their successors, that neither the said territories, limits, and places hereby granted, as aforesaid, nor any part thereof, nor the islands, havens, ports, cities, towns, or places thereof, or therein contained, shall be visited, frequented, or haunted by any of the subjects of us, our heirs, and successors, contrary to the true meaning of these presents, and by virtue of our prerogative royal, which we will not have in that behalf argued or brought into question : we straightly charge, command, and prohibit for us, our heirs, and successors, of what degree or quality soever they be, that none of them, directly or indirectly, do visit, haunt, frequent, or trade, traffic, or adventure, by way of merchandise, into or from any of the said territories, limits, or places hereby granted, or any or either of them, other than the said Governor and Company, and such particular persons as now be, or hereafter shall be, of that Company, their agents, factors, and assigns, unless it be by the licence and agreement of the said Governor and Company in writing, first had and obtained under their common seal, to be granted, upon pain that every such person or persons that shall trade or traffic into or from any of the countries, territories, or limits aforesaid, other than the said Governor and Company, and their successors, shall incur our indignation and the forfeiture and loss of the goods, merchandizes, and other things whatsoever, which so shall be brought into this realm of England, or any the dominions of the same, contrary to our said prohibition, or the purport or true meaning of these presents, for which the said Governor and Company shall find, take, and seize; and these places out of our dominions, where the said Company, their agents, factors, or ministers shall trade, traffic, or inhabit, by virtue of these our letters patent, as also the ship and ships, with the furniture thereof, wherein such goods may be found; the one-half of all the said forfeitures to be to us, our heirs, and successors, and the other half thereof we do, by these presents, give and grant unto the said Governor and Company. And, further, we have condescended and granted, and by these presents do grant unto the said Governor and Company and their successors, that we, our heirs, and successors, will not grant liberty, license, or power to any person or persons whatsoever, contrary to the tenour of these our letters patent, to trade, traffic, or inhabit unto or upon any the territories, limits, or places afore specified, contrary to the true meaning of these presents, without the consent of the said Governor and Company, or the most part of them.

[*Some unimportant matter solely relating to the Company's minor bye laws omitted.*]

And further, our will and pleasure is, and by these presents for us, our heirs and successors, we do grant unto the said Governor and Company and their successors that it shall and may he lawful in all elections and byelaws to be made by the General Court of the Adventurers of the said Company that every person shall have a number of votes according to his stock, that is to say for every hundred pounds by him subscribed or brought into the present stock, one vote, and that any of those that have subscribed less than one hundred pounds may join their respective sums to make up one hundred pounds, and have one vote jointly for the same, and not otherwise. And further of our especial grace we do for us, our heirs and successors grant to and with the said Company of Adventurers of England trading into Hudson's Bay that all lands, islands, territories, plantations, forts, fortifications, factories, or colonies, where the said Company's factories and trade are or shall be within any the ports or places afore limited shall be immediately and from henceforth under the power and command of the said Governor and Company, their successors and assigns, swearing the faith and allegiance due to be performed to us, our heirs and successors aforesaid; and that the said Governor and Company shall have liberty, full power and authority to appoint and establish Governors and all other officers to govern them, and that the Governor and his council of the several and respective places where the said Company shall have plantations, forts, factories, colonies or places of trade, within any the countries, lands, or territories hereby granted, may have power to judge all persons belonging to the said Governor and Company, or that shall live under them, in all causes whether civil or criminal, according to the laws of this kingdom, and to execute justice accordingly; and in case any crime or misdemeanor shall be committed in any of the said Company's plantations, forts, factories, or places of trade within the limits aforesaid, where judicature cannot be executed for want of a governor and council there, then in such case it shall and may be lawful for the Chief Factor of that place and his council to transmit the party together with the offence to such other plantation, factory or fort, where there shall be a Governor and council, where justice may be executed, or into this kingdom of England as shall be thought most convenient, there to receive such punishment as his offences shall deserve: and moreover, our will and pleasure is, and by these presents for us, our heirs and successors, we do give and grant unto the said Governor and Company and their successors, free liberty and licence in case they conceive it necessary to send either ships of war, men or ammunition into any their plantations, forts, factories, or places of trade aforesaid, for the security and defence of the same, and to choose commanders and officers over them, and to give them power and authority by commissions, under their common seal, or otherwise, to continue or make peace or war with any prince or people whatsoever, that are not Christians, in any places where the said Company shall have any plantations, forts, or factories, or adjacent thereto as shall be most for the advantage and benefit of the said Governor and Company and of their trade: and also to right and recompense themselves upon the goods estates, or people of those parts by whom the said Governor

S

and Company shall sustain any injury, loss, or damage, or upon any other people whatsoever, that shall anyway, contrary to the intent of these presents interrupt, wrong, or injure them in their said trade, within the said places, territories, and limits, granted by this charter : And that it shall and may be lawful to and for the said Governor and Company and their successors from time to time and at all times from henceforth to erect and build such castles, fortifications, forts, garrisons, colonies, or plantations, towns or villages in any parts or places within the limits and bounds granted before in these presents unto the said Governor and Company, as they in their discretion shall think fit and requisite and for the supply of such as shall be needful and convenient to keep and be in the same, to send out of this kingdom, to the said castles, towns, or villages, all kinds of clothing, provision of victuals, ammunition, and implements necessary for such purpose, paying the duties and customs for the same as also to transport and carry over such number of men being willing thereunto or not prohibited, as they shall think fit, and also to govern them in such legal and reasonable manner as the said Governor and Company shall think best, and to inflict punishment for misdemeanors or impose such fines upon them for breach of their orders, as in these presents are formerly expressed : And further our will and pleasure is, and by these presents for us our heirs and successors, we do grant unto the said Governor and Company, and to their successors full power and lawful authority to seize upon the persons of all such English or any other our subjects which shall sail into Hudson's Bay or inhabit in any of the countries, islands, or territories hereby granted to the said Governor and Company without their leave and licence in that behalf first had and obtained, or that shall contemn or disobey their orders, and send them to England ; and that all and every person or persons being our subjects, anyways employed by the said Governor and Company within any the parts, places, or limits aforesaid shall be liable unto and suffer such punishment for any offences by them committed in the parts aforesaid as the President and

Council for the said Governor and Company there shall
think fit and the merit of the offence shall require as
aforesaid ; and in case any person or persons being con-
victed and sentenced by the President and Council of the
said Governor and Company in the countries, lands, or
limits aforesaid, their factors or agents there, for any
offence by them done shall appeal from the same, and
then and in such case it shall and may be lawful to and
for the said President and Council, factors or agents, to
seize upon him or them and to carry him or them home
prisoners into England, to the said Governor and Company, there to receive such condign punishment as his
cause shall require and the law of this nation allow of ;
and for the better discovery of abuses and injuries to be
done unto the said Governor and Company or their successors, by any servant by them to be employed in the
said voyages and plantations, it shall and may be lawful
to and for the said Governor and Company, and their
respective president, chief, agent, or governor in the parts
aforesaid to examine upon oath all factors, masters,
pursers, supercargoes, commanders of castles, forts, fortifications, plantations, or colonies, or other persons,
touching or concerning any matter or thing in which by
land or usage an oath may be administered, so as the said
oath and the matter therein contained be not repugnant
but agreeable to the laws of this realm ; And we do
hereby straightly charge and command all and singular
our admirals, vice-admirals, justices, mayors, sheriffs,
constables, bailiffs and all and singular other our officers,
ministers, liegemen, and subjects whatsoever to be
aiding, favouring, helping, and assisting the said
Governor and Company and to their successors, and to
their deputies and every of them in executing and enjoying the premises as well on land as on sea from
time to time, when any of you shall thereunto be required ; any statute, act, ordinance, proviso, proclamation
or restraint heretofore had, made, set forth, ordained, or
provided, or any other matter, cause, or thing whatsoever
to the contrary in anywise notwithstanding. In wit-

ness whereof we have caused these our letters to be made patent.

Witness ourself at Westminster, the second day of May, in the two and twentieth year of our reign.

By writ of Privy Seal,

PIGOTT.

No. VII.

EXTRACT FROM THE CROWN GRANT CHARTER OF 1838, CON-
FERRING THE PRIVILEGE OF EXCLUSIVE TRADE WITH THE
INDIANS UPON THE SURRENDER OF A FORMER GRANT TO
THE HUDSON'S BAY COMPANY BY KING GEORGE IV. IN
1821.

"Now know ye, that in consideration of the surrender made to us of the said recited Grant, and being desirous of encouraging the said trade, and of preventing as much as possible a recurrence of the evils mentioned or referred to in the said recited Grant, we do hereby grant and give our license under the hand and seal of one of our principal secretaries of state to the said Governor and Company and their successors for the exclusive privilege of trading with the Indians in all such parts of North America to the northward and to the westward of the lands and territories belonging to the United States of America as shall not form any part of our provinces in North America, or of any lands or territories belonging to the said United States of America or to any European Government, state, or power : And we do by these presents give, grant, and secure to the said Governor and Company and their successors the sole and exclusive privilege for the full period of twenty-one years from the date of this our Grant, of trading with the Indians in all such parts of North America as aforesaid."

By virtue of this and the former license granted by George IV., the terms of the original charter were ostensibly, although not technically, revoked, and the

trade of the Hudson's Bay Company very properly confined solely to and with the Indians. Under what
authority, therefore, the Company now claim and enforce
an absolute monopoly and exclusive power and privilege
of trading with the imported white population, and imposing other restrictions, to the exclusion of every other
trafficker, is not apparent, and, indeed, seems as hard to
define as their proclamations issued at Victoria have
been injurious and perhaps unjustifiable.

No. VIII.

COPY OF THE TREATY BETWEEN HER MAJESTY QUEEN VIC-
TORIA AND THE UNITED STATES OF AMERICA FOR THE
SETTLEMENT OF THE OREGON BOUNDARY. SIGNED AT
WASHINGTON JUNE THE 15TH, 1846. RATIFICATIONS
EXCHANGED AT LONDON, JULY 17TH, 1846. PRESENTED
TO BOTH HOUSES OF PARLIAMENT BY COMMAND OF HER
MAJESTY, 1846.

Her Majesty the Queen of the United Kingdom of
Great Britain and Ireland, and the United States of
America, deeming it to be desirable for the future welfare of both countries, that the state of doubt and uncertainty which has hitherto prevailed respecting the
sovereignty and government of the territory on the
north-west coast of America lying westward of the
Rocky or Stony Mountains, should be finally terminated
by an amicable compromise of the rights mutually asserted by the two parties over the said territory, have
respectively named plenipotentiaries to treat and agree
concerning the terms of such settlement, that is to say:
Her Majesty the Queen of the United Kingdom of
Great Britain and Ireland has, on her part, appointed
the Right Honourable Richard Pakenham, a member of
Her Majesty's most Honourable Privy Council and Her
Majesty's Envoy Extraordinary and Minister Plenipotentiary to the United States; and the President of the

United States of America has, on his part, furnished
with full powers James Buchanan, Secretary of State of
the United States, who, after having communicated to
each other their respective full powers found in good
and due form, have agreed upon and concluded the following articles :

ARTICLE I.

From the point on the forty-ninth parallel of north
latitude, where the boundary laid down in existing
treaties and conventions between Great Britain and the
United States terminates, the line of boundary between
the territories of her Britannic Majesty and those of the
United States, that shall be continued westward along the
said forty-ninth parallel of north latitude to the middle
of the channel which separates the continent from Vancouver's Island, and thence southerly through the middle of the said channel and of Fuca's Straits to the
Pacific Ocean : provided, however, that the navigation
of the whole of the said channel and straits south of the
forty-ninth parallel of north latitude remain free and
open to both parties.

ARTICLE II.

From the point at which the forty-ninth parallel of
north latitude shall be found to intersect the great
northern branch of the Columbia River, the navigation
of the said branch shall be free and open to the Hudson's Bay Company and to all British subjects trading
with the same to the point where the said branch meets
the main stream of the Columbia, and thence down the
said main stream to the ocean, with free access into and
through the said river or rivers, it being understood that
all the usual portages along the line thus described shall
in like manner be free and open.

In navigating the said river or rivers, British subjects
with their goods and produce shall be treated on the
same footing as citizens of the United States, it being,
however, always understood that nothing in this Article
shall be construed as preventing or intended to prevent

the Government of the United States from making any regulations respecting the navigation of the said river or rivers not inconsistent with the present treaty.

ARTICLE III.

In the future appropriation of the territory south of the forty-ninth parallel of north latitude as provided in the First Article of this Treaty, the possessing rights of the Hudson's Bay Company and of all British subjects who may be already in the occupation of land or other property lawfully acquired within the said territory, shall be respected.

ARTICLE IV.

The farms, lands, and other property of every description belonging to the Puget's Sound Agricultural Company on the north side of the Columbia River, shall be confirmed to the said Company. In case, however, the situation of those farms and lands should be considered by the United States to be of public and political importance, and the United States Government should signify a desire to obtain possession of the whole or of any part thereof, the property so required shall be transferred to the said Government at a proper valuation to be agreed upon between the parties.

ARTICLE V.

The present treaty shall be ratified by her Britannic Majesty and by the President of the United States, by and with the advice and consent of the senate thereof; and the ratifications shall be exchanged at London at the expiration of six months from the date hereof, or sooner, if possible.

In witness whereof the respective Plenipotentiaries have signed the same, and have affixed thereto the seals of their arms.

Done at Washington the fifteenth day of June, in the year of our Lord one thousand eight hundred and forty-six.

RICHARD PAKENHAM (L.S.)
JAMES BUCHANAN (L.S.)

No. IX.

The matter of opening Vancouver Island and Frazer
River to free trade and unrestricted navigation, is already
attracting the attention of the people there, who evidently fully appreciate the importance of the question,
as affecting the future prospects of that country.

By the following correspondence, it will be seen that
the citizens of Victoria are already stirring themselves
in the premises. The bill spoken of in the first petition
following, was presented to the House of Representatives of Vancouver Island, but not finding, as yet, any
support, fell to the ground. To the appeal made to
Governor Douglas His Excellency gave a verbal reply,
which being afterwards taken down and presented to
him (as appended below), he approved it by affixing
his initials. What the Governor says about the future
policy of the Government is highly important. Here is
the correspondence referred to :—

5th June, 1858.

*To the Honourable the House of Representatives of Van-
couver Island, now convened :—*

We, your petitioners, having understood that a bill
for the purpose of levying duties on goods imported into
the Colony of Vancouver Island will be shortly laid before you, do hereby pray your honourable House to give
particular attention to our united wishes against the
passage of such a measure.

We beg to represent to your honourable House that
such a course at any time, and more especially at the
present, would be highly injurious to the welfare of this
Colony, and retard the well-known prosperity resulting
from commercial freedom.

It must be apparent to your honourable House, that one great reason why this Colony has been so retarded in its advancement is the need of a more numerous population. The recent discoveries of gold on the adjacent continent, inducing such a large immigration, the importance of which cannot be over-estimated, will vastly tend to develope the unexampled resources of this fine country, hitherto lying dormant; and no one measure is more necessary to carry out this object than unrestricted commerce.

We urgently recommend that, if the present revenue derived from the sale of public lands is insufficient to defray the expenses of the government of the Colony, that a *direct* tax be imposed, which we consider to be the most equalizing and just method of raising a revenue.

C. A. BAGLEY, President.

J. A. R. Horner, J. H. Doane, James Thorne, George Johnston, James M. Reid—Committee.

To His Excellency, James Douglas, Governor and Commander in Chief of the Colony of Vancouver Island and its Dependencies, and Vice-Admiral of the same, &c. &c.

SIR—At a public meeting, held on the 5th instant, the following resolution was unanimously adopted, viz. :

"That a Committee be appointed to draw up an address to his Excellency, James Douglas, Governor of Vancouver Island, and Chief Factor of the Hudson's Bay Company, for the purpose of obtaining free trade with the mining population on Frazer River, and also that steamers and other vessels be allowed to run between Victoria and the head of navigation on Frazer River and its tributaries."

We, the undersigned, having been named to carry out the above resolution, beg respectfully to solicit your Excellency's earnest attention to the following important points :—

First—It is notorious that the stock of provisions in the mining districts is utterly inadequate for the supply even of the present population, many individuals having been compelled to abandon their labours and return to this and other ports, to obtain the common necessaries of life. Many settlers on this island are most anxious to carry supplies to their countrymen at the mines, but are prevented by the obstacles interposed by the Hudson's Bay Company, who have already seized goods to a considerable amount, on their way up the river. We cannot, therefore, consider, without serious apprehension, the state of confusion and distress which must ensue, when the vast numbers now swelling the tide of immigration shall have settled on these shores, should the present restrictions imposed upon trade by the Hudson's Bay Company continue in force.

Second—We beg to draw your Excellency's attention to the great inconvenience that is suffered by all classes, and by the mining population in particular, from the want of a reliable steam communication between this port and the mining districts, a want which has already caused the loss of many valuable lives. Such a state of things is deplorable in this age, and the more to be regretted when we consider that the means are at hand and freely offered of supplying that want, but are rejected by the exclusive policy of the Hudson's Bay Company.

It was with great satisfaction that the public learned that on the 5th instant, your Excellency had given permission to the American steamers Surprise and Sea Bird to carry passengers from this port up Frazer River, but it heard with deep regret that this permission was granted for one trip only.

Thirdly—We would especially point out for your Excellency's most serious consideration, how highly injurious is that state of things to the interests and progress of this important colony. Many British subjects have recently come here, anxious to make this their home, and have invested in property to a considerable amount, and numbers of their countrymen are only waiting their advices to follow, but they find their ardour dampened and their operations checked by the monopolizing policy of the Hudson's Bay Company ; in the meantime, thousands of emigrants from California are passing by this beautiful island to settle upon American soil, because they see no fair field offered to their enterprise under the British flag.

We feel assured that your Excellency will at once perceive that in bringing the objects of this memorial so prominently before you, we are actuated solely by an earnest desire to advance the interests of this colony by providing for the welfare of settlers and holding out inducements to early emigration, convinced that this is duly to be obtained by the speedy adoption of the liberal measures embodied in the resolution we have submitted.

Requesting that your Excellency will favour us with an early reply,

We have the honour to subscribe ourselves,

Your Excellency's most obedient servants,

JAMES YATES,
J. W. NAGLE,
JAS. R. HOMER,
C. A. BAYLEY,
J. H. DOANE,
EDW. GREENE.

His Excellency's Reply to the Address.

On the important question of allowing free trade with the mining population on Frazer River, his Excellency states that it is quite beyond his authority to do so—that he is simply the executive of the Hudson's Bay Company, whose privileges he is bound to protect, and can only act upon special instructions from home; but he has already written explaining the anomalous state of things existing here, and expects that, in the course of two or three months, instructions will be received authorising such changes as the exigencies of the case may demand. It is very probable, he states, that the government will shortly take the territory into their own hands, and compensate the Hudson's Bay Company for any sacrifices they may make.

As regards the free navigation of Frazer River and its tributaries, he replies. that it is not the Hudson's Bay Company who are accountable for the existing prohibition, but the Customs-law of Great Britain, according to which this river must be closed for the present to foreign vessels; that certain conditions had been offered to the Pacific Mail Company, and subsequently to the owner of the Surprise steamer—one of which conditions was to run under the British flag — and if declined by these, arrangements will be made as early as possible for other steamers.

His excellency further declared that the progress of this country occupied his careful attention, and whatever might be done, the growing interests of the colony would be carefully protected. He would also forward the address to England with his own despatches by the next steamer.

No. X.

RIGHTS OF THE HUDSON'S BAY COMPANY—OPENING UP FRAZER RIVER TO FREE TRADE.

Report of a "Meeting of Conference," held at the Government House, Victoria, on 10th June, at which Governor Douglas, Councillors John Work and Roderick Finlayson, and five members, viz. : T. J. Skinner, J. Yates, J. D. Pemberton, Speaker Helmcken, and J. W. McKay, of the Colonial House of Assembly, were present. The Governor, on this occasion, gave some important information as to the supposed rights of the Hudson's Bay Company, and the probability of the Frazer River country being soon opened to free trade.

His Excellency commenced the Conference by stating that any information in his possession would be cordially given to those present, but that a portion of it must be considered confidential, and not to be made public.

1. *With regard to the rights of the Hudson's Bay Company.*

These rights were granted to them by licence.

The Speaker (Helmcken) suggested that this licence referred to trade with Indians only, and not with white men.

His Excellency replied that at the time of the granting of the licence there were no white men resident in the territory; and added, that he had received advices from the Home Government which left no doubt that the Hudson's Bay Company did possess the exclusive right of navigation and trade.

2. *Whether the Executive had assumed any authority over Frazer River.*

His Excellency replied that he had not assumed any such authority; but as the representative of the Crown, had taken measures to preserve law and order, and had made regulations enforcing the navigation laws of Great Britain. He had allowed persons to go up the river, and had granted them licences to mine; had appointed custom-house officers and justices of the peace, and had called upon H.M.S. "Satellite" to assist in preventing any violation of the navigation laws.

The Speaker desired to know whether, having taken, or undertaken the government of Frazer River, this act in itself did not abrogate the right of the Hudson's Bay Company to exclusive navigation.

His Excellency replied that it was entirely out of his power to abrogate any of the rights or privileges of the Hudson's Bay Company. In fact, so far as he had gone, he had received the sanction of the officers of that body in this region. Moreover, that the British government regarded treaties as sacred and binding in all cases.

3. *Touching the point by whose authority the "sufferances" to Frazer River navigation are granted:*

His Excellency stated that they were granted by virtue of the power vested in him as representative of the Crown, as well as by consent of the agents of the Hudson's Bay Company. The exclusive right of the

Company to trade and navigation, necessarily excludes the transportation of any property save theirs, except by their permission.

The Speaker suggested that the miners having been allowed to go up the river, and the Government having in a greater or less degree assumed control of the stream, it would follow that these people had a right to be supplied with provisions, exclusive of the Company's monopoly, and therefore that British vessels, duly cleared here, had a right to proceed up the river for that purpose.

His Excellency replied that he must repeat that he had no authority to diminish or interfere with the Company's rights and privileges.

The Speaker suggested that the Hudson's Bay Company had not the means of supplying the large number of people that would be at the mines within a short time, and that it appeared probable that starvation, or calamities equally serious, would ensue. It would therefore be necessary and proper to allow vessels to carry provisions.

His Excellency replied, that the matter had given rise to serious deliberation and attention. Already permission had been granted to two American steamers to carry passengers and provision under certain restrictions. Necessity had compelled this action, and had also forced him to act more or less illegally, but not unjustly. *Should an emergency arise, permits would of course be granted to other vessels for like purposes, and every possible means be adopted for the prevention of suffering in the mining region.*

The Speaker suggested that merchants in England, in view of the restrictions put upon trade, would not be likely to send out supplies and emigrants; thus inflicting a double injury, first on our country, next on our colony. It was also to be feared that merchants would presume from the fact of the Company's being the only large purchaser, that they would be more or less at the latter's mercy, who would buy only at a price fixed by themselves; that is to say, the ships would have no other market than the Company, to which they might take their supplies.

His Excellency replied, that far from having the effect feared by the Speaker, the Company's privileges would produce a result exactly the contrary. He thought the present condition of trade offered greater inducements to British merchants than an open traffic would do. Touching the price of articles, that depended entirely on supply and demand. He was quite sure, and the House must also know, that the Hudson's Bay Company were upright and honourable, and not likely to stoop to unfair dealing.

4. *Touching the future government of Frazer River.*

His Excellency said, that as this was a matter at present under negotiation, he could not make any facts known, save in conference; and, that the House might know the general outline of his policy, he would read extracts from his last despatches to the Home Government.

The Speaker wished to inquire whether the Hudson's Bay Company, having the exclusive right to trade, could transfer any part of their right to others; that is to say, whether they could grant sufferances to any other parties to trade.

The Governor suggested, that in issuing sufferances, the Company did not transfer their rights; in fact, that the regulations and stipulations did not interfere with them. The House must recollect that it was the conjoint act of the Governor as Executive, and the Governor as part of the Hudson's Bay Company. His Excellency added, that he has been actuated by two motives: 1st. To do full justice to the Hudson's Bay Company. 2d. To promote by every legitimate means the welfare and prosperity of the colony. He was always willing to impart information to the House, and was pleased that this Conference had been asked.

The Speaker replied, that the Conference was asked, 1st, for the sake of information; it being the misfortune of the House of Assembly not to possess any government members; that is to say, any one to supply information upon the acts and intentions of the Governor and Council. 2d, that the information furnished verbally would save his Excellency an immense amount of trouble in writing, which this House, aware of the pressing demands upon his time, were desirous of obviating. They did not wish to add unnecessarily to the cares of office, but had a duty to perform in endeavouring to promote the interest and welfare of their constituents and the colony. Therefore, they had taken this means of obtaining the desired information. In the name of the House, he begged to thank his Excellency for the courtesy shown, and was pleased to find that the explanations resulted in showing that little difference of opinion existed between the House and the Governor.

The deputation then withdrew.

No. XI.

MISCELLANEOUS.

LEGISLATION FOR DEBTORS IN VANCOUVER ISLAND.—Judge Cameron, the judge-advocate of the supreme court of civil jurisdiction of the colony, has furnished the following information :

Debts due by persons who are living here can be collected by process of law in the supreme court of civil jurisdiction, when sued upon in the usual manner, and the Statute of Limitations runs against debts which have been outlawed by the statute in the country where the contract was made. Persons who owed debts in New York and then went to California, although the New York debts could not be collected in California, because of the Statute of Limitations, yet those debts can now be collected unless the statute of New York has run against the debt, and the statute can only run against it when a person is within the jurisdiction of that state. Judgments obtained in foreign states can be sued upon here and enforced, if properly exemplified, and also notes, debts, and other contracts made abroad.

There is no court of bankruptcy on the island, and if there were it would only apply to debts accrued within the jurisdiction of the court.

The old common law rules of pleadings are not in full force, but I am informed that the court has established certain rules for the procedure therein, with a view to simplify the complicated forms, inasmuch as no counsel existed in the colony, and the judge said it would soon be published for the information of persons, in book form.

LICENCES FOR LIQUOR-SELLING AT VICTORIA.—A licence for retailing beer alone costs 50*l.* For retailing all kinds of liquors the charge is 120*l.* For dealing wholesale in liquors, 100*l.*

FOUNTAIN'S DIGGINGS—(Frazer River, at 51 deg. 30 min. north).

Five rockers worked by half breed Canadians.

June 1.	2.	3.	4.	5.
1....38 dols.	50 dols.	42 dols.	40 dols.	50 dols.
2....40	51	38	29	51
3....41		29	51	52
4....28	55	18	33	56
5....32	60	54	54	58
6....64	62	39	58	55
7....52	58	48	52	64
Total 295	389	268	327	381
Ave. 42.14	55.50	38.70	46.72	54.40

Copy of the latest issue of Miners' License.   June 1858.

NOT TRANSFERABLE.

No. ——   185—

The bearer, —— ——, having paid to me the sum of Twenty-One Shillings, on account of the Territorial Revenue, I hereby License him to dig, search for, and remove gold on and from any such Crown Lands, within the Couteau and Frazer River districts, as shall be assigned to him for that purpose by any one duly authorised in that behalf.

This license to be in force for three months, ending
———— and no longer.
Received   ———— ————.
Received   ———— ————.
Received   ———— ————.

*Regulations to be observed by the Persons digging for
Gold, or otherwise employed in the Gold Fields :*

1. This License is to be carried on the person, to be
produced whenever demanded by any Commissioner,
Peace Officer, or other duly authorized person.

2. It is especially to be observed that this License is
not transferable, and that the holder of a transferred
License is liable to the penalty for misdemeanor.

3. No mining will be permitted where it would be
destructive of any line of road which it is necessary to
maintain, and which shall be determined by any Commissioner, nor within such distance around any store
as it may be necessary to reserve for access to it.

4. It is enjoined that all persons on the Gold Fields
maintain a due and proper observance of Sundays.

5. The extent of claim allowed to each Licensed
Miner, is 12 feet square, or 144 square feet.

6. To a party consisting of two miners 12 feet by 24,
or 288 square feet.

7. To a party consisting of three miners, 18 feet by 24,
or 432 square feet.

8. To a party consisting of four miners, 24 feet by 24,
or 576 square feet, beyond which no greater area will be
allowed in one claim.

Copy of Resolutions adopted by a party of miners at
Fort Yale Bar, showing that an attempt is being made
to manage matters in California style, despite the regulations of the government.

MINERS' RESOLUTIONS.

Resolved, That this place shall be known by the name

of Fort Yale Bar, with boundaries as follows: Commencing at the head of the island below Fort Yale, and extending up the river to a certain big rock at the mouth of the first cañon above Fort Yale, and from the centre of the river to high-water mark on its west side.

Resolved, That all mining claims within the boundaries of this bar shall consist of twenty-five feet front, extending backward from the channel of the river to high-water mark.

Resolved, That no person shall be allowed to hold more than one mining claim within the boundaries of this bar, at any time.

Resolved, That the owner of every mining claim shall work upon, or cause to be worked upon his claim, one good and ample day's labour, within the period of five days, or forfeit his right to said claim; *provided* said claim be in a workable condition, and the owner is not prevented by sickness or public business.

Resolved, That a Recorder shall be elected by the miners, whose duty it shall be to record all claims and keep such record open to the inspection of the public. Said Recorder shall receive a fee of fifty cents for each claim recorded by him.

Resolved, That all mining claims shall be considered workable after five days from the passage of these resolutions.

No. XI.

THE WAY THERE.

From England to British Colombia and Vancouver there are four existing routes.

1. By the Isthmus of Panama, *viâ* the West India Steamers and the Island of Saint Thomas.
2. By the Isthmus of Panama, *viâ* New York.

3. Through Canada, or the United States, across the Rocky Mountains.

4. By sailing vessel round Cape Horn.

The first route is, geographically, the most preferable, being the shortest, and consequently the most direct of any of the others. The journey to Aspinwall (Colon) under present arrangements, which, however, are capable of great improvement, occupies twenty-two days, inclusive of the day of sailing and arrival, the steamers leaving Southampton on the 2nd and 17th of each month, and the fares, first-class, ranging from 38*l.* 10*s.* to 66*l.*; and second-class from 20*l.* to 25*l.*

The fares to New York, as every one knows, range from 26*l.* (the Cunard line having recently reduced their scale) to 7*l.* 10*s.* From New York, American mail steamers run in conjunction, also fortnightly, between New York and Aspinwall, and Panama and San Francisco, at through fares from 150 dollars up, the entire journey from New York to California occupying about twenty-eight days.

As is detailed in the body of the work, trains run daily across the Isthmus of Panama, a distance of but little more than forty miles, and from that port to San Francisco the fares, by the steamers mentioned, to those not having through tickets, range from 100 dollars up. Steamers run from San Francisco several times a week, as also numerous sailing vessels, to the mouth of Frazer River, touching at Victoria on the way for licenses, the fares ranging from 18 to 60 dollars.

From thence to Fort Hope steamers ply frequently, the fare being uniformly 20 dollars a-head.

By the third route, passengers may take a through-ticket in London, at the Grand Trunk Railway of Canada office by steamer to Quebec, and thence by railway to St. Paul, Minnesota, near the head of Lake Superior, the fares ranging from 13*l.* to 27*l.*, and the time occupied in the performance of the journey being about sixteen days. The route beyond, across the Rocky Mountains, will be found fully detailed in Chapter VIII., p. 66.

Of the fourth route round Cape Horn the reader can himself judge. While he contemplates the misery of being cooped up and pitched about on board a floating prison for four months, he must also remember that he will not be troubled with transhipment of any kind between his embarkation in England and his arrival at Vancouver. The fares range from 72*l.* to 25*l.*

THE END.

ERRATUM.

Page 23, line 12, *for* " information," *read* " reformation."

J. Billing, Printer and Stereotyper, Guildford, Surrey.

The Far Western Frontier

An Arno Press Collection

[Angel, Myron, editor]. **History of Nevada.** 1881.

Barnes, Demas. **From the Atlantic to the Pacific, Overland.** 1866.

Beadle, J[ohn] H[anson]. **The Undeveloped West; Or, Five Years in the Territories.** [1873].

Bidwell, John. **Echoes of the Past:** An Account of the First Emigrant Train to California. [1914].

Bowles, Samuel. **Our New West.** 1869.

Browne, J[ohn] Ross. **Adventures in the Apache Country.** 1871.

Browne, J[ohn] Ross. **Report of the Debates in the Convention of California, on the Formation of the State Constitution.** 1850.

Byers, W[illiam] N. and J[ohn] H. Kellom. **Hand Book to the Gold Fields of Nebraska and Kansas.** 1859.

Carvalho, S[olomon] N. **Incidents of Travel and Adventure in the Far West; with Col. Fremont's Last Expedition Across the Rocky Mountains.** 1857.

Clayton, William. **William Clayton's Journal.** 1921.

Cooke, P[hilip] St. G[eorge]. **Scenes and Adventures in the Army.** 1857.

Cornwallis, Kinahan. **The New El Dorado; Or, British Columbia.** 1858.

Davis, W[illiam] W. H. **El Gringo; Or, New Mexico and Her People.** 1857.

De Quille, Dan. (William Wright). **A History of the Comstock Silver Lode & Mines.** 1889.

Delano, A[lonzo]. **Life on the Plains and Among the Diggings;** Being Scenes and Adventures of an Overland Journey to California. 1854.

Ferguson, Charles D. **The Experiences of a Forty-niner in California.** (Originally published as *The Experiences of a Forty-niner During Thirty-four Years' Residence in California and Australia*). 1888.

Forbes, Alexander. **California:** A History of Upper and Lower California. 1839.

Fossett, Frank. **Colorado:** Its Gold and Silver Mines, Farms and Stock Ranges, and Health and Pleasure Resorts. 1879.

The Gold Mines of California: Two Guidebooks. 1973.

Gray, W[illiam] H[enry]. **A History of Oregon, 1792–1849.** 1870.

Green, Thomas J. **Journal of the Texian Expedition Against Mier.** 1845.

Henry, W[illiam] S[eaton]. **Campaign Sketches of the War with Mexico.** 1847.

[Hildreth, James]. **Dragoon Campaigns to the Rocky Mountains.** 1836.

Hines, Gustavus. **Oregon:** Its History, Condition and Prospects. 1851.

Holley, Mary Austin. **Texas:** Observations, Historical, Geographical and Descriptive. 1833.

Hollister, Ovando J[ames]. **The Mines of Colorado.** 1867.

Hughes, John T. **Doniphan's Expedition.** 1847.

Johnston, W[illiam] G. **Experiences of a Forty-niner.** 1892.

Jones, Anson. **Memoranda and Official Correspondence Relating to the Republic of Texas, Its History and Annexation.** 1859.

Kelly, William. **An Excursion to California Over the Prairie, Rocky Mountains, and Great Sierra Nevada.** 1851. 2 Volumes in 1.

Lee, D[aniel] and J[oseph] H. Frost. **Ten Years in Oregon.** 1844.

Macfie, Matthew. **Vancouver Island and British Columbia.** 1865.

Marsh, James B. **Four Years in the Rockies; Or, the Adventures of Isaac P. Rose.** 1884.

Mowry, Sylvester. **Arizona and Sonora:** The Geography, History, and Resources of the Silver Region of North America. 1864.

Mullan, John. **Miners and Travelers' Guide to Oregon, Washington, Idaho, Montana, Wyoming, and Colorado.** 1865.

Newell, C[hester]. **History of the Revolution in Texas.** 1838.

Parker, A[mos] A[ndrew]. **Trip to the West and Texas.** 1835.

Pattie, James O[hio]. **The Personal Narrative of James O. Pattie, of Kentucky.** 1831.

Rae, W[illiam] F[raser]. **Westward by Rail:** The New Route to the East. 1871.

Ryan, William Redmond. **Personal Adventures in Upper and Lower California, in 1848–9.** 1850/1851. 2 Volumes in 1.

Shaw, William. **Golden Dreams and Waking Realities:** Being the Adventures of a Gold-Seeker in California and the Pacific Islands. 1851.

Stuart, Granville. **Montana As It Is:** Being a General Description of its Resources. 1865.

Texas in 1840, Or the Emigrant's Guide to the New Republic. 1840.

Thornton, J. Quinn. **Oregon and California in 1848.** 1849. 2 Volumes in 1.

Upham, Samuel C. **Notes of a Voyage to California via Cape Horn, Together with Scenes in El Dorado, in the Years 1849–'50.** 1878.

Woods, Daniel B. **Sixteen Months at the Gold Diggings.** 1851.

Young, F[rank] G., editor. **The Correspondence and Journals of Captain Nathaniel J. Wyeth, 1831–6.** 1899.